Poems from the Heart

by

Eric Royston Harvey

Published in 2014 by FeedARead.com Publishing

First Edition

A CIP catalogue record for this title is available from the British
Library.

Of Mice and Men

We had a little visitor,
his fur was brown and white,
He ran into our lounge one day
and gave the wife a fright.

He popped out of the skirting board,
and scurried 'cross the floor,
The wife has said she does not want
to live here anymore.

I said 'He was just curious-
a gentle little mouse'
She said, 'Then let him poke around
in someone else's house!

If he's not gone by Friday night
I'm going back to Mum's,'
I thought about it long and hard
and fed the mouse some crumbs.

I bought myself a humane trap
to catch my furry friend,
and placed it where I knew he ran,
so I could apprehend.

Next morning when I checked the trap
my little mouse was there,
I tried to pick him up but he
just zig zagged everywhere.

I took him to the garden shed,
where my wife never went,
My sanctuary from nagging voice
where happy hours were spent!

Went to the shop and bought a cage,
to keep my new friend in,
We got to know each other as
I taught him discipline.

The wife began to rant and rave,
when I went to my shed,
Suggested I should pack my clothes
and move in there instead.

I'd had enough, she drove me mad,
she tried to spoil my life,
That's when I went back to the shop
and bought my mouse a wife!

Needless to say, they got on well,
if you know what I mean!
Within six weeks the babies came,
I counted them - FIFTEEN!

Then five weeks later...more arrived,
I was inundated
Words In my book 'How mice can breed'
are very understated!

And so my master-plan was born,
I let them loose inside
the house that she had made her own,
since she became my bride.

I sat there in my male retreat,
and waited for the screams,
Sure enough, they deafened me,
but fulfilled all my dreams.

She didn't even pack her bags, she
ran back home to mother,
A pair of whingers - it was clear,
they deserved each other!

And me? I love it on my own,
surrounded by my mice,
It's great that she's not here to moan
it really is so nice.

I cut my toenails in the lounge,
walk bare around the house,
No one to nag, in fact, it's just
as quiet as a mouse!

This is one of my nostalgic poems, set in the late fifties

Back in time

We didn't have a lot when I was quite small
the country was still recovering from war,
Families stayed loyal to their neighbours and all
and would leave their key on a string by the door.

So mostly, front doors remained open to all
everyone the same with nothing worth stealing,
Right there on the mantle should the rent man call
a tin stood next to old wallpaper peeling.

We didn't wear posh clothes, some food still on ration
no fizzy drinks, crisps, biscuits or sweets,
Easter and Whitsun were treated with passion
Christmas was a time for some special treats.

A clip round the ear if we had been naughty
or answered back – which a child never did,
Always down to earth we were never haughty
and to steal or lie – well- heaven forbid!

TV was luxurious in old black and white
but kids didn't care – they just played in the street,
From early morning to the fading light
when the street lamps lit we were quick on our feet.

Before Mum shouted us or Father came back
from the pub at the bottom of our road,
If you didn't make it you'd have a quick whack
on your head or backside not where it showed.

No health and safety – no children's rights
we had our own rules within our own heads,
The blackouts went up on light Summer nights
kids under eight years would be in their beds-

- to listen to mates playing out in the streets
screaming and shouting having a good time,
Sticking their heads under crisp cotton sheet
faces and hands smeared with the days grime!

A teaspoon of malt and cod liver oil
kept the doctor away, according to Mum,
We just knew that it tasted really vile
and left us with faces both sad and glum.

We'd go walking for miles o'er hill and dale
with nothing but a bottle of cold tea,
No matter how far we would never fail
to be back in time to watch some TV.

We'd gather old tins and use them as toys
use them as stilts with some well tied string,
Cans scraped on the tarmac – a horrible noise
but being so tall was a wonderful thing.

War was central in our imaginations
with a stick that looked like a rifle or gun,
Got rid of anger and pent up frustrations
like our dad's who'd fought, we were second to none!

With Mums old stockings we made fishing nets
then down to the brook to catch sticklebacks,
Paddling in water was as good as it gets
with fish paste sarnies for lunchtime snacks.

We had home made ice-cream from over the shop
rubbed dirt off new carrots and ate them raw,
Drinking from a hose was our council pop
on special days we sipped Vimto through a straw.

Kids of today will never understand
how we made our enjoyment back then,
We had no computers or phones in our hand
it's so sad those days can't return again.

When the air was filled with children's laughter
we had holes in our shoes, patches on our jeans,
We always looked poor, though Dad was a grafter
and we had a great life, well into our teens.

A Lifetime of love.

She took it from the proffered tray
A pile of dirt held in her hand
Why God had taken him this way
Dolly could never understand.

She threw it softly on the lid
As if afraid to waken him
A crumpled rose from view was hid
Her future now looked very grim

Saying goodbye to his two friends
Thanked them for attending today
George said that 'friendship never ends'
And he'd nothing to do anyway!

Dolly scowled at him, shook her head
Adjusted the old black hat she'd found
In the dusty box beneath the bed
Then heading homeward, she was bound

What would she do without her Ted
He had always seen to everything
How would she sleep alone in bed
Would she hear the alarm bell ring.

Turning the key in the front door
It seemed so quiet in the hall
The noise of ticking, Nothing more
That ticking clock upon the wall.

Filling the kettle making tea
Reaching up for the silver tray

Placing two cups absent-mindedly
Taking one, putting it away

Hands trembling she sat in the chair
Tears made tracks down her wrinkled face
She needed Ted, wished he was there
Placing cup on doily of lace

She took off her glasses, rubbed her eyes
She'd had a long day and was tired
Two turning up had been a surprise
Both men that Ted had admired

They'd fought together during the war
Watched out for each other in life
They were with Ted the night before
He had taken her for his wife.

She fell into a slumber so deep
A deep sleep that was unplanned
She could see a staircase very steep
Ted stood there, holding out his hand

Their eyes met and fingers touched
Holding each other they kissed
Turning around hands tightly clutched
Climbed the stairway into the mist

She was found dead ten days later
she had passed away in her sleep
She was sent alone to her creator
There was no one else left to weep.

This is dedicated to my beautiful daughter Vickie, whom we lost to cancer on 10/12/2018, a lot of my poetry is written around her.

The Garden of Life.

Allow me to take you on a journey
A loving journey of our life
A journey that started many years ago
when you became my wife

But let me set this beautiful journey
In a place that we both treasure
I'll take your hand and lead you through
a garden to give you pleasure.

The gate is the start where we first met
more than fourty years ago
When my eyes glanced across at a gorgeous girl
and my love began to grow

During our courtship we had our strife
at the open gate we tarried
but we strengthened our stems and walked right through
On the day that we got married

We trod our path of different textures
the cobbles were our stormy seas
Flat flagstones were our calmer times
and on gravel we were ill at ease

We travelled along our meandering path
planted shrubs along the way
Put in our bulbs and planted the seeds
and tended them day after day

As years passed by the shrubs all matured
We watched as they grew tall
They got so strong and began to spread
over winter spring summer and fall

We erected our Greenhouses, built our walls
to keep our plants safe and sound
We nursed them till they were strong enough
To stand on their own firm ground

Gazebos and pergolas reached up to the sky
all built by my own loving hand
You filled hanging baskets, planted more flowers
and we watched our garden expand

The daffodils, tulips and bedding plants
all just came and went
But the shrubs were there year after year
surely money well spent

Some years they would droop, not flower at all
but we nursed them with loving care
Next year they would be blooming again
raising their heads up to the air

And from those shrubs tiny shoots grew
all different sizes and years
They bring us such pleasure, memories too
but some have brought us tears

It wasn't always good, we had a beautiful
rose that faded and died
We knelt together on a camomile lawn
held hands together and cried

When a beautiful rose dies you try to get on
with tending your other roses
You attempt to be strong and carry on as a bad
chapter in your life closes

But you just can't replace a beautiful rose
it will never ever be the same
For the rose that you lost is the rose that you loved
a rose by any other name

But as we grow older so will our garden
It'll mature just like us
We'll carry on tending the shrubs as they grow
give lots of love and little fuss.

Fred the Lighthouse Keeper

Fred kept a lighthouse down on Beachy head,
A sixty year old Yorkshireman, born and bred,
It were a lonely life especially in bed,
Fred always regretted he'd never been wed,
One day the Postman turned to Fred and said,
'Get thee a Thai bride for company Fred',
'Nay, I'm sixty year old and nearly half dead,
just five foot six , from me toe to me head'.

Over the weeks it remained in Fred's head,
Could he get a bride to come and wed,
He sent a photo when he were twenty, instead-
-of an up to date photo looking half dead,
Well it soon happened, like the Postman had said,
that a letter and photo winged its way back to Fred,
Not the slightest bit of guilt for the way he'd misled,
She was a lovely young lass to fill his old bed.

He sent two hundred pounds to the young aforesaid,
With the help of the Postman his news was widespread,
That he'd sent for a Thai bride to be his masthead,
Or would it be her tying him to the bed,
Well the time finally came that on Beachy Head,
The bride would arrive and meet old Fred,
But what she might think never entered his head,
as the taxi pulled up at the old homestead.

As she alighted poor Fred's face turned red,
She were hardly a toy bride and hardly unfed!
Over twenty stone from toe to head,
'That'll be forty quid' the taxi driver said,
As she got out of the car both legs were well spread,
Her backside still in there but tummy well ahead,
She smiled, teeth were missing, hardly well bred,
'Thee's nowt like thee picture,' said a sorry old Fred.

'Well neither are you, I must have misread,
That you were twenty years old and good in bed,
But we'll make the most of it, today we'll get wed,
and tonight we'll have fun on your lovely bedstead'
So off to get married they both duly sped,
That night his Thai bride her clothes she shed,
The sight of her wobbling, filled Fred with dread,
By the time it were morning he was nearly half dead.

As the months passed by she got more widespread,
She'd order five Fish n chips and eat em in bed,
The whole of her nose was a massive blackhead,
Cheekbones shone in the dark, as if infra red,
Her skin was leathery, like the boot of a skinhead,
The thought of kissing her filled him with dread,
So he started to think how he'd get rid instead,
It was then evil thoughts entered Fred's head.

He lured her to the cliff at Beachy Head,
As she got to the edge his arms were outspread,
She toppled o'er the edge and split her fat head,
Now she lies quiet under the new damp bed,
When people asked, where was the Hogshead,
'Oh she's run off back home' says a frowning Fred
'I were too much for her in that old bedstead'
And he smiles at the Daisies in his new flowerbed.

Friends Forever

Bad people are tedious, boring and dull
Sad people will drag you down every day
Good people live life to the very full
Great people are so happy and gay

Bad friends will abandon you, you'll scream and frown
Sad friends will torture and torment your soul
Good friends bring cheer, acting the clown
Great friends will pull you, from a black hole

Bad pals will rile you, drive you around the bend
Sad pals will surely take you to the brink
Good pals will stay with you, to the end
Great pals hold you, if you start to sink

Bad people will abuse their friends without care
Sad friends will forever stand their ground
Good pals will surround you everywhere
Great people, Great friends, Great pals I've found

Blind ambition

Her nostrils filled with wondrous scents
as she strolled down cinder path,
For loss, her mind does not lament
it shows no sign of hate or wrath,
She hears the wasp buzz on the apple
brushes hands on lavender tips,
Opens the gate leading to the chapel
down gravel path to where it dips,
Turns rusting handle enters in
to the place where God she'll find,
Kneels and confesses all her sin
her only sin was being blind.

Have you ever wondered how that morning honey on your toast was made?

The Busy Bee

The honey bee buzzes, the honey bee stings
has real good antennae, and two pairs of wings,
Makes honey from nectar, by regurgitation
followed quite closely by evaporation.

To make just one jar, a bee travels afar,
three times around the world is just about par,
He'll settle on the calyx, suck from the bud,
extract the nectar, as a honey bee should.

Then fly back to the beehive, cap it with wax
as queen and male drones, protect from attack,
The Beekeeper arrives, resplendent in white
to extract the honey, well not all, not quite.

Smoke from the smoker, to pacify the bees,
lifts out the honeycomb, as nature decrees,
He'll take what he wants, return it to the hive
leave the poor bee enough, to just stay alive.

It's sent to a factory, somewhere afar,
shaken, shifted and stirred, put into a jar.
Sent out to Supermarkets, from coast to coast
and that's how you get honey on nice hot toast

First day

She rose at 5am that morn,
Plain cotton blouse did not adorn
the long black dress, which first time worn
o'er black laced boots and tender corn.

Opened the drapes , caught early sun,
Combed long black hair into a bun.
First day at school would be such fun,
her duties there she would not shun.

Threw cotton nightdress on bedpost,
down squeaking stairs to waiting host,
Her mother in pride overdosed,
awaited her with tea and toast.

Excitement built on her first day,
spent all breakfast chatting away.
Mother said "It will be okay"
hoping her face did not betray.

Then out into the cobbled street,
past terraced houses nice and neat,
nodding politely to the sweet
playing children, new shoes on feet.

Her heart was pounding oh so fast!
as eyes upon rough places cast,
past children of a different caste,
and then - she saw the school at last!

Inside - the dark green bottle walls,
where the cockroach lives and crawls,
But she knew well that duty calls
as she entered those hallowed halls.

The children looked her up and down,
then with a smile - not with a frown,
Spoke these first words in her home town,
"Good morning class - now settle down".

Grandad's House

They're tearing it down, my old granddad's house,
evicting the snails and the resident mouse.
I took one last look,-- just a few weeks ago,--
it wasn't long after a light fall of snow.
But my body felt warm and my heart beat real fast,
when, to a long gone era, my mind was cast.

On shelves in the pantry rows of pickling jars,
the platter used for carving that held the scars.
The lovely crock chicken full of newly laid eggs,
the muddy red tiles where the dog sat and begged
for his bone shaped biscuits and nice leathery chews,
next to dear old granddad's brown gardening shoes.

The marble slab was eternally cold,
the old rolling pin that Grandma would hold
while flattening the pastry for her apple pie,
not long on the plate and not long on the eye.
The little mesh window was opposite the door,
and enamel white flour bin sat on the floor.

Out in the scullery the hot copper sat,
next to a steel bucket, below Granddads hat
With the Belfast sink always sparkling white,
and the big green mangle to squeeze those sheets tight,
I can see Gran at the sink giving clothes a scrub,
but more stubborn garments went into the tub.

In the nice warm parlour Grandma's rag - made rug
ensured that Granddad was as snug as a bug;
Ever boiling kettle on the black lead grate,--
so any nice visitors didn't have to wait,

for homemade cake and a cup of PG tips--
a moment in the mouth, a lifetime on the hips!

The front room was best and the flooring brand new,
the cold damp corner where the aspidistra grew.
Tins of ready cash on the mantle shelf,
waiting for the rent man, who would help himself.
Photos of family hung from the picture rail
in Nan's best room where she'd always regale.

Up winding stairs to the bedroom above,
each creaking stair holds a memory of love.
I stare through the window, across to the town,
kneel on the bed and the feather eiderdown;
I can feel the warmth as I'm lying here,
snuggling between my grandparents so dear.

I make my way down with a tear in my eye.
I'm still reminiscing of great times gone by.
My dear Gran and Granddad are now laid to rest,
and now I'm a Granddad, with Grandchildren blessed.
I turn - look behind me, as I hear a sigh-
was that my dear Grandparents whispering goodbye?

<u>A Fathers Day wish</u>

How can I touch you when you're far away
How does my heart cope with each passing day,
You're here in my head every hour every minute
You're deep in my heart – but I want you in it.

You were a great teacher and taught me well
If I ever erred you would never yell,
You taught me the rules of right and wrong
'Just be a good person' was your swansong.

My heart still aches as I think of you
Your wonderful ways, the things you would do,
Standing on your shoes when I was so small
Dancing round the front room having a ball.

Sat up on your shoulders, so high off the ground
Life was exciting when you were around,
You sowed all the seeds and showed me the way
You made me the person that I am today.

I look up to heaven and think of you Dad
On this special day I feel a bit sad,
I know you're beside me to show me the way
As I send lots of love on Fathers day.

Light and Shade in the Woodland

There's a lovely woodland, quite close to me,
where I, in awe, would wonder at the sight.
A place where the shrews and the mice run free,
while the trees, stripped bare, now let in the light.

The thrushes swirling in grey winter skies
and tracks of the fox on snow-laden glade.
Hedgehogs and dormice have now closed their eyes--
all of them snuggled beneath winter shade.

Soon, sunny days, much warmer and lighter,
bring shoots springing forth from the earth below.
A wavy sea of blue that gets brighter;
as trees let in light for bluebells to grow.

And now, where bare trees of winter had stood,
are leafy green arbours of dappled shade,
Where butterflies in abundance will flood,
and - at morning light - dawn's chorus is played.

Ferns are unfurling within forest shade;
they're the oldest plants on our Mother Earth.
Thistles and foxgloves, gracefully displayed,
as the woodland light entices new birth.

In summer, a lovely canopy's made,
its majesty hiding the forest from view.
Throwing out different light and shade,
covering the floor, with shadows bestrew.

Then, all too soon, the warm summer has gone,
as leaves fall again, and birds fly away.
Inspiring how nature's cycle goes on,
creating its own 'fifty shades of grey'.

Autumnal shades of orange and brown,
in the far distance a shimmer of green.
The pine, now wearing the 'prince of trees' crown,
by two great firs stand - the King and the Queen.

A living cathedral here in this place,
letting in the soft beams of shaded light.
God's own creation, interwoven in lace,
where everything is beautiful and bright.

The Captains Girl

Out of the sea the Black Marie,
popped up like a cork held under.
From cannon holes poured murky sea,
her rigging was torn asunder.

The old ship's crew was ill at ease,
breeches and shirts all torn to shreds.
Now tossed around on stormy seas,
woken from their watery beds.

Captain stood steadfast at the mast,
one eye missing and one arm, too
Both taken by a cannon blast,
whilst in the arms of his love true.

Her beauty pure gave eyes pleasure,
he thought to take her as his wife.
She was his world - his own treasure,
then a Naval ship took her life.

Now rusting guns of the Galleon,
seen only every twenty years.
Searching for gems and bullion,
the ship and its grisly crew appears.

Captain's sweetheart and counterpart,
standing bravely there at his side.
For he could never ever part,
from the woman to be his bride.

He made a pact, a selfish act,
with the devil beneath the sea.
He sold his soul, signed a contract,
Now they'd sail for eternity.

Included too, were his motley crew,
who were not happy with the deal.
They hated him and each one knew,
with the devil they couldn't appeal.

Captain shouts orders at the boarders,
beneath the flag of skull and bones.
Sharing spoils with ragged hoarders,
in the locker of Davy Jones.

He walks the deck of his ancient wreck,
splintered boards beneath his feet.
Keeping the scurvy dogs in check,
with measured rum and salted meat.

And with devil's bride there at his side,
he's as happy as happy can be.
His ship will travel far and wide,
destined to sail the seven seas.

First cut is the deepest.

I look into your deep sad eyes,
There's nothing there, that's no surprise,
Those marks that cover both your arms,
Make me aware that you self harm.

You tell me life is not too good,
You're never heard, misunderstood,
You tell of trouble, tell of strife,
Tell of turmoil in your life.

How when at home you're filled with gloom,
Up there alone in your bedroom,
You have to live by father's rule,
So started cutting while at school.

If you were bullied, then you'd cut,
Up in your room, the door tight shut,
If someone slapped you didn't cry,
You'd cut yourself, hoped you would die.

You'd cut your arms, self harm again,
To rid your mind of emotional pain,
No friends to help, there's no one there,
No one to love, no mother's care.

But cuttings not the answer friend,
Self harm won't bring it to an end,
That pain you feel inside your heart,
I'll help you make a brand new start.

I'll walk right there, right by your side,
Return your faith, restore your pride,
I'll stem your anger, feel your pain,
And help you see the light again.

For I too have sensed great loss,
As I was nailed upon that cross.

An Angel Visits

If you get a feeling of deja vu,
that sort of feeling, you're just passing through,
Don't get yourself weepy, don't get yourself blue,
it means an Angel has just touched you.

If you're at your lowest and feeling meek,
you're aching all over, feeling very weak,
Then suddenly you feel like you're at your peak,
It just means an Angel, has kissed your cheek.

If you and your loved ones can't be apart,
you call them your lover, darling, sweetheart,
You've got this 'love thing' down to a fine art,
It means that an Angel has touched your heart.

So don't be despondent, live for today,
make love and understanding, your mainstay,
Be sensual and lush like creme brulee
or you'll drive your darling Angel away.

This is an epic poem and tells of the forbidden love of a young couple in a village of the 17th century

Thomas and Martha.

Thomas was a popular man
Blacksmith being his trade,
Twenty three years his life did span,
As Methodist he prayed.

A handsome man, all girls adored
His smooth clean shaven face,
But when Martha passed, his heart it soared
No one could take her place.

Their love it grew each time they met,
They never were apart,
Each night he kissed her at sunset
She vowed to him her heart.

Her parents scorned upon their lust
Said he was bad for her,
He wasn't a man that they could trust
On that they did concur.

They banished Thomas from their home
Discouraged them to meet,
In deep self pity Martha roamed
Her life was incomplete.

One Sunday Thomas missed his church
Martha could not be found,
They'd left her parents in the lurch
For loving they were bound.

They walked the moors, up hills they toiled
Then reached a tranquil place,
He took her hand, she turned, she smiled
He welcomed her embrace.

They lay down there that summer day
He took her in his arms,
His kisses drew her breathe away
Succumbing to his charms.

Her beauty smoothed his furrowed brow
As they consummated bliss,
His powerful love he did avow
Within a sweethearts kiss.

For hours they made love on the moor
Till moon rose high above
Twas dark as they got to her door
To tell them of their love.

The door flew open, father stood
His hand raised high to harm,
This maddened Thomas, flared his blood
He grabbed the old man's arm.

"Just one hair on her head you touch
And I will hang for you!
You hurt, but only insomuch
That I have hurt you too".

The mother pushed between the men
Forcing them both apart,
Father went for Martha again
For she had broken his heart.

"I'll gladly go" Thomas called out
"If you will stay your hand,"
The older man, so small and stout
Released on his command.

And so a peace descended on
The village where they met,
Thomas remembered times long gone
Though neither would forget.

Near eight months passed in which they'd meet
Though ne'er a word was spoken,
A silent vigil on the street
Smiles were but a token.

Yet Martha's life was in turmoil
Her stress began to show,
To talk to mother would embroil
In things she should not know.

She'd kept her secret very well
Hidden beneath loose dress,
Under that dress there was a swell
Her life was in a mess.

Then one night her drunken father
Pushed past her swollen frame,
His face was in a state of lather
As he realised her shame.

She fled from him, his swinging fist
Ran out into the dark,
Although his words did not desist
They did not find their mark.

She stumbled o'er the darkened moors
On that cold stormy night,
No sign of light or cottage doors
To end the poor girls plight.

Pain etched upon her pale young face
The hurt beneath the cloak,
Her breath was short and heart did race
Strong spirit now was broke.

She clutched her stomach, called his name
The wind blew words away,
Then she set down her weary frame
Upon wet grass she lay.

Her screams of agony were wasted
On that desolate moor,
The feel of death on tongue she tasted
Like nevermore before.

The rain swept down, battered her face
As baby's head appeared,
To die alone in this grey place
The only thing she feared.

She pushed and bore the baby out
And held his little head,
But sting of death she could not flout
By daylight she was dead!

Found by Thomas that very day
Where they first made sweet love
He fell to his knees, began to pray
For two lost souls above.

Now on a dark cold winter night
Where loving once occurred,
Across the moors on winds so light
A mother's screams are heard.

Poor as a church mouse.

I bustle along the old wooden pews,
With their splinters of wood and rusting screws,
Scurrying, hurrying, sniffing around,
Searching for food in this haven I've found,
Food is so scarce, in God's humble house,
That's why I'm so poor, a lowly church mouse.

I run free down the aisle in darkness of night,
When no one's around, not a soul in sight,
O'er well worn inscriptions written on tombs,
Into the transept and quiet little rooms,
Rooms where old cassocks are neatly racked,
And velvety hassocks haphazardly stacked.

No one comes into this church any more,
The bells never ring - no one opens the door,
The choir doesn't meet for practise each night,
The old vicar calling is a rare sight,
It seems they've abandoned God's lovely house,
And I'm doomed to die, a lonely church mouse.

This is another nostalgia poem and it really happened, when we moved in to a new house my Mum heard one of the onlookers say, 'Ooh they haven't got a telly' Mother went straight into town the next day and bought one on the never never, (hire purchase)

The Television

I recall our first telly, two men brought it in,
It looked like a coffin, it was long, brown and thin,
The screen was quite small and difficult to see,
But the day it arrived - we all jumped with glee,
I remember we moved to our house in that street,
The neighbours all gathered to meet and to greet,
As the van was unloaded by the man with beer belly,
We heard someone shout 'Cor, they ain't got a telly!'
Mum got one delivered from local shop's stock,
She couldn't pay for it so it came on the knock!

Well, a big burly fellow turned up with his mate,
His seventeen stone frame almost broke our gate,
As he barged his way through toting ladders and all,
he nearly broke the window and scraped the front wall,
Up the ladder he climbed, the aerial rigger,
The chimney was big, but the aerial was bigger,
He grappled and grunted for over an hour,
While downstairs his thin mate was fixing the power!
The wooden rungs creaked as he came down the ladder,
I felt glad he was down.. but the neighbours were gladder!

He swivelled the black knob as we froze on the spot,
There was a crackle - a hiss- and a great white dot
appeared on the screen.. then a girl with long hair,
she didn't do anything but we still sat and stared,
An interlude came and a potters wheel appeared,
We knew nowt about telly - but this seemed a bit weird,
Our joy turned to sadness as the younger man said,
'By the time programmes start, you'll be tucked up in bed,
but Mothers hour's on tomorrow, from one till two,
with Woodentops , Andy Pandy and Looby Lou.

We were all so excited that none of us slept,
But when one o clock came.. well, I could have wept!
It wasn't the Woodentops - Andy or Looby Lou,
It was Rag, Tag and Bobtail who came on till two!
Next day was no better - it was the Flowerpot Men,
There was some sort of weed with pots Bill and Ben,
But at night we had Robin Hood and Crackerjack,
with Double or Drop and a cabbage if you slacked.
We also had Picturebook and Muffin the Mule,
Then I reached five years and had to go to school!

_____

I Love the coming of Spring and have written quite a few poems on the subject, this is one.

Spring is Born.

I woke this early April morn,
to find that Spring again was born,
Imagine now - this English scene,
with fresh ploughed fields and hills of green.

The stream flows gently past the Mill,
and oak stands strong upon the hill,
New budding leaves unfurl on trees,
as young lambs bounce around with ease.

I hear the sound of birds up high,
among white clouds up in the sky,
New life and splendour of new spring,
and all new life that it will bring.

The stunning snowdrops and bluebells,
beneath the forest as it swells,
Chasing away the winter gloom,
replacing it with light and bloom.

The ploughman lets horse harness yield,
as seedsman sows the new turned field,
Brown furrows deep upon God's earth,
sown to produce the soil's new birth.

My wooden planter stands outside
just three feet long and one foot wide.
Now showing long awaited flowers,
brought to life by April showers.

Fresh blossoms overhang the wall,
from where I hear the cuckoo's call,
Bells in the hamlets start to ring,
ring out you bells... welcome the spring!

_____

Love Story.

My heart with pleasure fills today,
Your wonderous smile you send my way.
Thine eyes they speak...so eloquent,
Reminding me of long nights spent.
In arms you wrapped around me tight,
Throughout the failing candlelight.

I kiss your lips and lose control,
Desire your love, body and soul,
Your face a work of art - those eyes
can love another - or despise,
Yet, those in love are not so blind,
When in another's arms entwined.

Seas ebb and flow when you are near,
My life, it fills, with thoughts sincere,
Where other men may speak of you,
approvingly... as prone to do,
Then, let me love you, stay the night
And we'll be one come morning light.

I have always loved the Enid Blyton books about the Famous Five, this was the inspiration to write this poem, whether I have been successful will be up to you.

Devon Tea

Down winding lanes with giant hedgerows,
we were wending our way on holiday,
Glimpses of fields, where golden wheat grows,
quickly spotted through passing gateways.

Those little roads, were not very wide,
should two cars meet along the way,
Both drivers would then have to decide,
who should now back up and then give way.

So Dad backed up, 'cause he was polite,
driver waving to us as he passed,
By now dear Dad was getting uptight,
getting so hot from being harassed.

Respite from tall hedgerows as we came,
to a village with a pub and store,
A row of white cottages all the same,
with tiny windows and old oak door.

Sat at a table, had Devon cream tea,
then it was back down the winding lane,
Got round a bend, first glimpse of the sea,
our great excitement we could not contain.

Over a panorama of rolling hills,
our modern car was struggling to climb,
Then a farm entrance with various spills
like horse manure, straw and white lime.

Over one more hill, then we were there,
the most beautiful cottage ever seen,
The smell of the sea was in the air,
overlooked pastures of brown and green.

Scent of roses around the front door
of the thatched old house where we'd spend,
the rest of the summer, just offshore,
in this place of peace, a real Godsend.

We soon unpacked and went for a stroll,
down the footpath that led through the trees,
Into a field, where Donkey and foal,
ignored us and our 'come on' pleas.

Over a stile, where a leaning signpost,
pointed the way to Bideford or Bude,
Both narrow paths led along the coast,
in green fields where cows lazily chewed.

We went toward Bude, over another stile,
into a lane with a silvery stream,
Alongside, brambles for half a mile,
bereft of it's black fruit it would seem-

-Blackberry pickers had been there before,
to make fruity jam and home-made wine,
Red Campion, Cow parsley for evermore
show their heads and with brambles entwine.

We thought it best to make our way back
past the Rectory and Old Smithy Inn,
Villagers here had this strange old knack,
of naming homes after what might have been.

As we sat down to tea, full of glee,
recounted our adventures to Mum,
As she tucked us in, we'd have to see,
what great adventures were yet to come.

First Morning.

To wake and to find you here at my side
In the cool stillness of early morn
You stir so softly, hand touches mine
Full of embrace and empty of scorn
Soft full red lips gently brush mine
In the cool and quiet of early morn
Your eyes slowly open, I reach out for you
As together once more our bodies are drawn

Oh soft warm embrace, I need you my love
In the cool stillness of this our first morn
In this moment forever I wish we could stay
I need you and love you my bride of the dawn

_____

Peace and Tranquility

Well, Sunday morn has come around,
I sincerely hope that you have found,
The peace and calm that you all seek,
A love so strong, you are at your peak,
If not, perhaps it'll be this week.

Perhaps this week you'll find your true
peace and quiet, just meant for you,
An inner peace, sent from our dear God,
A peace of sorts, that will feel odd,
Upon that rocky path you trod.

We all need to think of others,
Fathers, Mothers, Sisters, Brothers,
Those whose faith has been sorely tried,
Those who have loved ones, who have died,
Those who are on a downward slide.

So, this week, as you go about,
try to keep calm, don't scream, don't shout,
Think of others and not yourself,
Those who are ill, or in poor health,
Then in your heart, you'll have great wealth.

I wrote this when it was becoming abundantly clear that many thousands of people were now fully dependent on food banks and handouts.

An Old English Town

Parallel Tram lines, trams all alike,
Those new fangled penny farthing bikes,
The old cobbled streets and horse drawn carts
where to and fro the wise cabby darts,
The hustle and bustle, an old English town,
where people don't smile, but wear a frown.

Black smoke, grey smoke, from dark chimney tops,
Brewers' drays strewn with barrels and hops,
Foul factories where poor children go
when moon is high, till the sun is low,
The feeling of an old English town,
where children slave, till the sun goes down.

Old market, where the bartering is done
money for food, but credit for none,
Waifs and strays stand at soup kitchen queues,
no money, no pride, no coat, no shoes,
Nothing left in this old English town
where cries for help, by laughter are drown.

Today it's different, so they say,
Children roam free, they run and play,
But look closely around, you'll still see
that famous adage, nothing's for free,
Hustle and bustle, of a new English town
Where sometimes a smile, but mostly a frown.

Old unused church is where people go,
Because bills are high, wages are low,
Memories return, soup kitchens of old,
where people are sitting, out of the cold,
Food for the hungry, an English town
where starving people, are badly let down.

The hungry, the helpless, on our streets,
Children with holes in shoes on their feet,
Rich folk running the country for you
how real people live, they haven't a clue,
They should all visit this new English town,
be damned ashamed, and hang their heads down!

On 1 November 1666 farm worker Abraham Morten gasped his final breath - the last of 260 people to die from bubonic plague in the remote Derbyshire village of Eyam. Their fate had been sealed four months earlier when the entire village made the remarkable decision to quarantine itself in an heroic attempt to halt the spread of the Great Plague. This is the story of the villagers who refused to run.

Eyam – The Plague Village

In the year of our Lord sixteen sixty five,
At the village of Eyam in Derbyshire Dale,
A bundle of cloth was delivered, alive
with fleas carrying plague, so goes the tale.

The first man to die from the dreaded black death,
Was an assistant who untied the bundle,
Unlucky George Viccars drew his last breath
and was transported away in a trundle.

Infection spread rapidly throughout the house,
Killing his stepsons, the Tailor and neighbours,
They all took precautions, with cleanser did douse
but it quickly spread, in spite of their labours.

It wiped out households yet left some others,
The plague hit the youngest and oldest the worst,
Young children buried by fathers and mothers
but inevitably whole families were cursed.

Doctors knew nothing and under their noses,
Ladies held flowers they kept around their gown,
'Ring a ring of roses, a pocket full of posies
Atishoo! atishoo, they all fall down'

During the cold winter there was some respite,
The fleas were fewer as rats lay in slumber.
People celebrated the end of their plight
but in Spring the rats returned in great number.

The Reverend Mompesson called people together,
'We must think of others, Isolate ourselves,
We must trust in God, we will brave the weather
you should look to God, in your hearts you must delve'

'If others should spurn us don't think them remiss,
Quote the gospel of John, the message he sends,
Just say; Greater love hath no man than this,
that a man lay down his life for his friends'

So the boundaries were drawn and lines well kept,
The cordon around the community strong,
Villagers knelt, they prayed and they slept
prayed that the plague would end before long.

Each family would quickly bury their own,
Close to their homes not on consecrated ground,
Nor anywhere by fields where crops would be grown
but as close to wherever the body was found.

Disinfected money was left on the well,
Soaked in vinegar to stay the infection,
Deposits for food to nourish, as well
as affording others safety and protection.

November sixty six the last person died,
Those selfless people with Christian conviction,
Had stayed together, the Black death defied
That terrible disease made its final eviction.

The price was high, two hundred and sixty dead,
Out of eight hundred people at the start,
So every villager raised up their head
gave thanks to God for keeping their heart.

Brock the Badger

The charming Brock we all love and know,
Made famous in most children's tales,
This beautiful creature puts on a show,
Around the country, o'er hills and dales.

Down in the copse or deep in the wood,
The badger lives freely 'neath the ground,
In ancient tunnels where Grandparents stood.
Is where this nocturnal animal's found.

With its elongated Weasel like head,
Part blindness but keen sense of hearing,
Good nose ensures its always well fed,
As it mooches for food in the clearing.

A diet of Hedgehogs or bulbs in the field,
Earthworms, berries or dropped fruit,
Most things that nature itself can yield,
Whatever the wily Badger can loot.

The sett can stretch more than a mile,
Where litters are nurtured and bred,
In underground tunnels so versatile,
They're a home, a birthplace, a bed.

Short stumpy legs with long reaching claws,
A great excavator of tunnels,
Strong sturdy animal with vice like jaws,
Now the subject of Government culls.

I pray the order to cull is repealed,
This wonderful creature, the places it lives,
In woodland, wetland, outlying fields,
And that Governments realise the pleasure it gives.

Leaving

I turned and looked from off the hill,
Onto the place where I was born,
The dark and dire satanic mill
Where Father toiled until it killed
his mind, leaving his life timeworn.

A working man , Weaver by trade
With principles that kept him true,
He was overworked and underpaid
By Masters who his life did raid,
Retirement was long overdue.

At age of almost sixty nine
Still working for his meagre pay,
Poor health was just on borderline
With weakened legs and bent old spine
Whilst walking home he lost his way.

Trod on loose stones upon the bank
And tumbled down toward the stream,
Under dark waters quickly sank
Down to the mud so dark and dank
His footing he could not redeem.

I buried him by my own hand
Next to Mother, a long time gone,
His funeral wasn't very grand
The Vicar's words were very bland
Those sad words written by anon.

Now I leave this dirty old town
Its blackened walls covered in grime,
My trophies I gladly lay down
Leaving behind my weary frown
Never to return in my lifetime.

Contradiction

Too many questions for one to survive,
Not enough answers for anyone alive,
Too many rules for people to comply,
not enough strictness so say you and I,
Too many people walking this earth,
not enough adults, to sustain future birth,
Far too much Autumn and Winter we fear,
Spring and Summer never seem to be here.

Too many rich people, who just sit and shirk,
not enough labourers to do all the work,
Too many man-wars that never will cease.
not enough loving and not enough peace,
Too many words written of all these dreams,
we don't do enough to help, so it seems,
Next time think, before you bemoan your lot,
be thankful, be grateful, for all you've got!

I wrote this after watching Derek Akora in an episode of Most Haunted, the scene where he supposedly shouted this in a trance went viral.

The Highwayman, Wife and Maid

A tale to tell I have for you,
About a Highwayman I knew,
He robbed the rich - gave to the poor,
Though lived a bad barbaric life,
And took up with the Squire's wife,
To sate delusions of grandeur.

The Squire knew but did not mind,
His wife being the hefty kind,
He liked them slimmer in his bed,
And took up with his servant Sue,
At night in chambers he would do,
Those naughty things to her instead.

The things she did just drove him wild,
With new positions she compiled,
She tied him up with silken rope,
One night while she was sat on top,
And tanning him with razor strop,
His heart gave out without much hope.

Within one week the Squire's wife,
With Highwayman began new life,
They made love afternoon and night,
But Dick her lover soon got bored,
Of loving Mary - being Lord,
And had young Sue within his sight.

But Mary she knew naught of this,
Each night would end with loving kiss,
Thought they were both of one accord,
But every night in dark and gloom
Dick visited Sue's own bedroom,
As Mary lay asleep and snored.

53

Once Mary had a real bad turn,
Ate chicken that gave her heartburn,
To find her man she wandered off,
Looking for cuddles... nothing more,
She passed outside Sue's bedroom door,
And heard as Dick plighted his troth.

She burst right in - tripped o'er Sue's cat,
The whole house shook as she fell flat!
She hit the floor and smashed her head,
Dick pulled away from young Sue's arms,
Said "don't be silly dear - stay calm"
But Mary lay there... very dead.

They panicked - buried her so deep,
And every night they tried to sleep,
They'd hear her shouting from the hall,
Those words made them feel very sick,
'Mary loves Dick - Mary loves Dick'
That's what the poor Squire's wife would call.

Metal, stone or wood?

Some things that are made from cold hard steel
Lead on to death and tells us beware!
The sharpened sword of Damocles is real,
Hanging from a thread - suspended there!

Armoured cars and suicidal tanks,
Atomic bombs in bright steel casing,
Spears and arrows projected from ranks,
Toward the enemy they were facing.

Hard stone does not fare any better,
Medusa could give people a glare,
When Poseidon set out to get her,
Venomous snakes replaced her blonde hair!

The Decalogue was written in stone,
And handed to Moses on Mount Sinai,
Tablets telling us we should atone,
Should worship one God - not sin or lie.

And stone will finish our lives for us,
Epitaph written on a cold tomb,
We leave as we came,- no fear no fuss,
Are re-united with mother's womb.

Jesus was born in wooden stable,
To a world of pity and pathos,
Wafers and wine on Altar table,
Remind us he died on a wooden cross.

So, bring forward the tables - the chairs!
Bring the Fiddles, the Guitar, the Harp,

The saw, the plane, the chisel that pares,
The spokeshave, the drills - lovely and sharp

For I'm a skilled man - mostly self made,
A God fearing man, Noble and good,
Like Joseph a carpenter by trade,
A lover of all things made from wood!

The Wall

With daring on this crumbling wall
the slugs and snails will slowly crawl
Through Buddleia's spread wide and tall
a few miles from the urban sprawl.

When skies are blue and breezes bland
and planting out is neatly planned
about fertile and luscious land
the Phlox and Hollyhocks are spanned.

The morning sun gives quite a boon
to Goats beard that will die at noon,
While skylarks in the trees will croon
and Daisies dance to summers tune.

A Rambling rector climbs the wall
its fragrant flowers white and small,
A frame for insects - dense and tall
that leave red hips in Autumns fall.

Borders crammed with budding flowers
shows someone's toiled for hours and hours,
Above - the Lily overpowers
as down below Lobelia cowers.

And here on fresh cut grass I lie
Just looking up at cloudless sky,
As hardened world flows quickly by
I breath a long contented sigh.

This was the very first serious poem I wrote so it holds a special place in my heart, I hope you enjoy it.

Antoinette

Twas a warm summer night by a soft flowing stream
I first met my love Antoinette
As she sat on the banks combing long flaxen hair
A lust o'er my whole body swept

'Good evening sire, she spake unto me
And she bade me sit down by her side
'Tis a strange sort of place for a maiden to be
At this hour of the day' I replied

As I sat down beside her I caught the sweet scent
Of her body like Lilies in spring
Her eyes were of sapphire Her lips were full red
And ruby dress to young curves it did cling

We sat and we talked till the oncoming night
Drove the hills all around from our view
The full moon rose high causing shadows to flit
And the course of true love to run true

Oh Antoinette, my dear Antoinette
How my fool heart she'd already captured
With her beauty, her charm, her exquisite form
My thoughts and mind were enraptured

These thoughts to myself I could not contain
'My darling' I started to say
But gently so gently her soft lips brushed mine
Throwing all thoughts into disarray

Her sweet tender body I draped with my own
That moment I'll never forget
For twas there on that bank by the soft flowing stream
I made love to my sweet Antoinette

I woke the next morning my clothes soaked with mist
As a woodsman stood at my side
I looked around hastily for my sweet Antoinette
'Where is she?' to the man I cried

'You were alone when I woke you' the woodsman replied
'Who do you seek around here?'
'A young girl, Antoinette whom I met here last night'
The man's face went white with fear

'You couldn't have seen her, for a year ago today
I came to the stream and I found
The daughter of my neighbours lay on this bank
She'd slipped into the stream and drowned

A new Red Dawn

Have you ever thought how red affects our lives,?
How throughout history, it ducks and dives,
A three letter word used for love, hate and rage,
Red hot off the press it's always front page.

Red is the colour if you're deeply in love,
Lay with your lover , red sunset above,
A dozen red roses will show her you care,
a good sign of passion is red flowing hair.

The Red Badge of Courage, about civil war,
blood a sign of bravery, and nothing more,
The angry red planet also known as Mars,
Man walks with Red flag, in front of cars.

If your looking for love one dark cold night,
Look for the door with a red shiny light,
Don't get embarrassed, you'll have a red face!
if you paint the town red with satin and lace.

Red is associated with pain and sin,
a sign of real evil, and the devil within,
Though your sins be scarlet, we all know
As Isaiah said, they'll be as white as snow.

The Antichrist always depicted in red,
Breathing fire and spouting horns from his head,
The book of revelation, a Red monster at one.
with Woman on his back, whore of Babylon.

A footballer who thinks he is brave and hard,
Fouls an opponent, shown a red card,
Red alert given, for an enemy attack,
Red eye on a photo, taken with a Kodak.

A red herring will throw them off the scent,
A red rag to a bull is anger to vent,
To catch them red handed, is caught in the act
To a Lawyer, red tape is a matter of fact.

In India, red sari, sign of the blood
offered by Father, signifying good,
Feet painted with henna, to show good order,
once married the sari will have a red border.

Old chairman Mao, had his little red book,
In Japan a red wedding dress brings good luck,
In Canada a Mounties red uniform awaits,
In the U.S the republicans hold all the red states.

So when you get angry, Don't just see red,
Think what you"re doing, be happy instead,
Change your own colours, change your bad ways,
and you'll surely have, lot's of red letter days!

---

*One of my favourite poets was Alfred Noyes, I read his poem
The Highwayman when I was about eight years old, it left a
lasting impression on me, so I have attempted to replicate the
style of the poem here.*

A Highwayman's Faux Pas

I sit here in the darkness, the gloom of Worcester gaol,
I sit alone in the darkness, yet within my head a tale,
A borrowed quill and paper, lone candle for my light,
I need to ease my conscience,
My conscience, my conscience,
I have need to ease my conscience, to you this stormy night.

Just seven days ago this night, no moon seen in the sky,
I waited 'neath the darkened woods, for travellers passing by,
I heard the wheels, the horses neigh, primed my pistols ready,
I waited for the carriage,
the unsuspecting carriage,
I waited for the carriage, my pistols hand was steady.

I jumped out from my hiding place, into the road from hell,
The horses reared, the voices screamed, and then I gave my
yell,
'Give your coins or lose your life, stand and give your purse'
Then those eyes I noticed'
Those dark ebony eyes,
Those ebony eyes I noticed, her beauty was my curse.

For while her beauty held my gaze, just seconds and no more,
A brave young lad jumped from the coach, looking to even
score,
My pistol primed, pointed at her, flashed in the dark of night,
She clasped her chest,
her blood red chest,
She clasped a hand up to her chest, eyes slowly losing light.

I turned my horse, headed back, to the Inn from whence I came,
My head it spun; my heart, it raged, my mind was full of blame,
My forehead damp, my hands they shook, as they cupped the

rum,
My hands, they were trembling,
trembling, trembling,
My hands they were trembling, my fingers were feeling numb.

'Twas just one hour when they arrived, bursting through the
door,
Those redcoats armed, the young lad pointing, eyes looked to
the floor
They wrenched me from that pitiful place, slamming me in
chain,
then brought me here to Worcester,
the old town of Worcester
They brought me back to Worcester, where I do now remain.

Till noon arrives tomorrow, when gallows are complete,
When high upon those gallows, my maker I shall meet,
But I meet him with a reverence, my heart shall be unladen,
For I never intended murder,
cold blooded murder,
I never intended to murder that enchanting lovely maiden.

Becky the Witch

Becky Swann was a witch, so the stories do tell,
lived in an old cottage down in Trimpley lane,
She had three old black cats, had four dogs as well,
they say when she drank, she was close to insane.

The sign o'er her door showed qualifications'
'Town and country writer to all known parts
no need to apply without recommendations,
I'm wrongly used and walk with God in my heart'

But she embezzled money from a young maid'
The stern Judge who tried her, sent her to gaol,
On sentence, she turned to the Judge and said,
'you'll die afore I'm out, your family will wail'

Just a few days later, the old Judge dropped dead,
Becky's reputation was spread far and wide,
Locals visited Becky, troubles they shed,
she could tell their future, but mostly, she lied.

Then one night a weird thing occurred in town.
A big black cat scared all the dogs with its din,
It scared the old witch, brought her confidence down,
the beast scratched at her door till she let it in.

After a time, the locals realized that,
she hadn't been sighted for three days or more
not since that dark night, she let in the black cat,
they gathered some men and broke down her door.

The black cat was sat by a pile of grey ash,
yet there was no smell of smoke in the room,
the beast disappeared up the flue in a flash,
and by looking around they could only assume-

-something eerie had happened the previous night
nothing else in the room was even singed,
Not one of her pets were anywhere in sight,
so they reckoned old Becky had boozed and binged-

-then tripped over the beast, fell into the fire
But no fuel had been lit within the fire grate,
was pointed out by the knowledgeable squire,
who left the townsfolk to sit and cogitate

They took her ashes to St Mary's churchyard,
but to enter the church would have been bad
They put them in the ground, frozen and hard
to see the end of Becky, people were glad

But on a full moon at night on Trimpley hill,
if you look carefully you'll see Owls and Bats,
and when it's freezing cold, you can see her still,
riding along on the back of a black cat!

_____

I remember with great fondness the Punch and Judy shows at the seaside when I was a child, but the audiences were becoming less and less with the advent of television etc.

The Punch and Judy Man.

Shuffling along, back bent with pain,
Mere walking has become a strain,
Trouser bottoms brushing the ground,
Old shoes are tied, taped and bound.

Deep rugged lines upon his face,
The furrowed brow time's put in place,
Sets out his stall where e'er he can,
The lonely Punch and Judy man.

His hair unkempt - greasy and long,
Though no one cares, he's still headstrong,
Puts on two matinees a day,
E'en though the crowds have gone away.

Hands so arthritic from the knocks,
Can't pull the puppets from the box,
A long greatcoat hides skin and bone,
Though you will never hear him moan.

The days of money now long gone,
Kids disappear in summer sun,
Tablets, computers, wi-fi game,
Today's technologies to blame.

Most kids think puppet shows puerile,
Not tempted by the crocodile,
The constable, the ghost, the clown,
Baby and Toby all let down.

And so he sets up on the streets,
A little toddler sucking sweets
is waiting for the twelve noon show,
But mum and dad just want to go.

"Come on Leo, let's not stop here,
We'll get an ice-cream down the pier"
But mother's pleas fell on deaf ears,
Drowned out by little Leo's cheers -

- as the curtain opened and Punch
hit the Croc with a splendid crunch,
The little lad giggled with glee,
Soon others stopped so they could see.

And before long the bench was full,
as Toby bit the constable,
Toddlers roared in fits of laughter,
This was what the kids were after!

Friendly violence - lots of fun,
Out there in the midday sun,
Inside the booth the old man sweat,
This was his best audience yet.

His fingers didn't feel numb at all,
His back was straight, he stood so tall,
His life was once again on track,
The Punch and Judy man was back!

I don't normally do environmental poems but something inside my head kept urging me on to write this.

The Eve of Destruction

What more can this world ever give,
than precious air that we may live,
The gift of sight that we may see,
what God has given us for free!

The power of speech... that we may talk,
the power of feet that we may walk,
Two arms to feel our way through life,
the power of words to end our strife.

But even God with all his power,
just cannot save us in our hour,
of self-destruction, pain and greed,
from man born of the devil's seed.

We soil pure air with factory smoke,
we sit and watch our children choke,
We've turned our world into a joke,
While 'neath the earth the fires are stoked.

We cut down forests, clear the land,
destroy his earth - don't understand,
What we are doing to his world,
while bullets fly, and bombs are hurled.

The oak stands tall for all to see,
why can't that oak be you and me?
It's roots are firmly 'neath the sod,
Its branches reach above to God.

Beneath that oak - two roads diverge,
but from which one will we emerge?
One lights the way, the other's black,
choose wisely world, You can't turn back!

End of Day.

When darkness falls upon the land
and all the work is done,
I sit here quiet - glass in hand
to watch the dying sun.

As shadows flit across the room
the cat jumps on my lap,
And purrs so softly in the gloom
a melancholy chap.

The clock stands on the mantlepiece
strikes nine with such fine tone,
Then as the chimes start to decrease
I prime the gramaphone.

And listen to Handels Messiah
sitting with arms unfurled,
With sleeping cat and roaring fire
all is well within my world.

Baby Talk

I'm not one for gossiping or spreading small talk,
But my big Sis told me I was brought by a stork.
It was seen with a bundle above our roof top,
Addressed to mum, almost ready to pop.

My big brother said I was born in a barn--
Trust me, dear reader - he was spinning me a yarn.
If I was born in a barn, surely I'd be a horse,
A bleating sheep, or a cow, of course!

Dad said I was born neath a gooseberry bush--
I don't mean to be rude, but that's a load of tush.
If I was born there, I'd have been pricked by a thorn,
and surely would have popped, perhaps never been born.

So I lie in my cot feeling nice and yummy,
With a rusk in my hand, and mouth full of dummy.
I found out the truth, I was told by my mummy:
She had great fun with dad - I came from her tummy!

Grandma's Cottage

An amber glow flickered all around the room
the smell of fresh baked bread filled the air
In the darkened corner among the old heirlooms
Granddad slumbered in his rustic rocking chair.

The fat cat lay purring softly on his lap
the shell finish pipe lay waiting on the rack
hanging on the hatstand was his worn flat cap
next to the immaculate Gaberdine mac.

His watch ticked quietly neath his black waistcoat
worn over the striped collarless shirt
dappled and splattered, with spots of Creosote
beneath, the polished boots of the old introvert.

The room was dominated by a black lead grate
with its side oven and trivet for the kettle
lying there on the rug, the dog would patiently wait
for his owner and master to wake and unsettle.

Out the back, in the kitchen, Grandma slaved away
pounding with a dolly in the aluminium tub
at the clothes which were gathered religiously on Monday
for Monday was wash day and made to wash, to scrub

The fireplace lay unlit, against a whitewashed wall
its mantlepiece enhanced with pelmet neath a fringe,
a tin contained the rent, should the rentman call
old iron on the hearth, too cold to press and singe.

Sleeves rolled up neatly and net upon her hair
Gran carefully fed the sheet through the mangle
once good sheets had now become threadbare
forced through the rollers they inevitably tangle.

Black on the concrete where Granddad polished boots
with brushes and brooms, or with any other means
trays of dirt on the windowsill, showing tiny shoots

hopefully lovely carrots and award winning beans.

The parlour was the best room, Grandma's pride and joy
it housed her three piece suite and oak dining table
next to a massive aspidistra which would lie
atop an old sideboard, always rocky and unstable.

At the bottom of the garden was the loo
with newspaper squares hanging neatly on a nail,
it was a terrible place when the north wind blew
or when you had to use it in the snow, sleet or hail.

I remember it as though it were only yesterday
In my minds eye - I see them standing there,
my reminiscences no-one will ever take away
but money talks and people now don't care.

The dust stirs in the memory of my mind,
a silent tear falls from my misted eyes
as I watch the cottage demolished, redefined
to make way for another great high rise.

The Telegram.

Alone she sits in dressing gown,
her world around her falling down,
The crumpled telegram in hand,
The words so blurred, so harsh, so bland.

The day had started really well,
The war was over so they tell,
In battlefields no more he'd roam,
In six weeks time he'd be back home.

Back home to sit in pastures green,
To hold the boy he'd never seen,
Now four years old, running around,
Not for him that merry-go round--

Of war, destruction, living hell
He wouldn't hear the bell's death knell,
The paper signed by foreign power,
Eleventh day, eleventh hour.

Then came the rap upon her door,
Her bones they shivered to the core,
Her legs went weak, had no control,
All hope gone from her empty soul.

He stood there quietly, alone,
That skinny boy, so barely grown,
Gave her the paper avoided her eye,
She opened it, cried 'No reply'

The words resounded in her head,
They've made a mistake, he can't be dead,
She read the name, Private Ian Pound,
Missing in action on foreign ground.

Despite her prayers he never returned,
Advances of suitors rejected, spurned,
Her heart knew no other, first true love,
Fitting together like hand in glove.

She raised her son to be a man,
He went off to war, was killed at Cannes,
A telegram once more received,
Another loved one to be grieved.

With bitter heart she struggled on,
In the shadow of World War one
and World War two, she lived her life,
Full of sorrow and full of strife.

Today she sits there, old and grand,
Two crumpled papers in her hand,
The telegrams of both her men,
She closed her eyes, joined them again.

Well that's it, my second book of poems finally completed, I sincerely hope you have enjoyed them, if you have please tell all your friends, if you know an Agent or better still a publisher then my life would be complete lol.

This book and the contents are dedicated to my Darling daughter

Vickie Harvey.

CROSSBILL GUIDES

North-east Poland
Biebrza, Białowieża, Narew and Wigry

Crossbill Guides: North-east Poland
First print: 2013

Initiative, text and research: Dirk Hilbers, Bouke ten Cate
Additional research, text and information: Kim Lotterman, Albert Vliegenthart,
Gino Smeulders, Lars Lachmann
Editing: John Cantelo, Brian Clews, Jack Folkers, Cees Hilbers, Riet Hilbers,
Kim Lotterman
Illustrations: Horst Wolter
Maps: Dirk Hilbers, Bouke ten Cate, Alex Tabak, Horst Wolter
Design: Sam Gobin, www.samgobin.nl
Print: Drukkerij Tienkamp, Groningen

ISBN 978 94 91648 00 7
© 2013 Crossbill Guides Foundation, Arnhem, The Netherlands

This book is produced with best practice methods ensuring lowest possible environ-
mental impact, using waterless offset, vegetable based inks and FSC-certified paper.

This book is created with the financial support of Swarovski Optik and
Polish tourist organisation Amsterdam.

SWAROVSKI
OPTIK

POLISH
TOURIST
ORGANISATION

Published by Crossbill Guides in association with KNNV Publishing.

KNNV Publishing

KNNV
vereniging
voor veldbiologie

SAXIFRAGA
foundation

www.crossbillguides.org
www.knnvpublishing.nl
www.saxifraga.nl

CROSSBILL
GUIDES
FOUNDATION

4

Highlights of North-east Poland

1 Visit the primeval forest of Białowieża, the benchmark of European nature.

2 Go birdwatching in Biebrza and Białowieża and enjoy close encounters with Aquatic Warblers, Great Snipe, White-winged Terns, Collared Flycatchers, White-backed Woodpeckers and all those other sought-after species.

3 Enjoy the wonderful tranquility of the traditional farmland, with its flowery meadows, the wooden houses, the families of White Storks, and the friendly people.

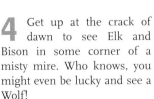

4 Get up at the crack of dawn to see Elk and Bison in some corner of a misty mire. Who knows, you might even be lucky and see a Wolf!

5 Search the little forest glades, bogs and calcareous swamps of the Biebrza and Wigry for the many rare wildflowers, butterflies and dragonflies that still occur here.

6 Rent a canoe and paddle into the true wilderness of Czarna Hańcza's endless river meanders and oxbows. Do so quietly and you may very well spot a Beaver, Otter, Elk or Crane by the river bank.

7 Go deep in the marsh of the Biebrza. Put on your wellies (or perhaps it is better to go barefoot) and wade through the wobbly peat layer to find out what the fen mires are really about.

8 Explore the culture of North-east Poland – that crossroads of Catholic and Russian Orthodox cultures, visit an ancient wooden Tatar Mosque and enjoy the fine Jewish food in Tykocin.

About this guide

This guide is meant for all those who enjoy being in and learning about nature, whether you already know all about it or not. It is set up a little differently from most guides. We focus on explaining the natural and ecological features of an area rather than merely describing the site. We choose this approach because the nature of an area is more interesting, enjoyable and valuable when seen in the context of its complex relationships. The interplay of different species with each other and with their environment is astonishing. The clever tricks and gimmicks that are put to use to beat life's challenges are as fascinating as they are countless.

Take our namesake the Crossbill: at first glance it's just a big finch with an awkward bill. But there is more to the Crossbill than meets the eye. This bill is beautifully adapted for life in coniferous forests. It is used like scissors to cut open pinecones and eat the seeds that are unobtainable for other birds. In the Scandinavian countries where Pine and Spruce take up the greater part of the forests, several Crossbill species have each managed to answer two of life's most pressing questions: how to get food and avoid direct competition. By evolving crossed bills, each differing subtly, they have secured a monopoly of the seeds produced by cones of varying sizes. So complex is this relationship that scientists are still debating exactly how many different species of Crossbill actually exist. Now this should heighten the appreciation of what at first glance was merely a plumb red bird with a beak that doesn't close properly. Once its interrelationships are seen, nature comes alive, wherever you are.

To some, impressed by the 'virtual' familiarity that television has granted to the wilderness of the Amazon, the vastness of the Serengeti or the sublimity of Yellowstone, European nature may seem a puny surrogate, good merely for the casual stroll. In short, the argument seems to be that if you haven't seen a Jaguar, Lion or Grizzly Bear, then you haven't seen the 'real thing'. Nonsense, of course.

But where to go? And how? What is there to see? That is where this guide comes in. We describe the how, the why, the when, the where and the how come of Europe's most beautiful areas. In clear and accessible language, we explain the nature of North-east Poland and refer extensively to routes where the area's features can be observed best. We try to make North-east Poland come alive. We hope that we succeed.

How to use this guide

This guidebook contains a descriptive and a practical section. The descriptive part comes first and gives you insight into the most striking and interesting natural features of the area. It provides an understanding of what you will see when you go out exploring. The descriptive part consists of a landscape section (marked with a red bar), describing the habitats, the history and the landscape in general, and of a flora and fauna section (marked with a green bar), which discusses the plants and animals that occur in the region.

The second part offers the practical information (marked with a purple bar). A series of routes (walks and car drives) are carefully selected to give you a good flavour of all the habitats, flora and fauna that Northeast Poland has to offer. At the start of each route description, a number of icons give a quick overview of the characteristics of each route. These icons are explained in the margin of this page. The final part of the book (marked with blue squares) provides some basic tourist information and some tips on finding plants, birds and other animals.

There is no need to read the book from cover to cover. Instead, each small chapter stands on its own and refers to the routes most suitable for viewing the particular features described in it. Conversely, descriptions of each route refer to the chapters that explain more in depth the most typical features that can be seen along the way.

In the back of the guide we have included a list of all the mentioned plant and animal species, with their scientific names and translations into German and Dutch. Some species names have an asterix (*) following them. This indicates that there is no official English name for this species and that we have taken the liberty of coining one. We realise this will meet with some reservations by those who are familiar with scientific names. For the sake of readability however, we have decided to translate the scientific name, or, when this made no sense, we gave a name that best describes the species' appearance or distribution. Please note that we do not want to claim these as the official names. We merely want to make the text easier to follow for those not familiar with scientific names. An overview of the area described in this book is given on the map on page 13. For your convenience we have also turned the inner side of the back flap into a map of the area indicating all the described routes. Descriptions in the explanatory text refer to these routes.

 car route

 bicycle route

 walking route

 beautiful scenery

 interesting history

 interesting geology

 interesting flora

 interesting invertebrate life

 interesting reptile and amphibian life

 interesting wildlife

 interesting birdlife

 visualising the ecological contexts described in this guide

Table of contents

List of text boxes

LANDSCAPE

The air resonates with the calls of Cranes which hide somewhere in the October fog that hangs thickly over the river. An Otter slips quietly out of the water hole on the mid winter ice. A herd of Bison breaks out of the forest cover to feast on the sprouting grass in early April. Hunderds of Black and White-winged terns flutter, turn and dive over a wet meadow where thousands of bright yellow Marsh Marigolds bloom in early May. The low evening sunbeams dance over the delicate flowers of the Creeping Lady's-tresses in the mossy forest floor of the vast and silent spruce forests... These, and thousands and thousands more of such scenes are the pixels that make up the image of north-east Poland's immense natural wealth.

The natural world of north-east Poland is extremely diverse, but has one salient feature: it is part of the so often undervalued natural treasure chest of temperate Europe – that broad belt between the Mediterranean and the northern eco-zones. All too often we admire the exotic corners of the world rather than the natural areas of 'our' part of Europe. And perhaps this is understandable, as in many places, natural areas have disappeared or are reduced to a small patch between two rapidly expanding cities. But not in North-east Poland. Here you'll find the highest concentration of large, more or less pristine habitat of temperate lowland Europe. The numbers and diversity of birds, the big mammals like Elks, Wolves, Beavers and Bison, the many rare butterflies, dragonflies and wildflowers you encounter, they are all testimony to how rich 'our' temperate European lowlands can be.

The superb old-growth forest of Białowieża (route 17).

Geographical overview

North-east Poland roughly coincides with Podlasia, a province to the north-east of Warsaw that borders, Russia, Lithuania and Belarus. The two most famous National Parks of Poland lie within its boundaries: Białowieża (pronounce Bja-wo-viè-shah) and Biebrza (pronounce Bièb-shah).
Białowieża is world-famous for being the last remaining primeval forest of lowland Europe (or nearly primeval, as you will see). It is also famous for being the final place where the last European Bison lived in the wild, and, after a short period, the first area to which it was reintroduced (see box on page 86). Białowieża is a must-see forest reserve for naturalists, birdwatchers and ecologists.
Gateway to Białowieża is the small loggers' town of Hajnowka. From here, a single road enters the forest to end at the village of Białowieża, which is the touristic centre of the National Park (oddly, Hajnowka has little to offer the many visitors that come for the great forest that begins right at its outskirts). A potholed dirt track connects Białowieża forest with the small villages and hamlets north of the National Park, which form an excellent alternative base to explore the forest.
Biebrza is Poland's largest National Park covering a huge area of floodplain of the Biebrza river. Within a European context, it is unique for harbouring a complete and largely intact river ecosystem over a huge length, and over its entire width from river channel through reed and willow swamps, to vast mires, groundwater fed swamps onto the dry moraines. Biebrza is Poland's top birdwatching region. The wide Biebrza floodplain has a narrow waist, where the provincial road 65 connects the small towns of Grajewo with Monki. On the east bank of this narrowest point, in the military settlement of Osowiec Twierdza, lies the Park's visitor's centre (where you need to buy entrance tickets to the Park). From here you can go down the Carska Droga (Tsar Road) to discover the south basin, which is the most popular part of the park. Alternatively you can explore the less visited middle and upper basin.
Mid-way between Białowieża and Biebrza (about 50 km between both) lies Białystok, the province's capital. And just west of it lies Narew National Park, covering an inland delta (see page 18 for more details) of the Narew River. Narew National Park is somewhat reminiscent of the Biebrza, which is a mere stone's throw away.
After Białowieża and the Biebrza-Narew combination, the region's third grand natural region lies north of the city of Augustów, which in turn lies a little north of the Biebrza. Here begins the hilly and lake-dotted region of Masuria which owes its picturesque landscape to the fact that it was

covered in ice during the last ice age. The huge forest of Augustów, with Wigry National Park in its outskirts is the most eyecatching feature. This *Puszcza* (which means vast-forest-with-primeval-character), which continues for many kilometres in Lithuania and Belarus, is much larger than its famous cousin Białowieża. Augustów forest is dominated by pine forest, which, although largely planted, is close enough to the northern taiga regions to have a northern atmosphere. North of Augustów lies the town of Suwałki, the last sizable town before the border. To the northwest of it the Suwałki Landscape Park is, besides being very pretty and picturesque, one of Poland's most attractive geological sites.

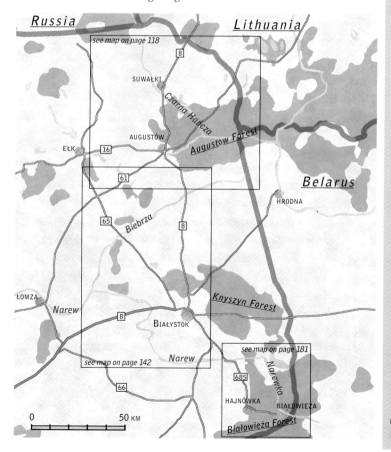

Overview of North-east Poland.

Geology

> The best route to get to know the glacial landscape is the Suwałki landscape park (route 1). Beautiful glacial lakes are present on routes 1, 2, 4 and 5. Pleistocene sand dunes feature on routes 7, 8, 9 and 12. To explore the anastomosing Narew and the meandering Biebrza, get into the canoe! See page 216.

North-east Poland is highly interesting from a geological point of view because it lies right on the edge of the southernmost limit of the land ice of the last glacial period. So part of the region (the area north of Augustów) is covered by a recent post-glacial landscape, while the region south of Augustów is much older, being formed instead by the penultimate ice age. Finally, the river sediments and peatlands, described in the hydrology chapter (page 18), are a third, and more recent, element shaping the landscape.

Ice age geology

Gentle and attractive as the landscape of north-east Poland may look on a bright spring day, it was created by the massive forces and extreme climate of the ice ages. During the second last glacial period, known as the Saalian (Wolstonian in Britain), which occurred 350–130,000 years ago, the whole of Poland was covered by ice. The last glacial, known as the Vistulian (Weichselian in Western Europe), saw its maximum extension

Upon the retreating of the ice sheet, melt water streams have created a complex pattern of deposited sediments and eroded gullies. This pattern is the base of the hilly landscape found today in the northern part of the region.

The Rutka boulder Field near Jeleniewo (route 1). Boulder-strewn fields are one of the geological features associated with ice ages.

of the ice sheet some 22,000 years ago, when it came to roughly where Augustów now lies.

Solid and immobile as such glaciers appear, on a geological time scale, they are neither immobile nor solid. Extreme pressure from the weight of the ice makes the lower part of the ice sheet semi-fluid, and even produces melt water. As the base of the glacier becomes lubricated by melt water, the glacier starts sliding over the surface. Where the ice is firmest, it scrapes the surface, leaving scars that are today the elongated lakes in the north of Poland.

When the climate warmed and the ice sheet started to melt, the torrents of melt water, still half underneath the sheet of ice, formed elaborate stream systems, which transported sediments from one place, and dumped them elsewhere. When the ice retreated and the streams dried up, it left a strongly undulating landscape, with hillocks of sediments, and fields of boulders where the finer-grained soil was washed away (see illustration on page 17). This is the landscape we find today north of Augustów (and further west in the Masurian Lake district) with the best example being the Suwałki Landscape Park (route 1). Here you'll find other ice-age related landscape features, like eskers, drumlins, moraines, pingos and kames (see box on page 17). It is quite astonishing that such elemental forces of ice, frost, torrents of melted snow – everything we find today in such raw landscapes of Iceland and Greenland – have created the lovely, flower-clad hills and peaceful blue lakes of Suwałki and Wigry!

GEOLOGY

16

The landscape south of Augustów

After the Saalien ice sheet retreated, most of north-east Poland must have
looked like the hilly landscape described just. But since then 130,000 years
of erosion and sedimentation have gone to work. Wind, rain and rivers,
continually changing their course, moderated the postglacial landscape.
Moraines and hills were flattened, while lakes, if not engulfed by large river
systems, filled up with peat and sediments. A much gentler landscape was
the result – the landscape you find south of Augustów.
Although this region did not receive another bulldozer treatment by a mul-
ti-tonned ice sheet, new landscape features were added during the last ice
age, which are still very visible today.
During the last ice age, the regions of the Biebrza and Białowieża had an
arctic climate. Plant cover was minimal, it was dry, and the wind, which
had a carte blanche in that open landscape, blew large amounts of sand
into the region. The sand was blown into dune complexes in a way that
can still be witnessed in the Sahara. These dune complexes, now covered
by dry pine forest, stands of juniper, lichens and dry, warmth-loving grass-
lands are present throughout the region, with particularly beautiful exam-
ples in the Biebrza river basin.

The creation of the marshes

After the glacial periods, north-east Poland consisted of a very softly undu-
lating landscape with a warm and humid climate, a lush vegetation and a
precipitation that was much higher than the evaporation. Ideal conditions
for large swamps, in which plant material accumulated, forming thick lay-
ers of peat. Isolated lakes are mostly fed by rainwater. Such nutrient-poor
conditions favour the growth of raised bogs dominated by peatmosses.
Since these lakes are mostly in the north, such as near Wigry, it is here
that the most beautiful examples of raised bogs, known locally as *Suchar*
(plural *Suchary*), are found.
Further south, the water formed large sluggish rivers, like the Biebrza and
the Narew. These rivers run through such wide and gently sloping valleys,
that they were able to create, over the years, huge swathes of peat. The pro-
cess is quite simple: the river (the Biebrza is a good example) has a single
peak discharge of water, namely in spring. The river spills its water over
a level floodplain, where it stagnates. Generations of marsh plants that
grow in these permanently wet conditions (even in summer, the floodplain
doesn't dry out) create a thick layer of peat. These peat layers are different
from the *Suchary*, being richer in minerals and nutrients.

Ice age geology

Glacial lake generally deep and large lakes, created by the underside of the land ice, which scarred the land. These scars, filled up with water, became glacial lakes which are now common in the northern part of the region.

Pingo ruin a small, often acidic lake (such as the suchary – see page 49), which was created when an ice lens (pingo) collapsed. In arctic conditions, ice grows in the soil, when groundwater migrates upward through cracks in the permafrost. It grows to form a small hillock, which collapses when temperatures rise or the ice breaks through the top soil.

Esker an (often kilometres) long sandy ridge, created by rivers of melt water that run in or underneath the ice sheet. Sediment silts up the waterway (like in a normal river) and after the disappearance of the ice, these sediments remain as a snake-shaped hill in the landscape.

Kame large sandy hill, created in much the same way as the Esker. A lake in the ice sheet silts up and, when the ice has disappeared, the sediments remain to form a hillock of sand.

Moraine An elongated, asymmetrical hill of unsorted sediments, pushed forward by the growing ice sheet, and left at the farthest expansion of the ice.

Boulder field large boulders were taken down south from Scandinavia when the land ice flowed south. They are everywhere in the ground, but in places where, when the climate was warming up, melt water streams were very strong, fine material eroded away, leaving the large boulders exposed.

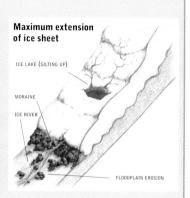

Maximum extension of ice sheet

ICE LAKE (SILTING UP)

MORAINE

ICE RIVER

FLOODPLAIN EROSION

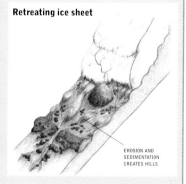

Retreating ice sheet

EROSION AND SEDIMENTATION CREATES HILLS

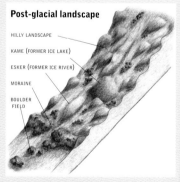

Post-glacial landscape

HILLY LANDSCAPE

KAME (FORMER ICE LAKE)

ESKER (FORMER ICE RIVER)

MORAINE

BOULDER FIELD

Hydrology

The key to much of the region's splendour lies in the fact that most rivers here have a pretty much intact hydrology. Both longitudinal (from source to mouth) and cross-sectional (from riverbed to hillside), the water follows its natural course. The Biebrza is deservedly famous for this, but the Rospuda and Czarna Hańza in the north, and large parts of the Narew and Narewka in the south are attractive for exactly the same reason.

Natural river from source to mouth

When you look at a map of the Biebrza you'll see a sharply meandering river, winding its way through the landscape. These slow moving rivers tend to flow around obstructions such as falling trees. In the curve that develops, the water on the outer edge of the arc flows faster and this force allows it to cut into and erode the outer bank. At the same time the water in the inner part of the curve slows, sometimes to a standstill, so that it can no longer carry sediments suspended in the water. Light soil particles can accumulate here in the inner part of the curve, and the original obstacle becomes a bulge in the river course. Thus loops in the river are created and accentuated. Where the river breaches the base of the loop, the isolated river arms, oxbows, are formed. These often impenetrable and quiet backwaters, form a natural world on their own (see page 35).

Canalised rivers (which applies to most of the central European rivers) largely lack the diversity of slow and faster flowing river stretches and bird-rich oxbow lakes. This is one of the natural treasures of the rivers of northeast Poland.

The Narew, an anastomosing river

Whist the Biebrza is the textbook example of a meandering river, the Narew, at least in the stretch of the Narew National Park, is an unscathed example of a much less well known and, in Europe, quite rare river type known as the anastomosing river.

An obstruction in a meandering river diverts the water flow, thereby creating the water pressure differences that inevitably start the process of meandering. In an anastomosing river, such an obstruction splits the flow, creating two river channels. They split again, and again, with some of the branches rejoining other side channels, creating an 'inland delta'.

In a way this process is like a braided river, but the difference is that braided rivers occur under conditions of highly erratic water levels. Such rivers are characterised by fairly small sand or pebble islands. An anastomosing river by contrast flows much slower and has large, marshy islands – in fact, the Narew inland delta is one huge complex of marshes, as you can see beautifully on the trail from Waniewo (route 14).

Cross-sectional hydrology

The source-to-mouth flow is only half the hydrology story. Just as important in understanding the tremendous natural wealth of the rivers of north-east Poland is the cross-sectional hydrology – the water flow from moraine to riverbed.

River water is rich in suspended nutrients and minerals, and functions as a liquid manure that is washed over the flood plain once a year. The

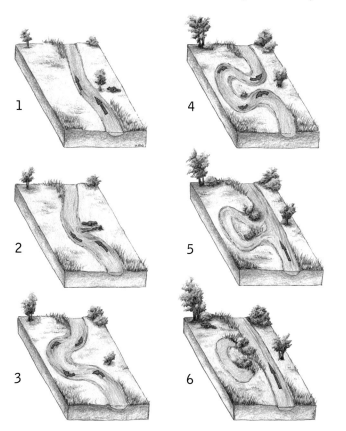

Creation of a meander
A gentle flow (1) is obstructed (by a tree for example; 2). The water needs to pass around it, whereby the flow in the outer curve is faster than that of the inner curve (3). The current slowly erodes the soft banks in the outer curves, while the inner banks silt up. The river creates a bend (4). This process continues until the curve is cut short (5). The river water takes the shortest way down and the old channel slowly fills up with marshland, until an oxbow lake has formed (6).

willows, reeds and tall herbs like nettles and willowherbs all love this kind of nutrient-rich water. But the many other species of plants, require their own water type. Thanks to an intact cross-sectional hydrology, there is plenty of space for these habitats.

Roughly 3 'types' of water can be found. Each supports a different flora and fauna. Nutrient and mineral rich river water is one. The second type is groundwater. and the third is rain water.

Rain falls on the sandy hillsides, where it quickly trickles below the surface. The sandy soils of the Biebrza are poor in minerals. But in the deeper

layers iron and calcium abound. In its unseen journey through the ground, the rainwater picks up these minerals. Locally this seepage water wells up in the floodplain, 'pushing' away the river water. Don't picture this as a dramatic and forceful interplay. Actually it is invisible to the eye, except for the difference in vegetation at these spots (and what a splendid difference this is for botanists – see page 73). Where ground water sur-

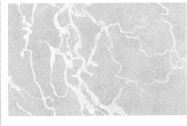

Aerial view of the Biebrza, a meandering river (top) and Narew, an anastomosing river (bottom).

faces, a special vegetation, typical in such mineral-rich circumstances, can be found. Calcium, for instance, plays an important role in plant physiology. And iron binds nutritious chemicals such as phosphate, making it impossible for plants to take these up. Instead of being harmful for the vegetation, this is actually favourable, as it benefits some of the more rare and often more beautiful flowers – especially orchids. It explains the large populations of rare orchids like Lady's-slipper in the lower Biebrza Basin. The Rospuda valley near Augustów, completely wild and impenetrable accept by canoe, is even known as 'the orchid valley' by Polish botanists – all thanks to mineral-rich, nutrient-poor seepage water!

In many river valleys, the balance between seepage and river water influence varies from place to place. River water is often (but not always) dominant closer to the river, and seepage close to the moraines. The ever-varying balance between these types of water creates the complicated and diverse pattern of vegetation types you find in these river valleys.

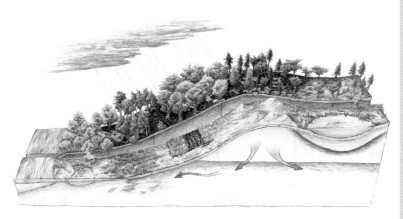

Flood forest	Alder carr and mire	Dry dunes and coniferous forest	Bog
Flooded by river water Nutrient-rich Mineral-rich	Seepage groundwater Moderately nutrient-rich Mineral-rich	Rain water sink Nutrient-poor Mineral-poor	Rain water Nutrient-poor Mineral-poor

The hydrology of North-east Poland in a nutshell. In isolated depressions, rain water stagnates and creates a nutrient and mineral poor environment. This is where you find bogs. On sandy hills, rain water sinks in the ground and reappears as ground water further down the slope. Depending on the course this ground water takes, the seepage water my be richer or poorer in suspended iron and calcium, and richer or poorer in nutrients. This is the realm of alder carr wood and (calcium-rich) fen mires. Closer to the river, temporary flooding creates an environment both rich in minerals and nutrients. Here, reeds and willow flood forests dominate the scene.

The third hydrology type is that of raised bogs. Where rainwater is unable to disappear through the surface (usually in isolated depressions) and no other type of water flows into the basin, the local environment is almost devoid of both nutrients and minerals. Here life revolves around the art of economising. Raised bogs therefore have their own unique flora and fauna. Raised bogs are fairly rare in river basins, but are frequently found fringing the smaller lakes in the post-glacial landscape of the north. There is even a name for such lakes in Polish: these are *Suchary* of which Wigry National Park is famous.

Climate

North-east Poland enjoys a continental temperate climate. The average high temperature is about 22°C – comparable to that of Amsterdam and London, although there is less precipitation with only 580 mm rain per year. Winters are much colder, with –2°C the average 'high' in January (compare +5°C in Amsterdam). It is markedly colder towards the north with Suwałki being the coldest place of Poland (–3°C the average maximum in January).

Habitats

For people from the Netherlands, Belgium, Germany and, to lesser extent, the UK, the habitats encountered in North-east Poland are familiar. The landscape is dominated by various types of deciduous and coniferous forests, marshes, mires, bogs and meadows. But their vast extent and their extraordinary unscathed state, make them special – so special in fact, that students and scholars from these countries come here to see 'their' nature in its pure and unspoilt form.

The large old-growth forests, impenetrable floodplains and freely meandering rivers are indeed two of the great draws of North-east Poland, but often people will find themselves just as enchanted by the picturesque countryside. The flowery meadows bloom, the orchards echo the calls of Grey-headed Woodpeckers and Wrynecks, wooden farms are topped by Storks' nests and larkspur-fringed fields visited by probing Hoopoes. The nature that co-evolved with mankind is just as impressive as the relics of primeval nature.

Cross-section of the habitats of North-east Poland in different stages of succession from river to ridge.

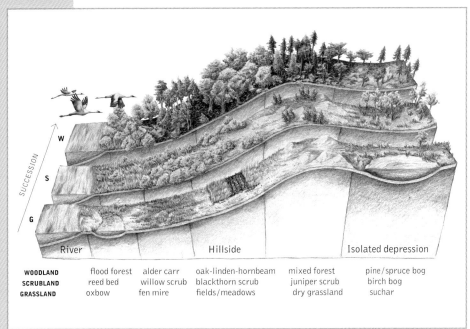

	River		Hillside		Isolated depression
WOODLAND	flood forest	alder carr	oak-linden-hornbeam	mixed forest	pine/spruce bog
SCRUBLAND	reed bed	willow scrub	blackthorn scrub	juniper scrub	birch bog
GRASSLAND	oxbow	fen mire	fields/meadows	dry grassland	suchar

The tranquil coun-
tryside of North-east
Poland. The Stork
come standard with
each farm.

We should hasten to add that this image of the natural areas is a little rose-tinted. On closer inspection, the primeval forests, swamps and mires will turn out not to be entirely free from human influence, and the idyll of a landscape evolved from an harmonious man-and-nature partnership is, perhaps, a little naïve. Moreover, the comparison with the original habitats of temperate western Europe is slightly skewed due to the presence of many strictly eastern and some northern species. But even with this in mind, North-east Poland, in particular the Biebrza, Narew and Białowieża National Parks, represents a benchmark in understanding intact temperate European habitats. Hence every naturalist ought to rush off to visit this magical place.

North-east Poland has a gently sloping terrain. One can make an idealised cross section of its habitats, going from wet depressions and river floodplains to dry sandy or loamy ridges, in which, locally, lakes and peatlands occur – see the illustration on the opposite page. Each spot on this cross-section sports its own types of habitat. Which one prevails depends on the stage of succession the particular spot has reached. A sandy moraine may be clad in a spruce-pine forest, but could just as well sport a dry grassland with juniper bushes. A soggy stream valley may be covered by alder carr, if unused by man, but if regularly cut and mown, will be a sedge marsh. Hence the illustration on the opposite page shows not one but three cross-sections – one showing forest types, one with bushes and one with various grasslands. In the 'field' you'll find a mix of all these habitats.

Forests

> The best examples of old-growth forest are in Białowieża (routes 15, 16, 17, 18 and the strict reserve – see page 207). But fitting examples can also be seen on routes 5 and 12. Large old alder carr woods are present on routes 8, 10, 12, 16, 17, 18 and 19. Oak-linden-hornbeam forests are present on routes 4, 12, 13, 15, 16, 17, 18, 19 and the strict reserve. Mixed forest and dry coniferous forest is part of routes 3, 4, 5, 8, 17, and 18. Small patches of birch carr forest is present on routes 5, 8 and 18. The best examples of pine and spruce bog forest is found on routes 2, 3, 5, 17 and 18.

Treading the mossy forest soil underneath a canopy of majestically tall trees, and watching the enormous trunks of fallen forest giants, it is not hard to understand that the forests of north-east Poland are something special. The large areas of undisturbed, natural forest are, together with the marshes, the most valuable and exciting habitat of the region.

A large part of north-east Poland is covered in forest, and the bulk of this is part of one of the three huge forest complexes: that of Białowieża, of Knyszyn and, the largest of them all, that of Augustów. In each of them, you can walk many kilometres before you break cover from the trees. And if you do enter an open area, it is only to cross a river or a forest glade.

North-east Poland is one of the more densely wooded regions of the north-European plain. Hence it seems only logical that there is such a rich flora and fauna of woodlands still present, which has become rare or extinct elsewhere. This is only partially true. The forest's natural, unscathed state contributes much more to the high biodiversity than its size.

Hey, where is the Beech?

You might have noticed that the most prominent and dominant tree species of many European forests has not been mentioned in the text.

Whereas the Beech is the ruling tree in many European forest types, it does not occur at all in the Białowieża forest and is, in fact, uncommon in all of eastern Poland. Beech thrives in Western Europe, more or less up to the German-Polish border. Towards the south and further east it becomes a species of mountain forests.

Although superficially similar to hornbeam, the ecological role (niche) of Beech is entirely different. Hornbeam is a species of the lower canopy and has nutritious leaves that enrich the forest floor. Beech, in contrast, creates an acidic, growth-inhibiting leaf litter and is an aggressive tree that can easily dominate forests elsewhere in Europe.

The absence of Beech in the Białowieża forest is one of several factors that make it difficult to take the Białowieża as a model for the natural vegetation of central Europe.

The stunning old-growth forests of the region are one of the prime attractions.

LANDSCAPE

Old-growth forest – what makes it special?

The great quality of the forests of north-east Poland is the large amount of old-growth woodland. Old-growth is not simply a collection of old trees. Rather, it is a forest that has remained undisturbed for longer than the life span of the individual trees, creating a mosaic forest of trees of all different ages. Comparing it with human society it is something very different from an old peoples' home, the human equivalent of a forest with only old trees. As in a mixed human society, old-growth has much more diversity, variety and more niches – in other words, it is much richer than single-aged stands.

There are a couple of features by which you can distinguish an old-growth forest. First there are trees of mixed, random ages. There are forest giants in the wood, certainly, but they are outnumbered by smaller trees which, in turn, are outnumbered by saplings.

Another striking element is the presence of lots of dead wood. In strictly commercial forests, a tree that dies before it is harvested equals an investment gone to waste. Dead wood on the ground is cleared to facilitate wood extraction. Yet from an ecological point of view, slowly rotting wood, whether as snags and branches, fallen or standing, is of tremendous value. The decay of wood is a reverse succession from hard and strong wood through various stages of decay, each of which is facilitated by a different set of fungi and invertebrates. In Białowieża, where the richest stands of old-growth forest occur, there are fungi and invertebrates that, within Europe, occur only here.

Uneven-aged stands – trees of all different ages – is one of the features of old-growth forest and a driving factor of the high bio-diversity found within such forests.

I'm lost in a forest...all alone

It was 1980 when the British band The Cure struck gold with their famous song 'A Forest'. Listening to the cold, mysterious sounds, typical of their music at that time, you can easily imagine yourself being lost and desperate in some moist, grim and dark forest.

Centuries earlier, the fable of Little Red Riding Hood warned hundreds of children of the dangers of the forest.

Forests are uncanny, but why?

Environmental psychologists often call upon our common descent to explain our fear of the forest. Our ancestors roamed the African savannahs, open country in which they could rely on their eyesight. Today, this is still by far our most used sense, in contrast to most other mammals, which rely on hearing and smell. That is, so it is claimed, why we generally do not like the forest.

Some sociologists have gone even further and researched the aesthetic preferences for landscapes. They discovered that, generally speaking, people like half-open landscapes with a lot of depth. They also explain this preference by referring to the favourite hunting and hiding grounds of our ancestors. This is a tempting conclusion but, whether it is true or just the speculative linking of two unrelated phenomena is difficult to prove.

Obviously, there are many more aspects involved in these psychological questions. Nevertheless it is interesting to test the applicability of the theory to your own feelings. For example, imagine yourself riding into the Białowieża forest one evening. (Why not try it while you're there?). Dump your bike somewhere alongside a dirt road and start walking into the forest. Tread the uneven soil, work your way through the haze of humming mosquitoes, and face the endless, sombre walls of trees. Will you not feel that tendril of fear that runs like a thread through the old folk stories about the dangers of the 'Great Wood'?

There is another dimension to this question that makes it still more interesting. If the primeval landscape of central-Europe after the last ice age resembles the extensive, dark forests of the Białowieża strict reserve, you might wonder whether you would have felt entirely comfortable there. Maybe modern society has indeed turned you – turned us all – into romantic souls that have come to idealise wild nature. Maybe when push comes to shove, you might indeed choose the open man-made landscape instead of nature's design. You might even choose to remain together with thousands of others in the asphalt jungle, instead of being lost in a forest all alone.

Although North-east Poland is deservedly famous for its natural landscapes, the small-scale agricultural land is just as attractive.

A decaying tree trunk. An entire food web revolves around dead wood – many fungi and invertebrates are specialised on feeding on dead wood and form in turn food for many birds and mammals.

Furthermore, be aware that although the big trees in old-growth forests have impressive girths, they are not as excessive as you might think. This is a feature of trees that grow up amongst other trees. Their struggle for life means growing in height to reach their little place in the sun. Forest trees do not need very broad trunks because their neighbours will protect them against the wind. This is in stark contrast with old trees in parks, which need to resist the elements, but are not in competition for light.

A hugely important feature of old-growth forests is their mosaic forest structure. When a forest giant comes down in a storm, it leaves a large gap, which is sometimes enlarged because it takes down other trees in its fall. (Since many old trees suffer from disease and decay, they come down at some point, which is the reason that you are not allowed in the forest during storms). Such a gap leaves space and light for a series of young saplings to grow.

Trees crashing to the ground takes place on a regular basis in a natural forest, and results in a patchy vegetation structure: there are spots with fairly young trees and underbrush, mixed with old trees with very few young trees at their base.

The mosaic structure is one of the key reasons that old-growth forest offers shelter to so many different species of flora and fauna: they offer home both to those species that seek out shelter of young underbrush, and those that thrive in tall, old trees.

In young, commercial forests, there is strong competition amongst the birds for nest sites. The fierce struggle is won by a few more aggressive species (Great Tit being one) which is one of the reasons for the low bird diversity in young forest. In old-growth, there are many holes, because old trees are prone to disease. Woodpeckers (mostly Black Woodpecker) drill holes in trees, and fungi and insects further enlarge them. In fact, nest holes form a special ecosystem within the forest, and there are even some invertebrate species that live exclusively in such holes.

The White-backed Woodpecker is a specialist of old-growth forest that benefits from the many cavities in old trees.

These holes not only provide sufficient shelter for the birds and smaller mammals, but also for their predators. The Pine Marten especially does very well in the forests of north-east Poland, and you have far more than just a theoretical chance of coming across one. Nest predation is an important limitation to the bird population of the old-growth forest. To such predators, a bird is a bird and a chick is a chick – they don't discriminate between species. Hence, the old-growth forest supports a large variety of bird species, even though their numbers are not necessarily very high.

Primeval forest – heated semantics

Often, primeval forests and old-growth forests are taken as synonyms. And when on holiday, why lose valuable time over hairsplitting about definitions? Yet officially, the forests of north-east Poland, even those of the strict reserve in Białowieża, are not truly primeval. People have tampered with them, even though this was over 70 years ago and not much more than taking out the occasional tree. Therefore, some puritan ecologists insist on calling it near-primeval forest (language puritans in turn, will discard this as an oxymoron – something is either primeval or it is not). However, such forests are certainly old-growth: the occasional extraction of trees in recent history does not affect the features that are typical of old-growth forest.

Last but not least, large old-growth forests consist of many different forest types, ranging from soaking wet alder carr wood and coniferous bog forests, to open woods on the dry ridges.

Needle versus leaf

Trees, like most plants, get their energy through their leaves which poses a problem in cold winters. North of the Mediterranean, winter is unsuitable for growth, and the cold is damaging for the leaves.

Perennial plants have two strategies to cope with this problem. Some shed the leaves in the autumn and produce new ones next season – this is the way of most broadleaved trees. Alternatively, the leaves are designed in such a way, that they can survive through winter. Hence the needle-shaped leaves of coniferous trees which go for this option.

The broad-leaved strategy is very energy-consuming, but offers the advantage of being able to 'outshade' the competitors during the most favourable months for growth – spring and summer. Carry needles and you will be able to grow in unfavourable, nutrient-poor, or very cold conditions.

Some climates favour one or the other of these strategies. You'll find coniferous trees only in very cold regions (the north) or very dry situations (Mediterranean mountains). Broad-leaved deciduous trees dominate in nutrient-rich, climatically favourable conditions, such as in temperate western Europe.

The continental climate of north-east Poland, with its long and harsh winters, is still favourable for broad-leaved trees, but not nearly as good as the mild climate of western Europe. Hence, both needle-bearing and leaf-carrying trees are part of the native flora. In the nutrient-rich places with lots of moisture, such as in the alder carr forests and oak-linden-hornbeam forests, coniferous trees are in disadvantage (although the odd spruce is still there). In more extreme conditions, like the nutrient-poor bog forests and dry sand dunes, Pine and Spruce are the dominant trees. Here the deciduous trees play second fiddle.

Various forest types

No less than sixteen types of forest have been identified in the region, which can be reduced to six major types. Two main physical conditions determine the type of forest that has developed in a certain location: the amount of water and nutrients in the soil.

The dominant forest type of the region is the oak-linden-hornbeam forest – a forest that is dominated by Pedunculate Oak and Small-leaved Linden, with Hornbeam a common tree in the lower canopy. In Białowieża, about 45% of the forest is of this type. Oak-linden-hornbeam dominates where soils are fairly rich in nutrients and where the soil is neither too wet nor too dry.

Where soils become wetter, the Ash appears and, with a further increase in soil moisture, the Alder. In swamps where water seeps out of the ground, such as in river catchments and so-called streaming swamps (slightly sloping terrain where water flows so slowly it cannot form a streambed), alder carr forests dominate the ground. Together with the oak-linden-hornbeam forest the alder carr wood is the most species-rich of the Białowieża forests. These two forest types, with their huge trees, are also the most impressive.

The Collared Flycatcher is a bird of old-growth deciduous forests.

As soon as soils become poorer in nutrients, trees become somewhat smaller. Alder, a demanding tree species when it comes to nutrients, rapidly throws in the towel and surrenders to Downy Birch, Norway Spruce and Scots Pine. This forest is typical of badly drained basins, where rain water accumulates and bogs occur. On peat bogs, spruce and pine are the dominant trees. Such sites are very poor in nutrients.

Interestingly, the very dry, sandy soils are also dominated by coniferous trees (see box on facing page). If you walk from an oak-linden-horbeam forest up on to a sandy ridge, you'll see the Linden and Hornbeams becoming scarce, and a little further uphill Pedunculate Oak as well. Silver Birch and Trembling Aspen become more common, but the number of Pine and Spruce increase. On the highest and driest places, it is the Scots Pine that is most common.

Spruce-pine and mixed forests

Occurrence Dry, sandy, nutrient-poor ridges
Dominant trees Norway Spruce, Scots Pine, Silver Birch
Others Trembling Aspen, Rowan, Goat Willow, Juniper

Characteristic This forest type has a different flora and fauna from deciduous forests. But be aware that not all forests dominated by spruce or pine are spruce-pine forests ecologically speaking. Commercial spruce or pine forests are often planted on soils which would have otherwise been covered by other forest types. Such plantations have mixed characteristics of both forest types.
Some typical species Crossbill, Pygmy Owl, Tengmalm's Owl, Hazel Grouse, Nutcracker, Stag's-horn Clubmoss, Creeping Lady's-tresses, Heather, Mountain Parsley
Routes 2, 5, 17, 18 / commercial coniferous forest: 2, 3, 4, 5, 7, 8

Spruce Bog and Pine Bog forest

Occurrence Permanently wet, nutrient poor, boggy places
Dominant trees Either Norway Spruce or Scots Pine
Others Downy Birch, Goat Willow
Characteristic This northern forest type is quite rare in North-east Poland, where it reaches its southern limit. Here it is restricted to peat-filled shallows and, especially, fringing bog lakes in Wigry and Augustów forest. The silence, rotting wood and half decayed snags make this an enchanting forest type.
Some typical species Hazel Grouse, Capercaillie, Interrupted Clubmoss, Labrador Tea, Hare's-tail Cottongrass.
Routes 2, 3, 5, 12, 15, 17, 18

Oak-linden-hornbeam forest

Occurrence Moderately moist, fairly nutrient-rich soils
Dominant trees Pedunculate Oak, Small-leaved Linden, Hornbeam
Others Norway Maple, Ash, Norway Spruce, Trembling Aspen
Characteristic This is the dominant forest type in NE-Poland. In well-developed forests (e.g. Białowieża strict reserve), trees can reach formidable heights. It is of great ecological importance.
Some typical species White-backed Woodpecker, Collared Flycatcher, Red-breasted Flycatcher, Hawfinch, Isopyrum, Peach-leaved Bellflower, Mezereon, Liverleaf
Routes 12, 13, 15, 16, 17, 18, 19

Alder carr wood

Occurrence permanently wet, nutrient-rich catchments
Dominant tree Alder
Others Norway Spruce, Ash, Grey Willow, Elm
Characteristic This is the most jungle-like forest type, due to the fact that trees are standing in water and that many trees have fallen down. The shallow-rooting spruce tips over relatively easily. Beaver activity (biting down trees and flooding the forest) creates lots of dead wood which attracts a lot of wildlife. Alder carr wood is a common forest type in Northeast Poland, but has decreased in western Europe, due to drainage.

Some typical species Crane, Green Sandpiper, Black Stork, Alpine Enchanter's-nightshade, Greater Spearwort, Touch-me-not Balsam
Routes 4, 7, 8, 10, 12, 16, 17, 18, 19

Lakes and rivers

The most beautiful rivers are the Biebrza (routes 6, 7 and 13) and Narew (route 14) in the centre, the Czarna Hańza (route 3 and 5) and Rospuda in the north, and the Narewka (route 15 and 18) and Lesna (route 17) in the Białowieża area. These routes give you a taste of the river ecosystem, but you need the canoe to fully explore them (see page 216).
Beautiful lakes are present along routes (1, 2, 4 and 5). Many artificial lakes, reservoirs and fishponds are also very rich. (route 20 and the Dojlidy fishponds of page 208). The *suchary* bog lakes (see page 48) are present on routes 2, 3 and 5.

Lake Wigry is, according to some, the most beautiful lake in Poland.

The aquatic habitats of this corner of Europe are among the richest of the continent. The crown jewel of the list of attractions is the Biebrza. It is Europe's last remaining river which flows almost completely freely from source to mouth.
The very insubstantial fall in elevation has made for slow-flowing rivers which meander widely in their broad flood plains. This meandering is caused by the way the current finds its way past obstacles in its path, like a tree felled by a beaver or a washed away chunk of peat. This process has created a myriad of old river-arms and oxbows (see hydrology section on page 18). The river ecosystem unfolds before your eyes in its full glory from

a high viewpoint like the bridge at Osowiec (route 6) or from the Burzyn watchtower (route 7), but to truly appreciate this maze of reed beds, flood forests, meanders and oxbows you'll have to explore such a river by canoe (see page 216). Narew National Park is a good spot to explore one of these mazes by canoe, although technically, this is not a meandering river but an anastomosing river (for more information on this hydrological oddity see page 18).

The river channel ecosystem

There are two salient features that make the land directly surrounding the river channel very different from the sedge marshes and swamps further away in the floodplain: nutrients and flooding. The continuous influx of nutrients from the river water favours a vegetation of strong, competitive plants rather than those able to economise. The vegetation also needs to be able to cope with continuous water level fluctuations. The two champions of this adaptive arms race are reeds and willows.

Reed beds that fringe the rivers (and in some places, lakes) are a very typical habitat, favoured by birds like Savi's, Reed and Great Reed Warblers and Bittern. Patches of willow flood forest can be found throughout most larger river basins, usually fringing the older

The slow flowing Biebrza with its peaty soils, oxbows and fields of Water-soldier provides a home to the Green Hawker.

oxbows. Only willow trees can survive the fluctuations of the water level here so other trees are rarely encountered. The flood forests create secluded and sheltered oxbows which are home to many species. The bark of the willow is a delicacy to Beavers. The Penduline Tits' elaborate nests dangle from their branches and Common Rosefinch is numerous in dense willow scrub.

After reed beds and willow thickets, the third element of the riverine ecosystem are the many oxbow lakes and river channels. Partly overgrown with Water-soldier, waterlilies and Arrow-head, they are true submerged jungles. They are the breeding and hunting ground of many different dragonflies, some of which are exclusive (and rare!) to the world of floating plants (e.g. Eurasian Baskettail, Lilypad Whiteface and Green Hawker). The floating vegetation is also where Black, Whiskered and White-winged Terns breed. The willow thickets surrounding the oxbows are mostly impenetrable. Hence they form and an important refuge for waterfowl and herons.

In places where water is pushed through a narrower valley or where the drop is a little less subtle, rivers flow faster and have a slightly different character. Peaty soils are replaced by sandy river beds and sedge marshes are replaced by arable land

The Narew near Strekowa Gora. The river's sandy soils make for a habitat suitable for the Green Snaketail.

or forest, making for a subtly different flora and fauna. A place where this difference is very visible is the mouth of the Biebrza. Here, the Biebrza with its peaty water flows out of its enormous sedge marshes and into the Narew with its sandy beds. The different populations of dragonflies that occur along both rivers are indicative of the changes in flora and fauna of the two rivers. The Green Hawker, which depends on large fields of Water-soldier, will be frequent along the Biebrza, while River Clubtail and Green Snaketail, which depend on sandy river beds, will be numerous along the Narew and almost absent along the Biebrza.

The region's smaller rivers like the Czarna Hańcza, Rospuda, Narewka and Lesna are like miniature versions of the Biebrza and the Narew. At some places slow-flowing, peaty and surrounded by sedge marshes, in other places fast-flowing, sandy and surrounded by woodland or farmland. Further north, the more recent glacial history has created a more undulating landscape (see geology section) where fast flowing streams are more frequent. The stronger current has eroded the soil, bringing the many boulders, also of glacial origin, to the surface. At some points, they bear more resemblance to mountain streams than to lowland rivers (route 1).

The Czarna Hańcza near Bachanowo. With its fast flow and its boulders it is reminiscent of a mountain stream. Here the Small Pincertail feels at home.

Lakes

The rolling glacial landscape north of Augustów has a high density of lakes. The streams flowing through the hills filled the depressions in this part of the region with water, dotting the landscape with lakes. Among them is Europe's deepest natural lowland lake, Lake Hancza in Suwałki Landscape Park (route 1). These lakes are moderately nutrient rich (mesotrophic in jargon) and in some places fringed by broad, but rather thin, reed beds.

In these, roughly the same species can be found as in the reeds beds in the river basins. Of course the lakes also harbour a lot of waterfowl. Some species that occur predominantly, or exclusively, in the northern lakes are Goldeneye, Whooper Swan and Goosander – although in true northern fashion and reflecting the relative scarcity of nutrients, these birds are spread rather thinly. Hobbies hunt over the lakes, gracefully plucking dragonflies out of the sky as if performing an aerial dance. The deeper and larger lakes regularly have Red-throated and Black-throated Diver in winter.

The Great Bittern occurs exclusively in well-developed reed beds.

The very small depressions are not fed by streams, but solely by rainwater. Such lakes are very poor in nutrients and are locally called *suchary*. They are sufficiently different from the other wetlands to justify spending a separate chapter on them. See page 49.

Fishponds and reservoirs

Finally, there are man-made wetlands: the reservoirs and fishponds. Some have developed into real pearls. Siemianowka reservoir is the most well-known example (route 20). Along its shallow shores, you'll find extensive reed beds and sedge marshes. Siemianowka reservoir is an excellent spot to look for waterfowl and herons (there is a large population of Great

White Egret) and one or two White-tailed Eagles are almost always seen when you visit the area.

The best reservoirs and ponds combine the nutrient-richness of the river ecosystems with the size of the northern lakes – hence they form an attractive cross between the two. Thick reed beds and patches of willow woodland, familiar to the river, are now easily scanned from small embankments (instead of when peering upwards into a wall of vegetation from a canoe on the river). The large extent of open water, like the northern lakes, are perfect for waterfowl, but the greater amount of nutrients support a larger number of birds. And there are fish. This seems commonplace when talking about fishponds, but for fish-eating birds, and for Otters, this is a big draw. Hence, various species of grebes and White-tailed Eagles are much more numerous here than elsewhere.

All this, of course, depends on how the ponds and reservoirs are managed. If the shores are too tidy, there is little to attract the birds, but many ponds, which are much larger and wilder places than the name would suggest, have a lot to offer.

Fishponds, like those at Dojlidy, have nutrient-rich waters that attract many species. Among them is the Red-necked Grebe, which is otherwise quite rare in the region.

Sedge marshes and Willow scrub

The best examples of sedge marshes are found in Biebrza NP and Narew NP. Routes 7, 8, 9, and 10 are especially good for exploring sedge marshes. The special vegetation of mires fed by mineral-rich seepage water are present on routes 10 and 13.

What goes for the forests, holds true for north-east Poland's marshes as well: the large swathes of wetlands that have disappeared throughout the north-European plain, still exist here. One very special type of wetland that covers a massive area in north-east Poland is the sedge marsh or fen mire. Only in Poland and Belarus do sizeable tracts of sedge marsh persist. It is the habitat for which the Biebrza National Park is famous. On a smaller scale, it is also present in some other river valleys, such as those of the Narew, Narewka and the Lesna in Białowieża, and the Czarna Hańza and Rospuda in the Augustów forest.

The sedge marshes form a vegetation zone that lies between the reedbed and willow zone close to the river, and the dry soils outside the floodplain. The sedge marshes are flooded by the river during the peak floods in spring, but for most of the year, they are dominated by standing water, often coming from seepage.

These mires are open, knee-high marshlands dominated by a sedge vegetation (mainly Fibrous Tussock-sedge and Slender Tufted-sedge). Dead plant material accumulates as the current in the broad river valley is not strong enough to carry it away, creating a layer of peat on which the sedge marshes develop.

Looking out over the Biebrza's enormous sedge marshes, you might come to the conclusion that this is one of the less interesting habitats. Endless plains of seemingly dull vegetation appearing to harbour little life. In reality, the opposite is true – the sedge marshes are of tremendous ecological value.

The undisputed highlight of the sedge marshes is the Aquatic Warbler (see box on page 99). It breeds exclusively in well-developed, large sedge marshes. Due to the disappearance of this habitat elsewhere, only the Biebrza, and two locations in Belarus, still support large populations. Other species that thrive in this habitat are the rare Great Snipe and Black Grouse, both of which use the inaccessible terrain as lekking and breeding grounds. Apart from these rarities, there are a large number of other birds that breed in the sedge marsh (see page 98).

The sedge Marshes at dusk. Lesser Butterfly Orchid is one of the flowers that thrives under the influence of calcareous ground-water swells and can be found locally in the extensive sedge marshes.

Next to various species of sedges, the vegetation consists of an attractive mixture of Milk Parsley, Marsh Fern, Marsh Cinquefoil, Marsh Lousewort, Water Horsetail, Bogbean and Early Marsh-orchid.

Amphibians too feel very much at home in this wet and sheltered environment. Apart from the widespread Grass Frog, the Moor Frog and Fire-bellied Toad are among the sedge marshes' common inhabitants. Even reptiles (Viviparous Lizard and Grass Snake) find a home here. The invertebrate enthusiast can also scan the marshes to their heart's content as a score of rare fritillaries can be found here because their host plant, Marsh Violet, occurs commonly in this habitat type.

The sedge marsh is not a uniform habitat type. The water level and quality differs from place to place, creating a mosaic of subtly different vegetations which takes a little practise to differentiate between. In places where river water has a greater influence, the vegetation is denser and taller, while in places where nutrient-poor ground water dominates, the more open types of sedge marsh come to the fore. Generally, as one moves away from the river towards the moraine, the influence of the river water diminishes and the influence of groundwater becomes more apparent.

The beautiful Bog Bean is frequent in the sedge marshes.

The Common Rosefinch is indeed common in willow scrub. It is easily recognised by its pleased-to-meet-you song.

The flora of the sedge marsh is locally influenced by base-rich underground streams of seepage water. These streams carry minerals with them and under their influence, some of the region's most rare and attractive plants occur, such as Lady's-slipper and Marsh Helleborine.

Sedge marshes as extensive as those in the Biebrza river valley are not entirely natural. The local farmers once cut the sedges annually, keeping them from developing into woodlands. The exploitation of the sedge marshes was done manually – a very strenuous labour. The soil is too soggy to support machinery and hay cutting was only done fairly late in summer when the soil is a bit firmer. With the rapid changes in agricultural practice, partly because of modern farming methods and European subsidies, this type of agriculture is no longer economically viable and many sedge marshes have been abandoned. This presents a new threat to the region's biodiversity as large swathes of sedge marsh are slowly turning into willow scrub and subsequently alder carr woods, resulting in the loss of a unique and very valuable ecosystem. Various organisations are battling this trend, one of which is the Polish Birdlife organisation OTOP, which has, with financial aid from the Austrian firm Swarovski Optik, just carried out a LIFE project to restore sedge marshes (see box on page 66).

In well-managed sedge marshes (e.g. routes 8, 9 and 10) there are patches with willow scrub. As long as the willows don't dominate, they enrich the natural value of the area. It is another tile in the mosaic of habitats which adds new qualities and benefits other species. The willows and the tall herbs that surround them are home to birds such as River, Barred and Grasshopper Warblers, Common Rosefinch and Red-backed Shrike. Elk and Beaver enjoy eating the saplings and young stems. Predators like Great Grey Shrike and Buzzards use the bushes as perches to scan the surrounding marshland so be sure to keep an eye out for them.

This mosaic of habitats that we collectively call the sedge marsh, stretches out for kilometres in the southern basin of the Biebrza, and forms the highlight of the National Park.

Fields and meadows – the traditional countryside

> Splendid traditional villages on mounds and sand dunes are along routes 5, 7, 11 and 19. The best examples of dry grasslands on sand dunes are on routes 7, 8, 9, 12 and 20. There are splendid flowery grasslands of loamy soils on route 1, but also on routes 4 and 5.

The fierce and cold gales that blew across Europe during the last ice age have deposited large amounts of sand all across the North-European plain. At this time, the landscape of north-east Poland, as much of Europe, was a tundra, over which the wind reigned supreme. It brought sand and other sediments from the largely dry area now occupied by the North Sea.

Today these sands are partially covered by sediments and peat from the many rivers and marshes that covered the region after the last ice age. But in many places sand dunes rise above the marsh. They form warm, dry and nutrient-poor environments with an attractive flora and fauna.

White Storks on the rooftop in Gugny.

Islands in marsh and forest

From an ecological perspective these sand dunes are like islands. In case of the Biebrza (e.g. routes 7, 9, 11 and 12) they are quite literally islands in a 'sea' of wet marshes. But more importantly, they are islands in a metaphorical sense, as they are isolated habitats surrounded by a hostile environment. This is where the large mammals, such as Elk, Red Deer and Wolf retreat to when the water level rises. The marsh-dwelling Grass Snake, of which there are many in the region, use the islands in the marsh to warm up. Like a natural Polish 'playa', they lay in the sand or dry grass, soaking up the warmth of the sun, before they are off to hunt in the marsh again. The sandy islands were also the places where people have built their villages and made clearings in the forest. This is very apparent on routes 11 and 12, the sand dunes of Kopytkowo and Grzedy in the Biebrza, which all used to support small villages. The hamlets in Białowieża forest are also built on elevations in the landscape.

Traditional villages

The traditional villages and hamlets are ecosystems in themselves. Most consist of only a handful of houses and a number of barns and sheds, all made from wood. They have small orchards and little plots of arable land around them which reach down to the meadows and marshes near the river below. This is the type of landscape we know from romantic paintings – the small parcels separated by hedgerows and old pollard willows, colourful, herb-rich grasslands with herds of grazing cattle and picturesque small villages.

Traditional farming methods play an important part in the conservation of North-east Poland's natural wealth.

The semi-open landscape is home to many birds, such as Serins, Spotted Flycatchers, Black Redstarts, Wrynecks, Green and Grey-headed Woodpeckers, Hoopoes and, above all, White Storks. The latter are the archetypical village birds. Indeed it would be difficult to find a village which does not have at least one pair of Storks on a chimney or roof somewhere.

The clearings within the traditional villages are also a big draw for birds and mammals from the forest. In Białowieża, the best place to see forest dwellers like Bison and Red Deer is in a corner of a forest clearing. They are drawn by the grass which provides food, but stay close to the cover of the forest. For birds of prey, such as Lesser Spotted Eagle, these clearings are important hunting grounds. The gradual closing of forest clearings around the hamlets in Białowieża has a direct negative impact on the population of this 'forest raptor'. Such an impact in fact, that the PTOP

– the regional organisation for the protection of birds – has launched a campaign to keep these clearings open.

Sand dunes

The highest, driest and nutrient-poorest dunes naturally support only a thin and open woodland of coniferous trees and juniper shrubs. In many places these woodlands were cleared and replaced with dry grasslands and a scatter of Junipers. If you come from western Europe, you'd say this was a heathland. And indeed, the ecological and physical conditions of such sites are like those of heathlands in Germany, the Netherlands, Belgium and the UK. However, in north-east Poland there is something problematic about this identification, because there is one vital element missing in these 'heathlands': Heath. On the sand dunes, there is no Heather nor any other species of the heath family – at least not in any numbers (Heather is quite common in coniferous forest in north-east Poland, but not in open landscapes). Instead, there is a thin vegetation of Grey Hair-grass, Mouse-ear Hawkweed, lots of lichens and a number of attractive wildflowers (see flora section). Another important component is Wild Thyme, which attracts many butterflies.

The warm conditions are much appreciated by grasshoppers (Blue-winged and various bush-crickets are common), butterflies and lizards. The big, green Sand Lizard in particular is a typical species of the dunes. The

Dry, exposed sand dunes form a special habitat where warmth-loving plants and animals feel at home.

birdlife of the sand dunes is not particularly rich, but there are some attractive species, such as Tawny and Tree Pipits, Woodlark and Great Grey Shrike.

Dry meadows

Most sand dunes are found south of Augustów, which was not covered in ice during the last ice age. North of Augustów, the ice produced rolling hills with a mixture of loam, boulders and sand – a blend that is richer in nutrients than sand alone. The south-facing slopes here sport dry meadows with

a stunning mixture of wildflowers. These are, above all, a botanical paradise, with attractive species like Bloody Crane's-bill, Common Rockrose, Snowdrop Anemone and various knapweeds (and many more – see flora section). The knapweeds are, like Thyme, butterfly magnets that draw many fritillaries, blues and other species. The large numbers of flowers and butterflies make these meadows somewhat reminiscent of Alpine meadows, although, in all honesty, they are not as rich in species.

The dry meadows of Suwalki Landscape Park are true butterfly magnets.

Wet meadows

Meadows are found everywhere in temperate Europe, but those in northeast Poland are of special interest. The region has not been hit as hard by the modernisation and development of agriculture as some other regions of the continent. Although Poland's entry into the European Union has brought about rapid change in the last decade, a lot of 'islands' of old fashioned meadowland still persist.

A major factor contributing to the ecological diversity of north-east Poland's farmland is the fact that many meadows lying on lower grounds are subjected to seasonal flooding. This in its turn is due to the fact that drainage is not (yet) as efficient as in the rest of Europe. The wet meadows are more akin to the sedge marshes in many respects, only they are richer in nutrients. They are soaking wet in early spring, when they attract lots of waterfowl and waders such as Ruff. Excellent examples of such meadows are found around Pulwy, Grądy-Woniecko and Zajki (routes 7 and 8). In early spring, they turn into yellow seas of Marsh Marigold, a truly spectacular sight! Later in the season, scores of Ragged Robin, Bistort and other wildflowers typically associated with 'unimproved' meadows, are a feast for the eye.

The wet meadows offer food and shelter to frogs and mice, which in turn attract many Storks and Cranes. Lesser Spotted Eagles fly above, or walk through the grass in search of frogs. After the hay is cut, suddenly the shelter the meadows provided is gone, and mice and frogs are easily caught. At this time, that is in the middle of summer, Lesser Spotted Eagles are frequently seen on haystacks, looking for prey in the recently cut meadows.

In spite of the high quality of the meadows from nature's point of view, typical meadow breeders like Black-tailed Godwit and Redshank are fairly scarce. Skylark and Corncrake in contrast, are very common.

North-east Poland also has its fair share of intensive agriculture. Fields of corn, potato, buckwheat and wheat are ecologically of lesser value despite the occasional Crane strolling through a recently ploughed field or a Montagu's Harrier hunting over the wheat.

The countryside of North-east Poland at its best: wet meadows that turn into seas of brightly coloured wildflowers in spring.

Raised bogs

The best examples of raised bogs are found in Wigry and Augustów, on routes 2, 4 and 5. Drier, less species-rich versions are present in Biebrza (route 8) and Białowieża (routes 17 and 18).

Raised bogs cover only a tiny surface of the area covered in this guidebook, but they are completely different from the other habitats in the region. Raised bogs are a breath of Scandinavia – a quiet and serene world, its silence broken only by the gentle whisper of the wings of dragonflies and the melancholy call of the cranes.

The raised bog as a habitat is defined by its soil. Like the soil of fen mires, it consists of peat; a thick layer of plant material where decay is strongly inhibited by the fact that it is waterlogged – hence little to no oxygen reaches the peat and decay is halted at an early stage. The important difference that sets it apart from fen mires, however, is that where low bogs are fed by mineral-rich seepage water and/or rivers, raised bogs are fed solely by mineral-poor rainwater, which is naturally acid.

Such conditions are found in cool, permanently wet areas with an isolated hydrology, such as depressions that are fed neither by river water nor by ground water. Rainwater will flow into the depression and remain stagnant. This makes for an extremely nutrient-poor environment in which only few species can meet life's demands.

A *suchar* or peat lake in Wigry National Park.

Tatar descendants still exist. Head to the villages of Bohoniki and Kruszyniany in north-east Podlasia to find the wooden mosques and a Muslim cemeteries that are testimony to the Tatar heritage.

Prosperity and the Golden Age

After two centuries of almost continuous warfare the population of the area was at an all-time low after the battle of Grunwald. But the Polish-Lithuanian victory heralded several decades of relative peace. A steady repopulation and economic development of the region followed, and several settlements were either founded or greatly expanded. Among them were Lomza, Tykocin, Knyszyn, Narew, Augustów, Lipsk, Waniewo, Goniądz, Sejny and Grajewo.

In 1569, the Polish-Lithuanian Commonwealth was established. It would emerge as one of the most powerful forces in Europe. At the peak of its power, its territories stretched from the Baltic to the Black Sea. This period in history is known as the Polish Golden Age. But as always, as the Commonwealth's power increased, so did the nervousness of its neighbours.

The extensive lands of the Commonwealth hosted many different ethnic groups, some of which lived at odds both with each other and the authorities. In 1648 the Cossacks, one of the peoples in the Polish-Lithuanian empire, revolted and ravaged the eastern half of the country. The enemies of the commonwealth seized the opportunity to declare war on Poland and Lithuania. The Tsardom of Moscow supported the Cossacks and occupied almost all of the Commonwealth's Ruthenian lands (parts of present-day Ukraine and Belarus). Meanwhile, the Kingdom of Sweden invaded from the west, starting a war which the commonwealth barely survived. The all but defeated King Jan Kazimierz was able to form some strategic alliances and scramble together an army with which he expelled the Swedes. However, the victory meant very little as the Commonwealth had sustained significant territorial losses. Many cities, castles and palaces had been destroyed and the retreating Swedish army had stolen everything of value they could lay their hands on, robbing the empire of complete libraries, countless works of art and most of its weaponry. One third of the empire's population was dead and the Commonwealth lost its status as a significant force in the region.

North-east Poland is a borderland of various cultures and religions. Within the region you will see Catholic churches (above), Orthodox churches (opposite, centre), Jewish Synagogues (opposite, bottom), and there are even a few Mosques of the Tatars (opposite, top). Entirely made out of wood, they are nothing like the typical mosques.

54

Podlasia was also hit hard. War casualties, famine and the plague had caused severe decrease in population of the area and many cities once renowned for their arts and crafts fell into ruin (Tykocin and Bielsk for example).

The three partitions of Poland

In the decades that followed, Białystok emerged as the cultural and administrative capital of the region. The relative freedom of religion in Poland attracted religious refugees from Russia. At the end of the seventeenth century, many 'Old Believers' (Russian Orthodox dissidents who rejected Patriarch Nikon's reforms) fled Russia and settled in Poland. Even today, some communities of practising Old Believers can still be found in the region (for example route 1 and Gabowe Grady village in the Biebrza).

The Commonwealth was still weak, and it did not take long before its neighbours laid their eyes on it once more. The Russian Empire, the Austrian Habsburgs and Prussia each claimed parts of the country in three invasions, none of which the Poles were able to repel. These invasions would become known as the three partitions of Poland. The final partition in 1795 divided the last remains of the

Traditional wooded villages are testimony to the rural history of North-east Poland.

Commonwealth's territory between the three 'superpowers' and terminated the Polish-Lithuanian Commonwealth as a sovereign state. The majority of Podlasia fell into the hands of the Prussians, although they would later cede most of the area to the Russians.

From the Tsar to Napoleon and back again

The next invasion came from an unexpected direction. French Emperor Napoleon Bonaparte, widely regarded as one of the greatest military geniuses in history, having conquered much of western and central Europe, turned his eyes to the east. In his march to Moscow, Napoleon made clever use of the anti-Russian sentiment among the Poles and employed many of them in his Grande Armée with which he soon expelled the Russians from the Polish territories. Napoleon proceeded to create the Duchy of Warsaw, a puppet state of the French Empire which the Polish nobility hoped would evolve into an independent kingdom after Napoleon's victory over Russia. In vain, however, as Napoleon's 1812 invasion of Russia (with a substantial contingent of Polish troops) failed miserably and the pursuing Russian armies recaptured most of the Duchy of Warsaw while the rest of the territory was restored to Prussia.

After Napoleon's final defeat, the Polish Kingdom was created in union with the Russian Empire. Although enjoying substantial autonomy on paper, this kingdom was very much a part of the Russian Empire.

The Russian Tsars who now ruled the eastern half of Podlasia were as beguiled by Białowieża Forest as the Polish Kings had once been and a royal palace was built on the site of Sigismund's hunting lodge. Bison and other large herbivores were bred in large numbers in the forest to ensure there would be plenty of animals to shoot on the increasingly decadent royal hunting parties. This is the first true crack in the reputation of Białowieża as a truly primeval forest.

Anti-russian sentiments – the partisans

The Polish state had very little power, but the Poles themselves were not so easily defeated. A long struggle ensued to free themselves from oppression. The first act was a reaction to Prussian authorities that imposed high customs duties for transit of Polish goods through their territories in 1821. This severely crippled the Polish economy, which had no seaports of its own. In response the Poles build a canal to bypass the Prussian Baltic seaports – the Augustów Canal (route 5) – which was to connect the Polish heartland to the Baltic Seaport of Ventspils. The canal started from the Biebrza river, making use of a glacial depression in the southern part of the Augustów Forest. The canal has been described as one of the technological marvels of its time because of an advanced system of 18 locks. Although the canal was never used for its intended purpose, its impending completion did force the Prussians to re-evaluate their customs tariffs, enabling the Polish traders to make use of their seaports once again.

In 1830, the Poles rebelled against the increasingly oppressive Russian regime. The November Uprising, as it would become known, spread through the country like wildfire and took the Russians by surprise. The Poles hoped to negotiate a peace treaty with Russia and sought diplomatic support abroad, but the Tsar refused to negotiate and the European powers were not eager to risk a falling-out with Russia. The Polish military fought vigorously, but proved incapable of holding off the numerically superior Russian army.

Podlasia was situated on the Russian border and was among the first provinces to be overrun by the Russian military. It was also still the wildest part of Poland, which was excellent for guerrilla warfare. The Partisans retreated to the forests of Białowieża and Augustów from which they attacked the Russian forces.

The Russians responded with severe reprisals upon the local population. They also began to raise heavy duties on trade in their Polish territories. As a result, many Polish merchants moved to Białystok, then on the Russian side of the border, to avoid the duties. In this period Białystok grew to become the industrial centre of the region.

The Poles never settled under Russian rule and in 1863, when the authorities ordered the conscription of young Poles into the Imperial Army, the January Uprising broke out. This insurgency did not escalate into open warfare like the November Uprising. Instead, loosely organised bands of rebels conducted guerrilla warfare from within inaccessible areas throughout Poland. In Podlasia the rebels found again refuge in the forests of Białowieża, Knyszyn, Augustów and Czerwone Bagno. The uprising was brutally suppressed in 1864, the Polish Kingdom was abolished and its lands incorporated into the Russian Empire. Lastly, a campaign to 'Russify' Poland was launched. Russian was adopted as the official language, the Polish language and the Latin alphabet were banned at public places, schools and administration offices. Catholic churches, schools and monasteries were closed, demolished or given to the Russian Orthodox Church.

World War I

When in 1914 World War I broke out, the three partitioning powers – Russia, Austria-Hungary and Prussia (now part of the German Empire) – found themselves on different sides of the conflict. Austria-Hungary and the German Empire were allied against the Russian Empire. Polish soldiers fought in the armies of all three powers and many battles were fought on Polish territory. The Biebrza was of particular importance since its broad strip of marsh was a natural barrier. The Russians recognised the strategic significance of the Biebrza river and marshes as an obstacle to advancing armies and had reinforced the only point where the marshes could be crossed, the bottleneck between Middle and Lower Basins of the river at Osowiec, with heavy fortifications (route 6 and 8). It was during construction of these fortifications that the famous *Carska Droga* (Tsar's Road) was

Bunker ruins near
Osowiec Twierdza
(route 8). The Biebrza
was an important
barrier in WWI. Its
narrowest point near
Osowiec was heavily
fortified.

built along the Biebrza's east bank. The Germans assaulted the Russian stronghold relentlessly and even used poison gas in an attempt to break the defence. The line held out until August 1915 when it was abandoned and the fortifications partially destroyed by the retreating Russian forces. Eventually, German and Austrian forces would conquer all of the former Polish territories. In the period that followed, the Germans extracted huge amounts of wood from the forests of Białowieża, Knyszyn and Augustów. Hundreds of kilometres of narrow-gauged railroad were constructed in the forests to carry millions of cubic metres of lumber out of the area (e.g. routes 17 and 18). Numerous lumber mills and wood processing plants were built and wildlife was hunted relentlessly to provide provisions for the troops. This was a huge assault on the naturalness of Białowieża – and its traces (narrow-gauged railways, a straight grid of forester's tracks) are still visible today.

By 1917, the Russian economy and its armies were on the verge of collapse and civil unrest was rife. With German help, revolution broke out in Russia, ultimately leading to the Tsar's abdication and civil war.

The Germans would not be able to enjoy their success on the eastern front for long. The situation on the western front became untenable after the American entry into the war on the side of the British and the French.

The Central Powers were forced to sign the very unfavourable peace treaty of Versailles. All three partitioning powers now lay in ruins and the American president actively campaigned for an independent Poland. In November 1918, the last German forces retreated and for the first time since 1795, Poland was an independent country again.

World War II

But Polish independence did not last for long. Hitler rose to power in Germany and the communists solidified power in former Russia (now the Soviet Union). Nazi Germany and the Soviet Union signed the Molotov-Ribbentrop Pact in August 1939 in which they secretly divided Poland between them. On September 1st 1939, Nazi Germany invaded Poland, sparking the beginning of World War II. Poland was quickly divided between Germany and the Soviet Union (which had invaded on 17th September). Hence Podlasia, except for the Suwałki region, was now occupied by the Soviet Union.

The Russian occupation lasted until June 1942 when the Germans conquered the region from the Soviets. Like in World War I, the region was ruthlessly exploited. The large forests were again subjected to extensive

timber extraction and wildlife was hunted for provisions. Poland's large population of Elk was brought to the brink of extinction apart for a small population that survived in the impenetrable marshes of the Czerwone Bagno. From here they later on recolonised the Biebrza and other parts of Podlasia.

During WWII the forests and marshes once again provided refuge for resistance fighters. Their partisan actions against the German invaders were often met with severe reprisals against the local civilians. Near Czerwone

You can still find ammunition from WWII in the sand dunes of the Biebrza.

Bagno, the entire village of Grzedy (route 12) was burned down and many inhabitants murdered because they were suspected of helping the resistance. Partisan fighters hiding on an island in the Biebrza marshes near Barwik suffered an horrific shelling (route 9). The enormous craters created by the explosions can still be seen today. The large Jewish communities of Białystok and Tykocin were all but eradicated in the Holocaust. In 1944, the Russians were on the offensive again and drove the Germans out of the province. The retreating German forces burned down the royal hunting palace in Białowieża.

Post-war developments

After the defeat of Nazi Germany, Poland became a satellite state of the Soviet Union. Poland's borders shifted far to the west as the Soviets annexed eastern areas whilst Poland annexed eastern Germany (including much of East Prussia). The Soviets introduced a planned, industrialised system of agriculture, revolving around large state farms (Kolkhoz). Needles to say this approach to farming is completely at loggerheads with the traditional farming typical in the region.

After the collapse of Soviet power in 1989 and the subsequent exit of Poland from the Warsaw Pact, the country looked to the west. Poland's state-planned economy was transformed into an open-market economy. The agrarian sector modernised once again, but the traditional agricultural landscape in a market-driven economy was no safer than it had been under Communist collectivisation. Problems of overexploitation and, paradoxically, abandonment, brought about a major threat to the hitherto so splendid natural countryside of the region.

The uniqueness of Białowieża forest was already known far and wide, but in this period, the region's other natural gem, the marshes of the Biebrza, finally started attracting the recognition they deserved. Western naturalists came over to discover the marvels of Białowieża forest and the Biebrza marshes. Both within the region and from abroad, nature and threats to it, were acknowledged and a nature conservation movement stood up to defend Podlasia's natural heritage.

The horse-drawn cart is one of the traditional farming methods that persisted well into the 21st century in North-east Poland.

Conservation

A unique feature of north-east Poland's natural heritage is that it harbours large areas of pristine habitat, which has largely disappeared elsewhere. The most well-known example is, of course, Białowieża forest, with its large tracts of near-natural forest. But the Biebrza and Narew valleys could justifiably be seen as near-natural rivers, harbouring the extensive sedge marshes, reed beds and alder carr woods that were once common through-out most of the continent. The fact that these pearls of ancient nature can still be found in Podlasia owes much to the efforts of many visionary people who strived to preserve them for future generations.

Nature conservation in Poland started early, with the recognition of Białowieża as a unique natural area (see box on page 64), but apart from this it has been rather quiet on the conservation front. And what else could

CONTEMPLATING THE PRIMEVAL LANDSCAPE OF EUROPE

A common belief among 'Greens' in Europe and especially in the US is that man's primary relationship with nature is an abusive and destructive one. Yet just about all of Europe's most important natural areas today – with the exception of the Białowieża – were made or in some way shaped by man. Most of our declining or threatened species are dependent on these semi-natural areas. Many birds, mammals, flowers, butterflies and so on do not live in forests, but in more open areas.

The history and formation of Europe's great woodlands are the subject of two competing theories. The traditional view suggests that central Europe was once a dense forest where most of these now endangered species could not live at all. They were restricted to a few treeless refuges in mountains and on some rocky, volcanic or salty soils near the coast. Some researchers say that even the large animals we now associate with big, undisturbed forests like Red Deer, Tarpan and Elk did not occur either. Climate change after the last ice age had, it was supposed, created a forest so dense that these grazers were forced towards more open forest types in southeastern Europe. They only reappeared in central and western Europe with the arrival of Neolithic man, who made gaps in the forest and introduced nutritious crops and grasslands.

So this theory means that we human beings were not so disastrous for the diversity of Europe's natural world after all. On the contrary, we've created it! Before the arrival of man, central Europe must have been a rather dull, monotonous place.

A competing view arose in 1996 when the Dutch ecologist Frans Vera came up with a rather controversial hypothesis. He credited large herbivores with a more prominent role by claiming that they were able to maintain a mosaic gap structure be expected from a region that was perpetually tossed and turned, and not infrequently squashed, between quarrelling super powers? Conservation measures weren't really needed either – the traditional land use, together with low population density, sustained a mix of small scale agricultural land, wild forests and marsh with an extremely high natural value. It is this mix, including the rich cultural traditions, that the Polish Nature conservation organisations try to preserve in 21st century.

Several national parks were established in the region. Białowieża was founded early. It was already a reserve in 1921. The others came about much later: Wigry National Park in 1989, Biebrza in 1993 and Narew in 1996. In the same year, the surface area of Białowieża National Park was almost doubled. In addition to the National Parks, several landscape parks and nature reserves (each with a different legal status) were established in the province.

---

in the vegetation and hence weren't forced out by the dense forest. In his view the primeval landscape of Europe wasn't a dense woodland at all, but a 'forest-meadow': a landscape with patches of woodland, individual trees, bushes and meadows. In other words, the pre-human landscape encompassed all the habitats needed to sustain all European plants and animals. In Vera's opinion it was not until Neolithic man arrived and killed most large herbivores that large stretches of deep forests – now largely ungrazed – were created.

The Białowieża forest formed an important area for his research. Here he collected evidence for his theory by focusing on the decline of oak and hazel that can only germinate where sufficient light for growth is available. Pollen analyses (the most reliable source of information of vegetation history) indicates that those species were always common throughout central Europe, suggesting the presence of large open areas. This gave him the idea that the now almost absent thermophile oak forest (see section on page #) comes much closer to the pristine European landscape than does the oak-linden-hornbeam forest, which is commonly taken as the model for Europe's original nature.

Fierce opposition to Vera's theories comes from many directions, not in the last place from specialists on his prime study area itself: the Białowieża forest. They state that oak and hazel are not declining at all and that many massive oaks in the forest have long stems and small crowns, indicating that they grew up under competitive circumstances and emerged victorious.

Whether Vera's theory is true or not, one thing is clear. Europe's natural history is far from uncontroversial. It is the source of ferocious debates and the Białowieża is the prime battle ground.

Changing agriculture

After WWII agricultural changes in the planned economy of the Soviets brought about changes in the small scale, traditional, 'unimproved' agriculture of north-east Poland. After the collapse of the Eastern Block intensification proceeded at a quickened pace, but still not to the extent to which it did in most other places in Europe. Farmland on the better soils was the first to be modernised. The marshy soils, especially those in the Biebrza, were too big a project to be easily 'improved'.

Until then, the Biebrza had been a 'bubble' where time had more or less stood still. Small farming communities made a living on the islands in the marsh and the moraines on both banks, the wet sedge marshes were cut for hay once a year while the higher and drier patches were used to graze cattle and grow some crops. But in Poland's changing economy, these

marginal farming communities could no longer compete with the intensive agriculture that was becoming the new norm, leading to an exodus of farmers and the abandonment of their lands.

Both intensification and land abandonment are a threat to the semi-natural (man-influenced) habitats such as wet meadows, fen mires, flowery fields and traditional hamlets. Intensification (a process

The striking difference between modern monoculture on the left and herb-rich hay lands on the right.

that is still going on) leads to the disappearance of the wildlfowers, insects and birds of cereal fields and meadows. Abandonment leads to willows, alders and birches overgrowing the valuable sedge marshes, and the disappearance of its inhabitants, including the globally threatened Aquatic Warbler. New ways to maintain at least the most valuable sedge marshes were sought, and quite successfully so. Farmers are now being paid by the EU to keep cutting the hay. Several organisations have set up an ambitious plan to restore some of the already overgrown sedge marshes to their former glory (see page 66). The sedge marshes that had provided for the people in the area for centuries now need to be managed for their own sake. (see box on page 66).

Connecting the dots, and keeping them connected

Fragmentation of large natural areas is high on the list of threats to nature Europe-wide. Small patches of good habitat cannot sustain viable populations of rare flora and fauna. It is a mathematical inevitability that in smaller areas, a relatively larger proportion of surface lies close to the edge. And since disturbance usually comes from outside the area, the undisturbed core is disproportionally smaller in small sites, making fragile populations much more prone to extinction.

One of the great strengths of north-east Poland is the fact that natural areas are relatively large, but there is a constant danger of fragmentation. In 2007, Podlasia made global headlines when local authorities planned the construction of the Augustów bypass (part of the new Via Baltica or E67 motorway) straight through the Rospuda valley. The Rospuda is like a small and completely natural version of the Biebrza, just north-west of Augustów. Local and national environmental organisations protested the plan and the European Union warned Poland it would be heavily fined for violation of Natura 2000 regulations. In spite of this, construction of the proposed route continued. In order to force the authorities to put a halt to the work, protesters set up a camp in the threatened area which drew a lot of attention. Under mounting pressure, both from within Poland and abroad, the project was abandoned and an alternative plan which bypasses the Rospuda valley entirely was adopted. A huge success!

Less successful, unfortunately, have been the efforts to raze the border fence between the Polish and Belarussian part of Białowieża, which would greatly benefit the large mammals in the forest. They would all of a sudden see their population doubled, since the artificial separation of the two populations would be no more. Unfortunately, the political tension between Belarus and the EU is hardly a good starting point for joining the two National Parks.

Within Poland, conservationists increasingly look towards the connection of the large forest complexes of Białowieża, Knyszyn and Augustów to facilitate migration of large mammals. The woodland of Las Trzyrzeczki on route 13 is an example. It is part of a corridor connecting Knyszyn and Augustów forests.

Construction on the infamous Augustow bypass of the Via Baltica motorway has been terminated in favour of a new plan that spares the unique Rospuda valley.

Timber industry in natural forest

In the large forest complexes, especially Białowieża, there is a tension between the loggers and the conservationists. While the importance and uniqueness of the Białowieża forest has been known for ages, the actual National Park still only comprises about one fifth of the Polish part of the forest complex. In the rest, the forest's prime use is as a timber resource. The timber industry is traditionally well represented in the villages in and around the forest and many families have worked in this business for generations. For the preservation of the unique old-growth forest, an extension of the preserved areas is called for, and conservationists have the growing tourism industry on their side. In 1996 the National Park was indeed enlarged and in 2012, new local legislation was adopted which states that only local people are allowed to extract timber from the forest and this only for personal use. Conservationists are, of course, excited about these developments, but it polarises the local communities. Opposition against the 1996 expansion was met by re-employing the loggers as foresters by the National Park.

The history of Białowieża National Park

King Władysław II Jagiełło retreated to a huge, ancient forest, while preparing for the upcoming battle of Grunwald. He was beguiled by the ancient, sacred atmosphere of the forest and the wondrous creatures that inhabited it (not least the many Bison!). When he returned from the battle victorious, he declared the forest a royal hunting estate and built a hunting lodge. This white tower (Biało Wieża) stood on the site that is today known as Stara Białowieża (route 19). It was 1410, and one of the first nature reserves in the world was born.

The Polish royal family was very proud of Białowieża forest and its unique herd of Bison (see box on page 86). In 1529, the Polish-Lithuanian King Sigismund I built a new hunting lodge in Białowieża, on the hill where the National Park headquarters is now situated. He also enacted several laws to protect the forest and its animals from harm. One of these measures was instating the death penalty for poaching a Bison as they were considered royal property. He also built a hunting lodge on the grounds of today's palace park, around which Białowieża village developed.

After the partitions of Poland (see page 54), Białowieża came into the hands of the Russian Tsar Alexander I. The forest lost its protection, until Tsar Alexander II re-established the protection of Bison with drastic measures. All Brown Bears, Wolves and Lynxes were shot, while large game were bred in vast numbers to cater to decadent Tsarist hunting parties. The absence of large predators and the artificially high number of large herbivores damaged the fragile ecology of Europe's last primeval forest.

In short, Podlasia's natural wealth is of an overwhelming beauty and value, but it is also under significant pressure. Although public awareness of its value is, thanks to the efforts of non-governmental organisations and authorities, changing, agriculture and expanding economic activities pose an ever-present threat. There are many groups (like O.T.O.P. and P.T.O.P. – the Polish National and Podlasia's regional bird conservation organisations respectively) that are working hard to keep Podlasia's natural gems safe. They have allies in local people who are fiercely proud of 'their' forests and marshes.

More and more these organisations do so not just by opposing threats, but working on economic alternatives that are respectful to nature and local traditions. One of these win-win alternatives involves you! You benefit from their activities because they enable you to enjoy the rich nature and local culture of the region. And in return, you (or ecotourism in general) support an economy that employs a growing number of local inhabitants. See page 221 to see how you can be involved!

The wood extraction and Bison poaching of WW1 were disastrous (see page 56 and box on page 86). Fortunately Professor Conwentz, a German scientist, was able to convince the military authorities to spare a large swathe of forest north of Białowieża village from the sawmills – the area that is today known as the Strict Reserve.

Shortly after the war, Polish scientists came to Białowieża to assess the damage. They called for the creation of a reserve, which was created in 1921 – just in time to save the most intact old-growth forest from a British logging company which had obtained a license for timber extraction. Simultaneously, an ambitious plan was devised to save the European Bison from extinction (see page 86).

World War II brought yet another round of chaos. Between 1939 and 1941 Białowieża was in Soviet hands and the forest was once again subject to ruthless timber extraction. This came to an end when the Germans took over (they wanted to turn Białowieża into a huge hunting estate). After the war, a brief period of chaos ensued in which large-scale illegal timber harvesting took place.

Order was quickly restored in the province but as the entire country of Poland shifted to the west, Białowieża Forest suddenly found itself on the border between Poland and the Soviet Union (subsequently Belarus). A border fence was erected, effectively cutting the forest in half, a situation which persists to this very day.

A historical moment came in 1952, when two young bulls were released from the breeding enclosure into the forest, ending the European Bison's extinction in the wild. In 1977 Białowieża Forest was listed as a UNESCO Biosphere Reserve and two years later it was designated a UNESCO World Heritage Site.

Active habitat management

The Biebrza Valley holds about 33,500 ha of open habitats. Much of it are peat meadows, including intact fen mires. These habitats are of the highest international nature conservation importance, with the Aquatic Warbler as flagship species (see box on page 99).

Since at least 300 years, the fens have traditionally been used as hay meadows. Slight man-made changes to the hydrology of the valley, increased eutrophication through water and air combined with slow natural succession of the peatland lead to them being overgrown with dense reeds and trees, especially birch, willow and alder. This process was inhibited by the traditional extensive hand-scything, but became apparent as soon as this type of land use ceased around 1970.

After earlier plans of full-scale drainage had been abandoned, eventually resulting in the creation of the Biebrza National Park in 1993, the successional overgrowth has become the main threat to this habitat. The establishment of

The Długa Łuka boardwalk, probably the most accessible site in Europe to observe Aquatic Warblers.

the National Park could not stop this negative development resulting in the loss of about a third of the area of open fen mire habitat. Since 2005, the Polish Society for the Protection of Birds (OTOP – BirdLife Poland) and partners, amongst them the Biebrza National Park, have been implementing a large-scale project funded by the EU LIFE Programme and Swarovski Optik targeting the conservation of Aquatic Warblers and their fen mire habitats. This project has catalysed the implementation of an innovative landscape-scale solution for the restoration and sustainable management of the peat meadows.

Extensive mowing has been reintroduced on several thousand hectares. Hand mowing at such a large scale is nowadays not possible any more. The solution was the development and introduction of prototype mowing machinery based on alpine piste-bashers on caterpillars (called *ratrak* in Polish), originally used for the preparation of ski runs, with very low ground pressure and fast working speed. As it can be used also during high water levels and – in contrast to previously tested traditional tractors with twin tyres – has a minimal impact on the delicate peat soil and vegetation. It is now used across the site.

Since 2009 financial support for the extensive mowing of fen mires is available through a targeted Aquatic Warbler agri-environment scheme. To enable local farmers and enterprises to use this scheme to implement the necessary habitat management the national park has made c. 12,000 ha of public land available

under lease agreements that guarantee the benefit for biodiversity. Within another project, OTOP has set up a facility that processes the biomass harvested from the mires to produce pellets as an alternative carbon-neutral fuel. The sale of this biomass product will contribute to the management costs in the future.

Careful research and monitoring of the effects of this large-scale mowing has shown that it was possible to reclaim most of the open habitat that had been lost since 1970 and that Aquatic Warblers return to the areas restored. However, it has also shown, that the bi-annual mowing rotation implemented initially is more than is actually needed at this site. For the majority of the site rotations between 4 and 20 years are most suitable, with central areas of the mire needing no management at all. The aim is to keep the mowing frequency to a minimum needed to prevent the area from overgrowing, thereby minimising the impact of the mowing machines on the vegetation and peat soil. Plans are now being established to ensure each area receives exactly the frequency of treatment it needs.

Locally, some controversy has developed since ratrak mowing machines can now be seen working away on the near-pristine sedge fens from August till February, leaving some noticeable traces at the points of access to the mire, which are at the same time the places first seen by visitors. Active management, especially if it is so obvious to the observer's eye, contradicts the romantic ideal of a pristine wilderness. On the other hand, it needs to be accepted, that even the open Biebrza mires that make the place so special are 'only' near-pristine and would largely be lost if not actively managed. Thanks to the management implemented, Biebrza now hosts the world's only population of Aquatic Warblers that is not declining,

and this special species can again be observed easily from places accessible to visitors. The detailed knowledge gained recently about the effects of large-scale mowing now makes it possible to reduce the active management to the minimum necessary to maintain the habitat and at the same time keep the pristine feeling of wilderness in the Biebrza Valley.

Sedge marshes need to be mown to prevent them from being overgrown. The Austrian optics brand Swarovski Optik was involved in setting up a LIFE project with the Polish Birdlife partner OTOP to restore large swathes of overgrown sedge marsh.

Modern machinery now does the work that used to be done with scythes. This type of mowing machine was especially developed for the sedge marshes with their fragile peaty soil.

FLORA AND FAUNA

The previous section of this book raved about the large swathes of intact natural areas in North-east Poland. Consequently, you can expect their flora and fauna to be rich, but you'll still be surprised though just how rich the biodiversity is.

If you'd make a field guide of the flora and fauna of temperate Europe and start ticking off those species that occur in North-east Poland, only a few would be missed out. Indeed, the flora and fauna of North-east Poland are probably the most complete collection of its type to be found in a single region. If you ever felt that the nature of the temperate zone just doesn't have the exotic touch of, say, the Mediterranean or the Arctic, then North-east Poland will set you straight.

Most species you'll come across in this region are typical of the temperate region. The familiar species are just as plentiful as they are back home (assuming for a moment your home is somewhere in temperate western Europe). But just as common are those species that have plummeted in recent decades in most of these countries (including other parts of Poland). For example, the butterflies Pearl-bordered and Small Pearl-bordered Fritillaries are now target species for nature conservation in 'the West' so their abundance here in North-east Poland is a 'quality mark' for the region. Many species that have declined dramatically throughout the continent, and even became extinct in many countries still have strong-holds in Podlasia province. To stick with butterflies, Scarce Fritillary, Violet Copper and Large Chequered Skipper are all good examples of this.

Those temperate species that don't occur in North-east Poland are frost sensitive and so largely have an Atlantic distribution. This is especially marked when looking at the orchid list (page 81). Here you will find no species of the delicate bee orchid genus *Ophrys*, and of the equally sensitive *Orchis* genus, only Early-purple Orchid occurs, and this species is extremely rare.

A Whinchat and a Bison in a single frame. A scene like this is only possible in Białowieża.

Instead, the flora and fauna of North-east Poland enjoys a strong element of distinctly Central and East European species, of which Eastern Pasqueflower, Dark Whiteface (a dragonfly) and Collared Flycatcher are just three examples. Moreover, North-east Poland is home to a few species that have their main distribution range much further east. Examples of such 'Russian' species are the rare Pink Frog Orchid and Pallas' Fritillary. Among the breeding birds, Greenish Warbler, Spotted Eagle and Citrine Wagtail are species that reach their western limits in our area.

But there is more than just flora and fauna of the temperate zone in North-east Poland. This region lies well within the northern sphere of influence, and many boreal species (the northern taiga forest zone) are found in the region. All species groups have their northern representatives, such as Elk and Mountain Hare among the mammals, Chickweed Wintergreen and Interrupted Clubmoss among the plants, and Baltic Grayling and Northern Emerald among the insects.

There is something odd about these northern species too. Many of them have a bipolar distribution range in Europe: they occur wherever the climate is right in both the vast taigas of Scandinavia and Russia, and in the Alps and Carpathian Mountains further south. Many plant species that add the 'northern' touch to the flora of North-east Poland, are in reality such *Arctic-alpine* species. Good examples are Creeping Lady's-tresses (among many other plants of the coniferous forest) and Ruby Whiteface – a dragonfly.

Although North-east Poland lies close to the natural range of the northern taigas, there are still quite a lot of species that are typical of the central European mountains and not of the true taigas. There are several dragonflies and butterflies that fit this box. They are mountain species in Europe and occupy the lowlands only in the east, such as in Russia, and North-east Poland.

The cherry on this already quite well-decorated cake are the so-called Pontic species: those plants and animals that are typical of the south-eastern steppes, where the summers are hot and dry. It would go too far to say that North-east Poland lies within the Pontic sphere of influence, but there are a few species – most of them quite rare in the region – that are more typical of the south-east. The exotic-looking Roller is one example, as are Booted and Short-toed Eagles. These species are rare and some of them declining (one example, the Lesser Grey Shrike, is now probably extinct), but they do add to the excitement of what is already an extremely diverse region.

Boreal region
Elk *(Alces alces)*
Swamps and marshes

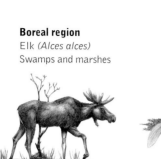

Atlantic region
Beech *(Fagus sylvatica)*
Deciduous forests

Siberian region
Pink Frog Orchid
Mossy coniferous forests

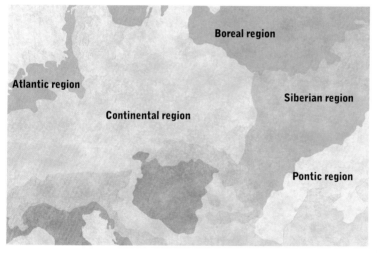

Pontic region
Citrine Wagtail
(Motacilla citreola)
Meadows

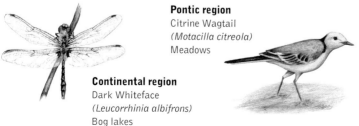

Continental region
Dark Whiteface
(Leucorrhinia albifrons)
Bog lakes

Flora

The aquatic flora is best explored from canoe (see page 216). The most attractive fen mire flora, including the species of calcareous seepage water, is found on routes 10 and 13. The wildflowers of bogs are easy to track down on routes 2, 3 and 5. The flora of deciduous forest is richest on routes 12, 16, 17 and 18 and in the strict reserve of Białowieża (see page 207). The flora of coniferous forest is most pronounced in the Augustów region, such as on routes 3 and 5. In Białowieża, the forest south of Stare Masiewo supports many northern species. The best routes for finding wildflowers of dry, sandy grasslands are route 5, 8 and 12. Explore the dry grasslands of loamy soils on routes 1, 4 and 20.

The flora of North-east Poland is exciting in two ways – first in terms of the wider landscape and vegetation and second in terms of the individual rarity and attractiveness of the plants concerned.

Looking at the landscape on the level of vegetation types, you may enjoy some of the finest examples of temperate European habitats. Marvel at the vast alder swamp forests, unscathed fen mires, hectare upon hectare of Marsh Marigold fields, oak-linden-hornbeam forests (with its fine spring flora), flowery dry grasslands, and so on. Both in terms of scale and conservation value it is pretty much unprecedented further west. From the UK

Wood Cow-wheat is very common, but no less attractive than any orchid. The purple top comprises 'ordinary' leaves that have evolved to help attract insects.

east to Germany, you'll find these habitats to be more fragmented, threatened, or degenerated. To see them here in North-east Poland in their full glory is utter joy. Moreover, they are complemented with more northern (boreal) vegetation of native spruce and pine forest and raised bog.

But if this is all too academic and your focus lies more on finding rare and attractive wildflowers, you have come to the right place too. North-east Poland harbours a lot of different wildflowers – the North-east is second only to the mountains of the south as the botanically richest part of Poland. This is truly

remarkable, given the fact that the landscape and soil is not highly varied, particularly in comparison with the soils in the mountains.
The reason for North-east Poland's richness lies in the presence of many unscathed habitats, but also in its fortunate position in the east, where boreal species reach their southern limit and where some 'typical' mountain species also occur. On a much more modest scale, some wildflowers from the Siberian and Pontic region (the Ukrainian steppes) just reach our region.

Some wildflowers of different ecoranges

North-European and Alpine species Chickweed Wintergreen *(Trientalis europaea)*, Creeping Lady's-tresses *(Goodyera repens)*, Beech Fern *(Phegopteris connectilis)*, Oak Fern *(Gymnocarpium dryopteris)*, Stag's-horn Clubmoss *(Lycopodium clavatum)*, Interrupted Clubmoss *(Lycopodium annotinum)*
East-European species Eastern Pasqueflower *(Pulsatilla patens)*, Small Pasqueflower *(Pulsatilla pratensis)*, Jacob's-ladder *(Polemonium caeruleum)*, Siberian Iris *(Iris sibirica)*
Widespread continental species Isopyrum *(Isopyrum thalictrum)*, Liverleaf *(Hepatica nobilis)*, Peach-leaved Bellflower *(Campanula persicifolia)*, Yellow Foxglove *(Digitalis grandiflora)*
Pontic species Yellow Scabious *(Scabiosa ochroleuca)*, Purple Mullein *(Verbascum phoeniceum)*

Wildflowers of the marshes

There are many different types of wetlands in North-east Poland, and they vary greatly in the attractiveness of their flora. The rivers and lakes sport a flora of aquatic plants, which is rich in attractive species, even though most of them are quite widespread in temperate Europe. White and Yellow Waterlilies are present on many oxbows and on rivers with standing or very gently flowing water. In the quieter parts, they are joined (or even pushed out) by Frogbit, Arrowhead, Flowering-rush, Water-soldier and the insectivorous Greater Bladderwort, whose delicate flowers pop out of the water every now and then. Altogether, they make the thick vegetable soup of lowland rivers in peaty soils, through which it is so wonderful to paddle (see page 216 for details on canoe rental). The river margins are cloaked in a thick layer of reeds, forming another marshland vegetation type, although extremely rich in nutrients, with strongly fluctuating water levels, it is decidedly less attractive in species.

Wildflowers of the marshes

Aquatic vegetation Frog-bit *(Hydrochaeris morsus-ranae)*, Fringed Water-lily *(Nymphoides peltata)*, Water-plantain *(Alisma plantago-aquatica)*, Flowering-rush *(Butomus umbellatus)*, Arrowhead *(Sagittaria sagittifolia)*, Water-soldier *(Stratiotes aloides)*, Yellow Iris *(Iris pseudacorus)*

Fen mires and wet meadows Common Meadow-rue *(Thalictrum flavum)*, Long-leaved Speedwell *(Veronica longifolia)*, Meadowsweet *(Filipendula ulmaria)*, Great Willowherb *(Epilobium hirsutum)*, Marsh Marigold *(Caltha palustris)*, Brook Thistle *(Cirsium rivulare)*, Tufted Loosestrife *(Lysimachia thyrsiflora)*, Water Avens *(Geum rivale)*, Bistort *(Persicaria bistorta)*, Marsh Cinquefoil *(Comarum palustre)*

Fen Marshes Marsh Lousewort *(Pedicularis palustris)*, Bogbean *(Menyanthes trifoliata)*, Marsh Fern *(Thelypteris palustris)*, Early Marsh-orchid *(Dactylorhiza incarnata)*, Milk Parsley *(Peucedanum palustre)*, Water Horsetail *(Equisetum fluviatile)*, Marsh Violet *(Viola palustris)*, Yellow Loosestrife *(Lysimachia vulgaris)*

Mineral-rich swells Grass-of-Parnassus *(Parnassia palustris)*, Marsh Helleborine *(Epipactis palustris)*, Lady's-slipper *(Cypripedium calceolus)*, Fen Orchid *(Liparis loeselii)*, Ruth's Marsh-orchid *(Dactylorhiza ruthei)*, Jacob's-ladder *(Polemonium caeruleum)*, Siberian Iris *(Iris sibirica)*

Raised bogs Bog Rosemary *(Andromeda polifolia)*, Bog Bilberry *(Vaccinium uliginosum)*, Cranberry *(Vaccinium oxycoccus)*, Labrador Tea *(Ledum palustre)*, Round-leaved Sundew *(Drosera rotundifolia)*, Great Sundew *(Drosera anglica,* rare), Rannoch-rush *(Scheuchzeria palustris)*, White Beak-sedge *(Rhynchospora alba)*, Milk Parsley *(Peucedanum palustre)*, Cowbane *(Cicuta virosa)*, Bog Arum *(Calla palustris)*

Further away from the river, where nutrients are limited due to permanent waterlogging and thereby lack of oxygen, the flora is at its most exciting. The most aggressive plants (such as Reed, Sweet-flag, Yellow Iris and Reed Canary-grass) are kept at bay, making room for the less dominant plants. On neutral soils, such fen mires support a variety of sedges, Marsh Fern, Marsh Cinquefoil, Marsh Marigold, Water Avens, Bogbean, Water Horsetail and Early Marsh-orchid. The list grows longer where alkaline water wells up. Most of these base-rich 'islands' are fairly small, and the species composition is never precisely the same, but always very interesting. Such sites are generally the orchid hotspots, with Marsh Helleborine, Lady's-slipper, Fen Orchid, and a variety of East-European marsh-orchids *(Dactylorhiza)* possible. Other attractive East-European plants are the blue Siberian Iris and Jacob's-ladder. Indeed, these alkaline fen mires are stunning places for botanists.

Siberian Iris, a flashy and fairly rare flower of calcareous marshes.

Wetlands which largely lack nutrients are bogs dominated by peat mosses. Bogs only develop under special conditions (see page 48) and support a very different flora, with key players such as Hare's-tail Cottongrass, Bog Bilberry, Cranberry, Bog Rosemary, Bog Aum, Round-leaved Sundew and Rannoch-rush. Most bogs are acidic, but there are a few places where alkaline ground water adds a few minerals, which allow some of the rarest species of the region to grow, such as the diminutive Bog Orchid and Marsh Saxifrage. Because of their extreme fragility, these sites are not included in the routes offered in this book.

Wildflowers of the deciduous forests

At the end of April, the forest floors in many deciduous forests in Northeast Poland burst into flower. Wood Anemone, Alternate-leaved Golden Saxifrage, Bird-in-a-bush and Liverleaf carpet the woodlands below the still leafless trees. Look carefully, because the richer places also support Yellow Anemone, Isopyrum (superficially like a taller, multi-flowered Wood Anemone), Asarabacca, Moschatel, Mezereon and Yellow Star-of-Bethlehem.

This spring flora is most pronounced in the deciduous forests with better soils, like oak-linden-hornbeam forest and the not-too-wet forests of Ash and Alder. Here, the rotting leaves provide plenty of nutrients and in spring the leafless canopy encourages early growth.

Wildflowers of the deciduous forests

Oak-linden-hornbeam Bastard Balm *(Melittis melissophyllum)*, Liverleaf *(Hepatica nobilis)*, Asarabacca *(Asarum europeum)*, Yellow Anemone *(Anemone ranunculoides)*, Wood Anemone *(Anemone nemorosa)*, Isopyrum *(Isopyrum thalictroides)*, Baneberry *(Actaea spicata)*, Early Dog-violet *(Viola reichenbachiana)*, Common Dog-violet *(Viola riviniana)*, Mezereon *(Daphne mezereum)*, Spring Pea *(Lathyrus vernus)*, Alternate-leaved Golden-saxifrage *(Chrysosplenium alternifolium)*, Woodruff *(Galium odoratum)*, Large-flowered Hemp-nettle *(Galeopsis speciosa)*, Toothwort *(Lathraea squamaria)*, Moschatel *(Adoxa moschatellina)*, Suffolk Lungwort *(Pulmonaria obscura)*, Sanicle *(Sanicula europaea)*, Narrow-leaved Everlasting-pea *(Lathyrus sylvatica)*, Betony *(Stachys officinalis)*, Ramsons *(Allium ursinum)*, Wood Cow-wheat *(Melampyrum nemorosum)*, Creeping Bellflower *(Campanula rapunculoides)*, Clustered Bellflower *(Campanula glomerata)*, Peach-leaved Bellflower *(Campanula persicifolia)*, Nettle-leaved Bellflower *(Campanula trachelium)*, Spiked Rampion *(Phyteuma alba)*, Wood Crane's-bill *(Geranium sylvaticum)*, Yellow Foxglove *(Digitalis grandiflora)*, Yellow Archangel *(Lamiastrum galeobdolon)*, Goldilocks Buttercup *(Ranunculus auricomus)*, Yellow Star-of-Bethlehem *(Gagea lutea)*, Bird-in-a-bush *(Corydalis solida)*

Alder carr woods Greater Spearwort *(Ranunculus lingua)*, Downy Current *(Ribes spicatum)*, Mountain Currant *(Ribes alpinum)*, Black Currant *(Ribes nigrum)*, Water-violet *(Hottonia palustris)*, Touch-me-not Balsam *(Impatiens noli-tangere)*, Wild Angelica *(Angelica sylvestris)*, Enchanter's-nightshade *(Circaea lutetiana)*, Alpine Enchanter's-nightshade *(Circaea alpina)*, Cabbage Thistle *(Cirsium oleraceum)*

A rich spring flora carpets the forest floors of the nutrient-rich forests, such as oak-linden-hornbeam and alder-ash stands.

The flora continues to develop when the leaves are slowly unfurling, but come June, when the wood is in shade, many wildflowers have already finished. This mid-spring (May–June) flowering consist of several attractive species like Common spotted-orchid, Ramsons, Woodruff, Wood Cow-wheat, Martagon Lily and Yellow Foxglove.

Very rich too, is the flora of the Alder carr woods. Here the pretty Touch-me-not Balsam is very common and grows alongside Water Avens, Greater Spearwort, Water-violet, Marsh Marigold and Alpine and Common Enchanter's-nightshade.

Wildflowers of the coniferous forests

The vast boreal coniferous forests extend into the extreme North-east of Poland. Many plant species typical of this forest type do not reach this far south, but in the forests around Augustów and Wigry, you are welcomed by a hint of the north. Walking through a silent, green coniferous forest through the soft mass of Interrupted and Staghorn Clubmosses, Wood Horsetail, Beech and Oak Ferns is an unforgettable experience. In between grow the delicate white flowers of Chickweed Wintergreen, May Lily and – later in summer – Creeping Lady's-tresses. These are the classic hallmarks of the silent northern forests.

An exotic rarity of exposed sandy slopes: the Eastern Pasqueflower.

Wildflowers of the coniferous forests

Coniferous forest Broad-leaved Sermountain *(Laserpitium latifolium),* Serrated Wintergreen *(Orthilia secunda),* Common Wintergreen *(Pyrola minor),* Umbellate Wintergreen *(Chimaphila umbellata),* Yellow Bird's-nest *(Monotropa hypopitys),* Creeping Lady's-tresses *(Goodyera repens),* Common Cow-wheat *(Melampyrum pratense),* Cowberry *(Vaccinium vitis-idea),* Heather *(Calluna vulgaris),* Chickweed Wintergreen *(Trientalis europaea),* Stag's-horn Clubmoss *(Lycopodium clavatum),* Interrupted Clubmoss *(Lycopodium annotinum),* May Lily *(Maianthemum bifolium)*
Dry sandy forest Small Pasqueflower *(Pulsatilla pratensis)* Eastern Pasqueflower *(Pulsatilla patens),* Mountain Parsley *(Peucedanum oreoselinum),* Swallowtail *(Vincetoxicum hirundinaria),* Heath Cudweed *(Gnaphalium sylvaticum),* Sand Pink *(Dianthus arenarius),* Thyme *(Thymus spec),* Bearberry *(Arctostaphylos uva-ursi,* rare)

Stag's-horn Clubmoss is one of the northern delights. It locally carpets the floor of coniferous forests.

Most pine plantations though, have a poorer vegetation in which Common Cow-wheat, Heather, Bilberry and Cowberry dominate. The undergrowth below Juniper bushes, very common in these forests, is also of interest. Coniferous forests are present not only on acidic, nutrient-poor and moist soils, but also, in a slightly different guise, on the very dry sand dunes. The latter is an open and warm woodland, which is rich in plant species of eastern and south-European ranges, so quite the opposite of the boreal forest type. This is another hot habitat for plant hunters, with some truly attractive species like Small and Eastern Pasqueflowers (late April and May), Mountain Parsley, Swallowtail, Heath Cudweed and Sand Pink flower. Because this forest type is so open, it shares many species with dry grasslands and juniper scrub. Often, the more interesting species grow right beside the trail, where most sunlight reaches the ground.

Wildflowers of dry grasslands

The final hotspot habitat of the region is that of the dry grasslands. They come in two forms – first those found on the mineral and nutrient poor sandy soils of the sand dunes and second, the grasslands of more nutrient rich loamy soils. The vegetation of the dunes are somewhat reminiscent of the heathlands of Western Europe. Interestingly, Heather, the dominant plant of sandy soils in western Europe, is here more typical of coniferous forest. Hence, they are not part of the north-east Poland's 'heathlands'. In fact, the heath family is absent from such grasslands. Instead, the

Wildflowers of dry grasland

Nutrient-poor (sandy) dry grasslands Heath Dog-violet *(Viola canina)*, Carthusian Pink *(Dianthus carthusianorum)*, Maiden Pink *(Dianthus deltoides)*, Small Scabious *(Scabiosa columbaria)*, Hoary Cinquefoil *(Potentilla argentea)*, Field Wormwood *(Artemisia campestris)*, Grey Hair-grass *(Corynephorus canescens)*, Jersey Cudweed *(Gnaphalium luteo-album)*, Sheep's-bit *(Jasione montana)*, Tormentil *(Potentilla erecta)*

Nutrient-rich (loamy) dry grasslands Burnet-saxifrage *(Pimpinella saxifraga)*, Snowdrop Anemone *(Anemone sylvestris)*, Lady Bedstraw *(Galium verum)*, Northern Bedstraw *(Galium boreale)*, White Cinquefoil *(Potentilla alba)*, Sainfoin *(Onobrychis viciifolia)*, Kidney Vetch *(Anthyllis vulneraria)*, Purple Milkvetch *(Astragalus danicus)*, Mountain Clover *(Trifolium montanum)*, Eastern Bastard-toadflax* *(Thesium ebracteatum)*, Bloody Crane's-bill *(Geranium sanguineum)*, Cowslip *(Primula veris)*, Pannonian Knapweed *(Centaurea pannonicum)*, Purple Mullein *(Verbascum phoenicum)*, Wild Basil *(Origanum vulgare)*, Common Rockrose *(Helianthemum nummelarium)*, Agrimony *(Agrimonia eupatoria)*, Common Restharrow *(Ononis repens)*

Fields, disturbed soils Yellow Scabious *(Scabiosa ochroleuca)*, Forking Larkspur *(Consolida regalis)*, Basil Thyme *(Acinos arvensis)*, Red Hemp-nettle *(Galeopsis angustifolia)*, Hare's-foot Clover *(Trifolium arvense)*, Common Toadflax *(Linaria vulgaris)*, Viper's-bugloss *(Echium vulgare)*, Bugloss *(Anchusa arvensis)*

typical species in Poland are Hoary Cinquefoil, Field Wormwood, Jersey Cudweed, Sheep's-bit, Tormentil and various lichens.

The grasslands on loamy soils, being richer in nutrients, are very different. Some very fine examples of these places are found in Suwałki landscape park, where the splash of wildflowers include Brown Knapweed, Pannonian Knapweed* *(Centaurea pannonicum)*, Burnet-saxifrage and Lady's Bedstraw. In combination with the glacial stones and steep slopes, it reminds one of the mountains of central Europe rather than the north European plain. Most species in these grasslands are not extreme rarities, but nevertheless, there is a lot to explore and admire.

Suwałki Landscape Park boasts many flowery, dry grasslands.

Finally, in abandoned or recently disturbed fields you'll find Stork's-bill, Common Toadflax, Red Hemp-nettle and Viper's-bugloss. In such habitats, you may also encounter the southern species Yellow Scabious and Purple Mullein.

Orchids

North-east Poland is neither outstandingly rich nor poor in orchid species. Nevertheless, the region has some 'goodies' to offer orchid enthusiasts. Hidden among the multitude of marsh orchids (*Dactylorhiza*) lurk a few true rarities, such as Baltic and Ruthe's Marsh-orchid* (*Dactylorhiza ruthei*), and a cream-flowered version of Early Marsh-orchid – *ochraleuca*. The true gem, though, is the Pink Frog Orchid – an essentially Siberian species with only four known localities in Europe, all four of which are in the Augustów forest (including Wigry National Parks).

Most orchids occur in the marshes, especially those that are influenced by mineral seepage water. Here Early Marsh-orchid and Marsh Helleborine flower in abundance in late May and early June. Red Helleborine and Lady's-slipper too, flower in this generally rare and localised habitat type which is mostly found in the southern basin of the Biebrza (route 10).

The rare white variant *ochrantha* of Early Marsh-orchid

Lady's-slipper, perhaps the most impressive of the European orchids, has its largest Polish population in the Biebrza marshes. Late May and June is also the period for the other Dactylorhiza species, like Broad-leaved, Ruthe's* (*Dactylorhiza ruthei*) and Baltic Marsh-orchids. Later in June, Common and Heath Spotted-orchids (both fairly rare), can be found.

July is another good month for orchid enthusiasts. Marsh Helleborine forms large drifts in open marshland, Broad-leaved Helleborine is common in wet forests and Dark-red Helleborine is present in slightly drier locations. Creeping Lady's-tresses is locally common in some of the coniferous forests. The Pink Frog Orchid closes the season, starting to bloom in the last days of July and on into August.

Konik horses freely
roam the sand dunes
of Grzędy.

for their meat. This brought the Polish population to the brink of extinction, with only a single remnant population remaining in the inaccessible Czerwone Bagno. Fortunately, other, healthy populations, untouched by war, remained in Scandinavia and elsewhere. Hence the plight of the Elk was never as severe as that of the Bison but it is still remarkable that after the war, the small remnant population was able to expand and recolonise much of the territory it had lost during the war.

Today it may be found in almost all the sizeable wetlands. Wigry, Białowieża and Biebrza each have their populations but if you really want to see them, the Biebrza remains the place to go. It is here that the best habitat is found, both in quantity and quality, and if you stay in the park for even a few days, you have a good chance of seeing one, especially in winter and spring.

Roe Deer, Wild Boar and Red Deer inhabit the forests of Podlasia, with Red Deer being especially frequent in Białowieża. The combination of large forests and plentiful forest clearings and wet grasslands on the river's edges, offer the so much preferred combination of food, shelter and tranquillity.

One major point of debate among nature conservationists and ecologists alike is to what extent large herbivores shaped the landscape by their grazing. Were grazing herds capable of maintaining an open, park-like landscape, or was this landscape type created by humans, thereby creating open spaces that attracted grazing animals (see box on page 60).

Without claiming to settle the outcome of this heated debate, we found little evidence in the field of open patches solely created by herbivores. But there is one exception: the Beaver.

Two Bison bulls grazing on the forest clearing of Olchówka in the northern part of Białowieża.

The decline and recovery of the European Bison

The word 'bison' is usually associated with the huge, prairie-dwelling American Bison, but an equally impressive relative of theirs is found in Europe. In fact, Europe was the bison's original home. During the ice age of the Pleistocene, sea levels dropped and the Bering Strait between Alaska and Russia fell dry, creating a bridge between Eurasia and the American continent. Some Bison crossed the strait and settled in America. At the end of the ice age the strait became inundated once more, and the Eurasian and American Bison populations were separated from each other. The animals that had moved to America largely settled on the continent's vast prairies, living exclusively off a diet of grasses, while their Eurasian relatives adapted to the primeval lowland forests that dominated the continent and became browsers with a more variable diet. The European Bison flourished in and around Europe's enormous forests and in prehistorical times it was found almost throughout the continent. Early European hunters celebrated bison in some of the most striking examples of Paleolithic *cave art in the world*. However, with the arrival of Man the forests increasingly made way for farmland, and suitable habitat for the Bison disappeared. Bison were also fiercely hunted, both as trophy and for meat. By the start of the 20th century, Bison only occurred in the primeval forest of Białowieża, and on the Northern slopes of the Caucasus, where another, slightly different subspecies lived.

Although the Bison's once huge range had been greatly reduced, for centuries the Polish and Russian monarchs, who controlled these two isolated populations, were fiercely proud of this majestic animal and protected it and its habitat vigorously (see page 64). But when WWI broke out, the protective hand which kept the population safe was gone. The German occupiers hunted the Bison without restraint, and in 1919 the last wild animal was shot in Białowieża (the last one in the Caucasus, victim to the chaos following the Russian revolution, followed several years later).

Fast action was called for to avoid the total extinction of the animal. In 1923, at an international conference on nature conservation in Paris, Jan Sztolcman, the deputy director of the State Zoological Museum in Warsaw, presented the case of the European Bison. All remaining animals in zoos the world over were inventoried and an ambitious breeding program was set up. Twelve animals started this program in 1929. Eventually, though, only seven animals of the lowland race provided offspring for today's free roaming animals. The most important breeding centre was built along the Hajnowka-Białowieża road. It is still there today.

The breeding program proved to be successful. Numbers increased and in spite of a second world war (during which the Germans, upon their retreat razed the fence around the breeding facility) the number of animals was on the rise again. In 1952, two bulls were released into the wild. After 33 years, the Białowieża Forest had free-ranging Bisons again!

Today, over 400 Bison roam the Polish part of the Białowieża forest, and there are also herds in the nearby Knyszyn forest and in the Belarusian part of Białowieża. In several other reserves in Europe, Bison were introduced. Success!

All in all, the Bison seems to be recovering from its low point in the early 20th century. There is reason to rejoice, but some grounds for concern remain. The fact that the population passed through a bottleneck of just seven individual animals means that the genetic diversity of today's Bisons is very limited. This severely impairs the animals' immune systems, exposing them to serious health risks. But a truly wonderful thing is that today, you can once again wander into the Białowieża forest with a chance of an encounter with a wild European Bison.

The Beaver's presence will not go unnoticed. Wherever a wetland is near, signs of its presence are plentiful. In early spring, when the vegetation is still low, you will see just how much this big rodent influences its environment. There are dams, lodges, felled trees, gnawed branches and flooded forests everywhere you go.

Beavers eat leaves and twigs, and enjoy a wet environment to build their lodges. Their teeth, which like finger nails never stop growing, are sharp

Beavers have, through their dam building and felling of trees, an enormous effect on the ecosystem.

enough to gnaw down entire trees. And they like to do so, because that is how they can reach the juiciest twigs high up in the canopy. The branches are used to build dams to flood marshy depressions so that they are wet enough to their liking. Beavers are big animals that do not hibernate, so they need to eat a lot in winter too, which is why they fell so many trees. If trees are not killed by gnawing them down, they die because of the sudden rise of the water due to the building of dams. As such, Beavers create many open, marshy gaps, as you will readily see in Białowieża when you come in summer, when the patches with dead trees are particularly visible

Early spring is the best time of year to see the magnificent Elks in the marshes.

Predators

Large, quiet and intact forests with lots of prey are ideal conditions for predators. Although predators have been hunted fiercely in North-east Poland, the remoteness of the region throughout history (see page 51) has secured the survival of most predator species.

Both Wolf and Lynx occur in fair numbers in Białowieża, Biebrza, Knyszyn and Augustow forests. Wolves hunt in packs, several of which at least occurs in each of these areas. They hunt for Red Deer primarly, but will take Wild Boar and young Elk as well. The Lynx is a very secretive animal. Their main prey is Roe Deer, which they apparently kill by ambush along a deer trail. Lynx are so difficult to find that their numbers are uncertain. They certainly occur in Białowieża and Biebrza.

The Otter is another elusive animal. It occurs in the rivers and fishponds throughout the province. Otters can only reliably be found in winter, when they occur in gaps in the ice.

Of the smaller predators, Red Fox, Badger, Beech Marten, Pine Marten, Weasel, Stoat and Polecat all occur, as do two invasive, non-native species – the American Mink and the Raccoon Dog. Many of these species occur throughout Europe but what's special about North-east Poland is that you actually have a fair chance of running into them. It may be the enormous size and sublime quality of the nature reserves but in this region you will see a lot more of these shy animals than you would in any other area in Europe known to us. For instance, without making a special effort we saw the Pine Marten, a predator normally only rarely encountered, on three different occasions during a two-week trip.

Of the smaller mammals like hares, mice, dormice, voles, shrews and bats, we ought to highlight the presence of the Mountain Hare. For this greyish hare from alpine and boreal regions, North-east Poland is its southernmost lowland haunt.

Wolves are not rare in the region, just difficult to see. Winter offers the best chance.

Birds

The best birdwatching routes are found in Biebrza and Białowieża. Birds of old-growth forest are best on routes 5, 15, 16, 17, 18 and in the strict reserve of Białowieża (see page 207). The rare birdlife of the fen mires are best on routes 8, 9 and 10. Wetland birds are best observed on routes 6, 7, 8, 9, 10 and 20. The birds related to traditional agricultural land are most easily found on routes 7, 8, 15, 19 and 20. Birds of dry sand dunes are found on routes 8, 11, and 12. There are but a few birds that are particularly related to northern-type ecosystems like boreal lakes and taiga-like forest. The best routes for those birds (e.g. Goosander) are routes 2 and 5. See page 225 for a detailed account of the best sites and routes to find each species.

Three-toed and White-backed Woodpeckers, Aquatic Warbler, Great Snipe, Pygmy Owl, Citrine Wagtail, Common Rosefinch, Spotted Eagle and many other mouth-watering species draw large numbers of birders to Northeast Poland. Birdwatching here is indeed nothing short of spectacular. The enormous area and great quality of near-primeval habitats makes for a list of species found scarcely anywhere else in Europe (with the Baltic states and Belarus being the only rivals).

The fact that the region lies on a 'crossroads' of climatic spheres of influence enriches the birdlife. On the one hand alpine-boreal ('northern') species like Three-toed Woodpecker and Pygmy Owl may be found, and on the other hand Pontic-Pannonian ('southern and south-eastern') species like Roller and Citrine Wagtail also occur. The presence of ecologically invaluable old-growth forests like Białowieża and Puszcza Augustówska also accounts for an enormous number of species that were presumably once more widespread in Europe but have declined drastically due to the disappearance of primeval forests. Red-breasted Flycatcher, Collared Flycatcher and White-backed Woodpecker are good examples.

The Biebrza National Park holds the highest diversity of birds. The unsurpassed quality and quantity of the Park's sedge marshes has made it one of the last major strongholds for Aquatic Warbler (see page 99) while the endangered Great Snipe still finds ample undisturbed patches of fen mire in which to lek (a communal form of display).

And then there is north-east Poland's last trump card: it's small-scale, traditional agriculture. Here you can still find species in fair numbers that have disappeared or are declining throughout most of Europe. Ortolan Bunting, Hoopoe, Red-backed Shrike and Common Rosefinch are some examples.

Old-growth forests

The main attraction of Białowieża forest and, to a lesser extent, Puszcza Augustówska are the large tracts of more or less primeval forest. It is here that many of the region's specialties may be found. Puszcza Augustówska even supports a remnant population of Capercaillie.

Some species occur throughout but others are associated with specific forest types (although there is a strong degree of overlap). The oak-linden-hornbeam forest, for instance, is home to Red-breasted and Collared Flycatchers, and White-backed woodpecker. Middle Spotted Woodpecker, with its penchant for old oaks also appreciates this forest type. Hawfinch is especially common in Białowieża but it reaches its highest densities in the oak-linden-hornbeam forest.

Mixed forests (especially with a lush undergrowth) are favoured by the Hazel Grouse. It is very common but it's elusive way of life makes it hard to find, except in early spring.

Coniferous stands of forest attract another suite of birds. Three-toed Woodpecker, Nutcracker, Bullfinch, Crested Tit and Coal Tit prefer this type of habitat although they may also occur in broad-leaved stands with

Great Snipes perform spectacular courting rituals that involve flutter-jumping, tail flicking and a plethora of odd sounds.

Specialities of North-east Poland

Lesser Spotted Eagle	Frequent, though declining in Biebrza and Białowieża.
Spotted Eagle	Rare but stable, especially the forested parts of Biebrza.
Black Stork	Fairly common in swamps.
Hazel Grouse	Common in large old forests, though only easily found in early spring and autumn.
Spotted Crake	Common in sedge marshes.
Corncrake	Very common in wet meadows and sedge marsh.
Crane	Emblematic and common, especially in Biebrza.
Great Snipe	Sought-after though difficult to find in Biebrza's sedge marshes.
Ruff	Spectacular spring migration and courtship in Biebrza.
White-winged Tern	The most common and gracious of the terns. Numbers fluctuate, but it is usually common.
Pygmy Owl	Fairly common in large mixed forest (e.g. Białowieża and Knyszyn forests).
White-backed Woodpecker	Typical of old growth deciduous forest.
Three-toed Woodpecker	The hardest to find of the woodpeckers – old mixed and coniferous forest in Białowieża and Augustów.
Citrine Wagtail	Localised but increasing bird of Siemianowka and Biebrza.
Common Rosefinch	Common!
Aquatic Warbler	Sedge marsh specialist, very local, but common.
Greenish Warbler	Parkland bird of the east, in fluctuating numbers near villages. Usually rare
Red-breasted Flycatcher	Specialist of old deciduous forest.
Collared Flycatcher	Specialist of old deciduous forest.

Three avian highlights of the forests of North-east Poland: Black Woodpecker (opposite, top), Tengmalm's Owl (middle), Hazel Grouse (bottom).

sufficient coniferous trees. Tengmalm's and Pygmy Owls are also at home in coniferous forests but in Białowieża they do equally well in mixed stands. The open Alder carr woods are inhabited by Cranes, who build their nests on the tussocks and islets in the swamp, out of reach from most predators. Another bird you are likely to encounter here is the Green Sandpiper, which breeds in tree holes. In the breeding season it quite often betrays its presence as it noisily tries to scare you off if you come too close to its nest. It is tempting to link birds solely to specific habitat types. But the reality in primeval forest is far more complex. Some birds don't necessarily exhibit a strong preference for a forest with a dominant tree type, as the age of the trees, the lack of forest management or the forest structure may be just as important. Black Woodpecker tends to favour larger older trees in which they excavate a nest. Such sites may be usurped by owls, which may also use the naturally formed holes found in older forests. Surprising is the case of the Swift which is usually assumed to be a cliff-dwelling bird which has adapted to using buildings. The fact that it is a cavity-breeder in Białowieża indicates that it may very well have been just as much at home in primeval forests as it is on cliffs and human settlements.

Old stands mean strong and sturdy canopies which are occupied by tree nesting birds like Black Stork and various eagles (including Lesser Spotted, Spotted, Booted and Short-toed Eagles – the latter two being least common). Although these birds are certainly forest dwellers, you'll have a better chance of seeing them in the places where they forage, like marshlands and agricultural land.

Other birds prefer either young stands or stands with sufficient undergrowth. Hazel Grouse is a good example. Although it thrives in large, old forests, it prefers younger stands within them. Many more species which are considered common throughout Europe (e.g Blackbird, Great, Willow and Blue Tits, Wren, and Robin), enjoy such young stands. Perhaps the relative lack of this habitat is the reason why they are several times more numerous in your own backyard than they are in North-east Poland's primeval forests.

Forest birds

Deciduous forest Middle Spotted Woodpecker, White-backed Woodpecker, Red-breasted Flycatcher, Collared Flycatcher, Green Sandpiper (in alder carr), Nuthatch, Golden Oriole (in wet forests), Hawfinch
Coniferous or mixed forests Capercaillie, Pygmy Owl, Tengmalm's Owl, Three-toed Woodpecker, Redwing, Crested Tit, Coal Tit, Nutcracker, Siskin, Crossbill
Forests in general Goshawk, Sparrowhawk, Hazel Grouse, Woodcock, Swift, Green Woodpecker, Grey-headed Woodpecker, Black Woodpecker, Lesser Spotted Woodpecker, Great Spotted Woodpecker, Redstart (only open forest), Song Thrush, Mistle Thrush, Wood Warbler, Treecreeper, Short-toed Treecreeper, Bullfinch (mostly wet forests)

And then there are the commuters: those species that require a different environment for breeding as for hunting or foraging. Take Pygmy Owls for example. They prefer old mixed or coniferous stands to breed, but hunt near young woods, forest glades and clear-cut edges.

Wetlands

The stunning, pristine rivers, with their wide, marshy floodplains, naturally support huge numbers of birds.
The alder carr wood is an important wetland for birds. It offers breeding ground to birds that forage closer to the river. Cranes seek the shelter of the carr to breed, as do Black Storks and various raptors which build their nests in the tree tops.
Once out of the forest, the open expanses of the sedge marshes appear. The sedge marshes or fen mires of Podlasia are among the most valu-

able of the world, and are prime birding habitat. In the middle of the day, the marshes appear rather devoid of birds, but during the morning and evening, they are alive with the sounds of Water Rails, Little and Spotted Crakes. A dusk in spring will reveal large numbers of 'comb-rasping' Corncrakes (their song is a strange sound, reminiscent of a finger nail running down a comb). This endangered bird

The Garganey is one of the rarer ducks you can encounter in the region's wetlands.

A Black Stork strolls leisurely through the flowery marshlands. Unlike its white cousin, the Black Stork lives in large quiet marshlands. Both Białowieża and Biebrza support healthy populations.

has its main European stronghold in this province and visiting suitable habitat in the early morning or late evening will probably be rewarded with a choir of 'rasping' corncrakes. Don't expect to see one though, they make a point of remaining hidden deep in the vegetation. Corncrakes occur in many low marshes and wet, rough meadows and are among the more common birds of the sedge marshes.

The true sedge marsh superstar is the Aquatic Warbler (see also box on page 99). Whereas the crakes are rarely seen, the Aquatic Warbler likes to perch in a clump of sedge to sing its song. In certain places and in the right season in Biebrza National Park (route 8 and 10) the likelihood of seeing at least one approaches certainty. Other frequent birds of the sedge marshes are Snipe, Sedge Warbler, Reed Bunting, Marsh and Montagu's Harriers and, in some years, Short-eared Owl. Another less common sedge specialist is the endangered Great Snipe. This bird also depends on large swathes of undisturbed sedge marsh in which to locate their lek (courting arena). In these special places the birds perform their odd ritual of standing upright, puffing themselves up and flashing their diagnostic white tail feathers whilst emitting clicking and drumming sounds. Give these rare birds plenty of space by remaining at distance and on designated paths.

The Black Grouse still holds its ground in the Biebrza river valley's extensive marshes, but it is rare and declining so rapidly that we do not advise visitors to go looking for them.

The willow scrub is home to many interesting species like Common Rosefinch, River Warbler, Barred Warbler and Thrush Nightingale. It is worth noting that this type of habitat is not exclusive to river valleys. It may also be found in wet meadows and around shallow lakes.

The willow scrub is usually part of some sort of marshy vegetation consisting of reeds, tall herbs or sedge marsh, and birds of those vegetations are usually not far away. This is a favourite haunt of the Grasshopper Warbler. Reedbeds hold another troop of birds: Bittern, Bluethroat, Penduline Tit and a host of warblers – Savi's, Reed, Great Reed and Sedge Warbler (the latter is easily mistaken for Aquatic Warbler so keep your field guide handy). Some of these birds may venture beyond the reeds to forage or collect nest material, but others hardly ever leave the cover of the reeds. Bittern is an oddity that is restricted to reed beds of considerable size. On some spring mornings you will hear its characteristic 'booming' call coming from several directions, but to see one you need either tremendous luck or perseverance (although heavy floods or a quick frost can improve your chances).

Although the graceful Crane is common in the region, it is never a dull sight.

As one approaches the river another habitat type enters the scene: the oxbow lake. These quiet, well vegetated, swampy lakes are favoured by a variety of birds. Black, White-winged and Whiskered Terns breed on oxbows where there is sufficient vegetation (e.g. Water-soldier or Water-lilies) on which to build their nests. These terns frequently hunt over the oxbows and the floated meadows. Black and White-winged are most common (although the latter's

In spring, Bluethroats like to perch up high in the vegetation to sing.

numbers fluctuate from year to year), but Whiskered and Common Tern are present as well. The Penduline Tits build their elaborate, hanging homes, from which they get their name, in the willow trees that sometimes fringe these little lakes. The oxbows and the river itself is where the region's herons live, but, as with most north and east European marshes, there are not many species of them. Grey Heron is common, as is, in recent times, Great White Egret. In 2012, Night Heron first bred in the region (route 8). Always keep an eye out when you come across a group of foraging White Storks in the wetlands, as sometimes one or two of their black cousins accompany them.

The ever-attractive Kingfisher, although not common, is found along rivers and around fishponds.

This brings us to another type of wetland that offers a different group of birds: Podlasia's lakes. The natural lakes, like the deep glacial lakes found north of Augustów, offer a different range of birds from the man-made lakes, like Siemianówka Reservoir or the Dojlidy fishponds.

The lakes in the northern part of the province are of glacial origin. Most are deep and fairly poor in nutrients, but in some shallow edges, reed beds develop where Bittern and Great Reed Warbler breed, and Great Crested Grebe, Teal, Garganey, Tufted Duck and Shoveler occur, albeit in small numbers. In keeping with the nutrient poor character of these lakes, wildfowl does not occur in large numbers. These lakes have a northern feel – something that is enhanced by the occurrence of boreal species like Goldeneye, Whooper Swan and Goosander, which breed here. These lakes are also the place to scan the sky for hunting Hobbies, which are far more

Birds of wetlands

Reedbeds and willow scrub Marsh Harrier, Water Rail, Little Crake, Bluethroat, Tree Pipit, Whinchat, Barred Warbler, Lesser Whitethroat, Reed Warbler, Great Reed Warbler, Sedge Warbler, Grasshopper Warbler, Savi's Warbler, River Warbler, Penduline Tit, Bearded Tit, Great Grey Shrike, Red-backed Shrike, Common Rosefinch, Reed Bunting

Fen mires and wet meadows Marsh Harrier, Montagu's Harrier, Lesser Spotted Eagle, Spotted Eagle, Water Rail, Spotted Crake, Corncrake, Crane, Snipe, Great Snipe, Ruff, other waders on migration, Aquatic Warbler, Grasshopper Warbler, Great Grey Shrike

Vegetated lakes, rivers and oxbows Mute Swan, Whooper Swan, Greylag Goose, Gadwall, Pintail, Teal, Garganey, Shoveler, Black Stork, Hobby, Whiskered Tern, Black Tern, White-winged Tern, Common Tern, White-tailed Eagle, Kingfisher

Open lakes Great Crested Grebe, Tufted Duck, Pochard, Goldeneye, Goosander, Mute Swan, White-tailed Eagle

common in the northern part of the province than they are to the south. In winter and early spring, Smew and Black-throated Diver seek out the larger lakes, like lake Wigry.

The small, boggy *Suchary* lakes are generally poor when it comes to birds although Goldeneye seems to prefer them as a safe place to rear its young. Cranes are also possible here. This may be said for most, if not all, of Podlasia's wetlands, but seeing them in the 'Scandinavian' setting of the *suchary* does lend an extra dimension to the observation.

The fishpond complexes are another very attractive place for birdwatching. They are shallow, rich in food and their edges are well vegetated so they harbour much larger numbers of wildfowl. Teal, Garganey, Pintail, Shoveler, Gadwall, Mallard, Mute Swan, and Greylag Goose are all common. In some fishpond complexes, such as the Dojlidy ponds near Białystok (see page 208), grebes are quite common and include good numbers of Red-necked, Black-necked and Little Grebes. White-tailed Eagles also frequent fishponds as they contain a high concentration of fish. The reeds and willow thickets offer close views of Penduline Tit, River Warbler, Common Rosefinch, Great Reed Warbler and Bluethroat, making many of these ponds a real treat for birdwatchers. Many fishpond complexes are private though. In fact the above-mentioned Dojlidy ponds are one of the few exceptions. Local birdwatching guides have arranged access for their customers, providing them close encounters with, for example, White-tailed Eagles (see page 218 for addresses of bird tour leaders).

Aquatic Warbler

On an international scale, the small Aquatic Warbler is by far the most significant bird featuring in the Biebrza Valley. It is the only globally threatened songbird of the European mainland, and at the same time the only migratory songbird in Europe with this status. The species even enjoys the protection of its own International Memorandum of Understanding signed by almost all countries in its breeding, migration and wintering range, making it the only little brown bird with its own international agreement.

The Biebrza Valley holds between 2600 and 4000 singing males of this species, representing a quarter to a third of the remaining world population, which nowadays is largely restricted to the peatland-rich lowlands shared between Belarus, Ukraine and Poland. Aquatic Warblers have evolved to live in groundwater-fed fen mires, which used to cover large areas in central Europe. But their numbers have dwindled by at least 95% within the past century, in line with the all but complete destruction of these habitats by drainage and conversion into arable or grazing land or for the extraction of peat for heating and gardening. The fen mires in the Biebrza Valley are the largest near-intact habitat left for this species. Due to its specialisation, the Aquatic Warbler serves as the umbrella species for all other animals and plants depending on fen mires, which can all be found in the same locations as this bird.

The cream-coloured crown stripe and the conspicuous dark streaks on the back distinguish Aquatic Warblers from the similar Sedge Warblers. The song consists of trills and whistles, like a simple version of the varied song of Sedge Warblers.

As soon as they arrive in early May from their only recently discovered wintering sites in wetlands of Senegal and Mali, the males start singing. They will do so until they leave at the end of July. They sing especially around sunset, which is unique amongst European songbirds. Also unique is that all other tasks of breeding and feeding young are done by the females – presumed to be an adaptation to the food-rich habitat they live in.

While the similar Sedge Warblers only occur where reed grows, Aquatic Warblers populate areas with sedges but no or fewer reeds. The world's best place to see the species is along the boardwalk Długu Łuka (route 8). Another good site, but requiring a longer walk, is the Honczarówska road (route 10). The OTOP reserve at the village of Mscichy in the west of the Lower Basin is another good place to get close to this special species (route 7).

Farmland and villages

The bulk of North-east Poland is agricultural land, consisting of meadows and fields. Throughout Europe the birds of this farmland are hit hard by habitat destruction caused by modern machinery, drainage and bio-industry. This holds true for North-east Poland too although on a much more modest scale. In many places, the more traditional forms of agriculture still persist and here White Storks and Cranes still search for frogs and mice in the meadows, while Lesser Spotted Eagles stake out prey from the top of a haystack.

The small fields and pastures, the hedgerows that separate them, the wet meadows, the pollarded willows and small villages create a mosaic of habitats that is favoured by a wide variety of species. Yellowhammers, Whinchats, Red-backed Shrikes, House and Tree Sparrows are especially common while Hoopoe, Corn and Ortolan Buntings, Great Grey Shrikes and Montagu's Harrier may also be found with some effort. Some specific areas of meadows harbour Black-tailed Godwit, Redshank, Lapwing and Corncrake.

Hoopoes (bottom) and Yellowhammer (facing page) are both common farmland birds.

Two sought-after species of the agricultural lands are the Roller and the Citrine Wagtail. Both are species for which north-east Poland is at the extreme of their range. The Roller, a bird of the Mediterranean and the east, is declining and becoming increasingly rare, but Citrine Wagtail, more a bird of central Asia, seems to increase by the year since first breeding in Poland in the late 1990s.

The wettest meadows are favoured by waders like Black-tailed Godwit, Redshank, Lapwing and the extravagant Ruff, the bird that graces the signs for the Biebrza National Park. The vast majority of birds only visit the area on passage but they do remain here for a considerable length of time to display. The Biebrza area is in fact one of the best places in the world to witness this spectacle (see box on page 103).

Agricultural land close to the marshes and forests are also of interest to some species that do not breed there. Although Black Stork, Lesser Spotted Eagle and Spotted Eagle breed deep in the forests, you are far more likely to see them in the fields or the

Yellowhammer

wetlands when they visit these places to feed. One place where this is es-
pecially true is in the forest glades around the hamlets of Teremiski and
Budy in Białowieża (route 19). These are the best places to see Black Stork
and Lesser Spotted Eagle.
The small villages in the province also have their own birdlife. Those
in and around the Białowieża forest are particularly interesting as they
boast an exotic set of garden birds. It is not uncommon to see Wryneck,
Green Woodpecker, Grey-headed Woodpecker, Hawfinch, Hoopoe, Black
Redstart and Spotted Flycatcher on a casual stroll through one of the vil-
lages of the area. And the many White Storks on the wooden houses are
always a pleasure to see. Along village lanes, the Ortolan Bunting still
breeds, although this bird has become rare over the last decades, even in
North-east Poland.

Birds of farmland and villages

Fields White Stork, Common Crane, White-fronted Goose, Bean Goose,
Montagu's Harrier, Lapwing, Curlew, Northern Wheatear
Meadows Corncrake, Black-tailed Godwit, Redshank, Skylark, Meadow Pipit,
Yellow Wagtail, Citrine Wagtail (localised),
Villages Barn Owl, Little Owl, Long-eared Owl, Hoopoe, Syrian Woodpecker
(very rare), Wryneck, Black Redstart, Spotted Flycatcher, Fieldfare, Tree
Sparrow, Serin, Yellowhammer

In the vast marshes of ancient East-Poland (see history section), villages on the drier sand dunes. These dunes are a final attraction for birdwatchers, with Woodlark, Tree Pipit, Hoopoe, Wheatear, Great Grey Shrike and, though rare, Tawny Pipit being typical species.

The birding year

As is the case in many eastern and northern parts of Europe, the outburst in bird activity is excessive and short-lived. The best time is from mid-April to mid-June. In mid-April to early May, most migratory birds arrive, whilst some wintering birds are still present. In the second half of April it is possible to see the last of the Rough-legged Buzzards, Smew and even Black-throated Diver, and at the same time the first Collared Flycatcher, Crane and White-winged Tern. This is also the perfect time to see the courting Ruffs, and track down the resident woodpeckers, grouse and owls.

Spring is in full swing from roughly the 10th to the end of May, when pretty much every bird is singing. The above-mentioned grouse, owls and woodpeckers are harder to find, but local guides know exactly where they are. This is the period that birdwatchers prefer. Come June, and the birds go quiet just as the vegetation rapidly grows to hide them from sight. In summer, nearly all the species are still present, just very hard to find. In the course of September, a huge exodus west and south takes place to flee from the chilly grip of an eastern European winter.

During migration, large flocks of Cranes gather in the wetlands.

The courting of the Ruff: dress to impress

Of all the wonderful sights the Biebrza has to offer in springtime, the courting of the Ruff is perhaps the most spectacular. The males of these migrant waders start to moult into an extravagant breeding plumage with brightly coloured tufts and ruffs (hence the name) before they leave their wintering quarters.

They start courting during migration. The Biebrza basin is an important way-point in the ruff's northward journey. Hence it is an excellent site to admire their colourful and elaborate plumage and witness the courting with its odd rituals, dances and battles. Groups of courting ruffs may be found throughout the National Park but the meadows between the *Carska Droga* (road of the Tsars), the hamlet of Zajki (route8) and the wet meadows of Grądy-Woniecko (route 7) are especially good.

Apart from the visual splendour, the ruff's reproduction process is riddled with evolutionary oddities. The dominant males (independent males) will defend a patch of territory in a larger lek. These males are easily identified by their chestnut and black tufts and ruffs.

A second, much smaller group of males does not occupy a territory. Instead, they visit leks and try to mate with females (reeves) when the nearby dominant males are distracted. These males are called satellites and their ruffs are predominantly white.

In addition to these two types, another category of males was recently discovered. This even smaller group has developed yet another strategy to pass on their genes. Instead of moulting into the extravagant breeding plumage, they moult into a plumage very similar to that of the reeves (females). These birds are called faeders and, like the satel-

lites, they don't occupy a territory but rather browse leks and wait for an opportune moment to 'steal' a mating. While it may seem logical to assume that these cross-dressers are not recognised as competitors by the independent males due to their reeve-like appearance, there is some evidence to suggest that the independent males are aware of their gender but tolerate their presence because a lek with other types of males present attracts more females than a lek with independent males only.

A Ruff in its spectacular courting plumage.

Reptiles and Amphibians

Moor Frog is most easily found the lakes in the Augustów and Biebrza areas (routes 3, 4, 5, 8). Tree Frogs are quite common in the Biebrza, but particularly easy to find in the Białowieża forest clearing (route 15). Search (by listening to their calls) for Fire-bellied Toad on routes 1, 7, 8, 20. Look for Sand Lizard on route 12. Grass Snake is often encountered along route 6, 8 and 20 and near the sand pits on near Masiewo (see map on page 181).

Both for amphibians and reptiles, early spring (April) is the best time, because then they are on the move to their mating waters. This is also the time that they are killed by traffic, especially on the minor roads you are likely to travel. So please take care!

Amphibians

As amphibians are intrinsically linked to wetlands, it should be no surprise that North-east Poland boasts enormous populations. Even though the number of amphibian species, eleven, is not very impressive, the sheer number of individuals certainly is. Strolling along minor roads in suitable habitat on warm rainy evenings in spring or summer you will encounter hordes of toads and frogs hopping or crawling to and fro. Many of the species found here occur throughout Europe and are by no means rare. Grass Frog, Edible Frog and Common Toad are the most numerous. The cute Tree Frog is also fairly common. It often betrays its presence when it starts croaking in choirs after sunset. The Moor Frog is another interesting species that is fairly easy to find in this area. Most of the time it is almost indistinguishable from the Grass Frog but during the mating season in early spring, the males turn bright blue, a feast for the eye! They may be found in reed beds on the edges of some of the larger lakes but the best places to look for them are the lakes in Puszcza Augustówska. Between late March to mid April, keep your ears open for their typical call which is slightly reminiscent of a gently boiling kettle of water. Natterjack Toad, Green Toad and Common Spadefoot are also present in the area although they are quite hard to find. The Green Toad is known to occur in Białowieża village. Taking a stroll from the first bridge on the Narew towards Skansen open air museum on a warm, rainy night in spring or summer might result in a sighting or two (see route 15). The Natterjack Toad and Spadefoot are restricted to sandy soils close to shallow water. Abandoned sand excavations are most likely to produce sightings on suitable nights.

The amphibian star of the area is the Fire-bellied Toad. This little wart-covered toad sports a belly with bright orange blotches – hence the name. If you find them (you need to develop an eye for them), don't miss looking at its beautiful, heart-shaped pupils. Although the Fire-bellied Toad is in decline, there

are still enough places where they may be found with relative ease in this region. Be aware of the fact that it is almost impossible to find without knowing its call, an odd, fluty *pjuup*-like sound.

Only two newts occur in the area. The Common Newt is, as the name suggests, common. The Crested Newt however is more tricky to find.

Reptiles

The harsh winters of north-east Poland make for conditions which only few reptiles can endure. So the number of species found in the area (seven, two of which are very rare) is relatively low. Of those that do occur only the Viviparous Lizard and the Grass Snake may be called common. They occur in almost all wet habitats, from the wettest alder carr woods to the soggiest sedge marshes. We even found Viviparous Lizards swimming in the waterlogged swamps of the Biebrza in spring!

The Slow Worm is not too rare either but its nocturnal way of life makes it hard to find. Most specimens you will come across are dead animals that have been hit by cars. Sand Lizard occurs only on exposed sandy moraines. Adder occurs even more locally and is very difficult to find. Smooth Snake and European European Pond Terrapin have also been recorded in the area, but are now likely extinct. The latter is an interesting example since it occurred in Białowieża only until the increasing woodlands around its breeding ponds apparently caused its disappearance. A case in which the increase of the natural forest has a negative effect.

Sand dunes near water are the favoured habitat of the Common Spadefoot (top). The adorable Fire-bellied Toads (bottom) live a hidden life. Listening for their fluty call is the easiest way of finding one.

Insects and other invertebrates

Good routes for butterflies of dry, flowery grasslands are route 1, 4, 12, 18 and 20. Better butterfly haunts are the wet marshes on routes 8, 9, 10 and 11 and 13. Great routes for finding dragonflies are routes 2, 3, 6, 7, 8, 9, 10 and 14.

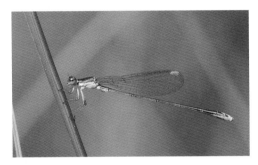

The Sedgling is Europe's smallest damselfly and a major draw for dragonfly specialists.

At the end of May, the insect season starts. This applies to both the annoying species, like mosquitoes and horseflies, and to the beautiful ones, such as butterflies and dragonflies. Little clouds of fritillaries flutter over the flowery meadows, while hundreds and thousands of dragonflies emerge from the waters. A feast for the eye for all, but a racing heart for those enthusiasts who catch their first glimpse of east European rarities like Sedgeling, Banded Darter, Scarce or Pallas's Fritillaries.

Butterflies

Europe's richest butterfly areas are generally in the mountains and in the south. Hence it may come as a surprise that North-east Poland is a butterfly hotspot. The region both excels in rare species (e.g. Scarce Fritillary, Purple Hairstreak) and in numbers. It is not rare to see 20+ Silver-washed Fritillaries on a single Angelica, 30-odd butterflies of eight species on a single patch of thyme or masses of White and Poplar Admirals along a single forest track.

The warm summers and the presence of large areas of unscathed habitat are the prime reasons for this abundance, but the location so far east in Europe is another factor. Many species (Cranberry Fritillary for example) have a distribution range that extends from the Alps to the east and then extending north. They are absent in lowland Europe except for the far eastern part, with north-east Poland their westernmost lowland area.

This odd distribution is strikingly evident in many species. It is thought to be a heritage from the last ice age, during which species adapted to cold winters and short warm summers gradually moved north and east with the retreat of the land ice. They subsequently disappeared in western Europe due to its mild and wet summers. Whether this theory is true or not, is not fully certain, but in any case, the number of eastern species that are known only as mountain species in the west is quite high. Hence it is quite easy to find butterflies of the central European hillsides, such as Chestnut Heath, Purple-edged Copper and Clouded Apollo in the flat, marshy expanses and Rock Grayling in an area where rocks are overall very rare!

Some of the butterflies of the raised bogs have a more restricted distribution range, and are confined to the bogs of the high Alps and the Scandinavian taigas. These are Large Heath, Cranberry Blue, Cranberry Fritillary and – very rare – Baltic Grayling. The bogs of north-east Poland are in their case the southernmost limit of their lowland range.

A great attraction for butterfly enthusiasts is the occurrence of some very demanding and rare central European species. Butterflies like Large Chequered Skipper, Large Copper, Violet Copper and Scarce Fritillary have become very rare, or very local in central Europe. They are not exactly common in North-east Poland either, but scattered over the various National Parks there are some good populations. This holds true too for the beautiful False Ringlet which occurs in Narew National Park despite being extremely rare across Europe (except for a small corner in southwest France).

Silver-washed Fritillaries swarming around Wild Angelica. In the middle of summer, it is not uncommon to see several tens of them around nectar plants. The rare Clouded Apollo is a much sought-after butterfly.

All over Europe these species have declined due to habitat destruction, so their presence is testimony to the splendid and intact habitats that are still widely present in the region. Butterflies such as Pearl-bordered and Small Pearl-bordered Fritillaries are still widespread in Europe, but show a marked decline in many countries (e.g. the UK and The Netherlands). Seeing great numbers of these beautiful butterflies glide over the mires in, for instance, the Biebrza is simply amazing. Many of the more attractive

Butterflies of north-east Poland

Widespread and conspicuous butterflies Swallowtail *(Papilio machaon)*, Pale Clouded Yellow *(Colias hyale)*, Wood White *(Leptidea sinapis)*, Sooty Copper *(Lycaena tityrus)*, Holly Blue *(Celastrina argiolus)*, Purple Emperor *(Apatura iris)*, Poplar Admiral *(Limenitis populi)*, White Admiral *(Limenitis camilla)*, Map Butterfly *(Araschnia levana)*, Camberwell Beauty *(Nymphalis antiopa)*, Silver-washed Fritillary *(Argynnis paphia)*, Dark Green Fritillary *(Argynnis aglaja)*, Queen of Spain Fritillary *(Issoria lathonia)*, High Brown Fritillary *(Argynnis ad-ippe)*, Heath Fritillary *(Melitaea athalia)*, Pearl-bordered Fritillary *(Boloria eu-phrosyne)*, Small Pearl-bordered Fritillary *(Boloria selene)*, Glanville Fritillary *(Melitaea cinxia)*, Ringlet *(Aphantopus hyperantus)*

Eastern, northern and 'mountain' butterflies Northern Chequered Skipper *(Carterocephalus silvicolus)*, Clouded Apollo *(Parnassius mnemos-yne)*, Moorland Clouded Yellow *(Colias palaeno)*, Eastern Bath White *(Pontia edusa)*, Scarce Copper *(Lycaena virgaureae)*, Purple-edged Copper *(Lycaena hippothoe)*, Geranium Argus *(Aricia eumedon)*, Mountain Argus *(Aricia artax-erxes)*, Amanda's Blue *(Polyommatus amandus)*, Cranberry Blue *(Plebejus op-tilete)*, Pallas' Fritillary *(Argynnis laodice)*, Lesser Marbled Fritillary *(Brenthis ino)*, Cranberry Fritillary *(Boloria aquilonaris)*, False Heath Fritillary *(Melitaea diamina)*, Assmann's Fritillary *(Melitaea britomartis)*, Nickerl's Fritillary *(Melitaea aurelia)*, Arran Brown (*Erebia ligea* – very rare), Baltic Grayling *(Oeneis jutta* – very rare), Dusky Meadow Brown *(Hyponephele lycaon)*, Scarce Heath *(Coenonympha hero)*, Chestnut Heath *(Coenonympha glycerion)*, Large Heath *(Coenonympha tullia)*

Southern or warmth-loving species Blue-spot Hairstreak *(Satyrium spini)*, Chalk-hill Blue *(Polyommatus coridon)*, Lesser Purple Emperor *(Apatura ilia)*, Weaver's Fritillary *(Boloria dia)*, Spotted Fritillary *(Melitaea didyma)*, Marbled White *(Melanargia galathea)*

Localised butterflies of central Europe Large Chequered Skipper *(Heteropterus morpheus)*, Violet Copper *(Lycaena helle)*, Large Copper *(Lycaena dispar)*, Short-tailed Blue *(Cupido argiades)*, Large Blue *(Phengaris arion)*, Scarce Fritillary *(Euphydryas maturna)*, Woodland Brown *(Lopinga achine)*, Large Wall Brown *(Lasiommata maera)*, Rock Grayling *(Hipparchia alcyone)*, Pearly Heath *(Coenonympha arcania)*, False Ringlet *(Coenonympha oedippus)*

Central and East-European species are unique to wetlands. Large Copper is typical of marshlands with a varied structure in which the larval food plant Water Dock occurs. Its smaller cousin, the Violet Copper, only spreads its wings around wet meadows with Bistort. Scarce Heath, Scarce Fritillary and Large Chequered Skipper are all specialists of damp meadows and clearings in wet forests.

There are also quite a few butterflies of dry grasslands. Look for them on the open sandy areas of the Biebrza, the slopes of Wigry and, above all, Suwałki Landscape Park. The Thyme patches are favoured haunts for Chestnut Heath, Sooty and Scarce Coppers. Here you can challenge yourself to tell apart the likes of Spotted, False Heath, Heath, Nickerl's, Pearl-bordered and Glanville Fritillaries. In June and July, all of these may be present. Marbled White is also frequent. It only recently started colonising the area from the south, and is frequent in Biebrza, Narew and Białowieża, but, at the time of writing, still absent from the northern parks. Easily the most common butterfly of such habitats, at least during the summer months, is the Ringlet.

Butterflies are not evenly spread over the region. The most diverse region is, without doubt, the Biebrza National Park. Its sedge marshes, wet meadows, flowery sand dunes and woodland glades offer a diversity of butterfly habitats. Yet it is Białowieża that, with 104 species, holds the formal record of numbers of butterflies recorded. Biebrza is only a little behind with 103 species (this compares to only 59 found on the British isles!). This immediately reveals a difficulty in interpreting these figures. Białowieża has a long tradition of systematic wild-

The Scarce Fritillary (top) and Large Chequered Skipper (bottom) are two of Biebrza's butterfly highlights.

life investigation and during this period many of the flowery forest glades have become overgrown, causing the disappearance of many butterfly species. In contrast, butterfly surveys of such a scale in the Biebrza have only recently been conducted for the first time. The areas of the Narew, Wigry and Suwałki are even less investigated, so you may even discover some new species here yourself! Wigry is famous for harbouring some of the country's populations of butterflies of raised bogs, including the country's only population of Baltic Grayling (on a site not accessible to the public).

Much more visible are the park's enormous populations of White Admiral, which fly along each forest track in summer.

The warm, flowery and stony slopes of Suwałki Landscape Park form a butterfly hotspot, with various fritillaries, Short-tailed and Small Blues and Swallowtails – in other words, butterflies of dry, flowery meadows. And they fly here by the hundreds!

Dragonflies

North-east Poland is, if not the very best, one of the best regions to watch dragonflies in Europe. There are approximately 60 species in the region, and many of those have a distinctly eastern European distribution and are often difficult to find elsewhere in Europe.

Many Dragonfly species are quite picky in their choice of breeding waters. Perhaps the richest waters are those of oxbows and still waters in river bends, which abound in the Biebrza and Narew. Such spots often hold large numbers of both Large and Small Redeyes, Yellow-spotted Whiteface and Hairy, Green-eyed and Brown Hawkers. On patches with Water-soldier, look for Green Hawker – a species that is very typical of areas with this plant and which can occur in large numbers. One very attractive species of oxbows (and to lesser extend also of peaty lakes), is the Yellow-spotted Whiteface. It is an early species that can emerge by the hundreds in course of May. Oxbows are also the sites of some of the rarest species of dragonflies, namely Eurasian Baskettail and Lilypad Whiteface. Both are very rare and because of their habit to fly over the central part of lakes and oxbows rather than close to the shore, quite difficult to find. There are only a handful of sightings of the Eurasian Baskettail in Biebrza while Lilypad Whiteface occurs on the lakes of the Wigry area.

The Yellow-spotted Whiteface is fairly common in oxbows and shallow, peaty lakes.

Still water bodies that heat up quickly, such as quarries and exposed, shallow oxbows, are the haunts of White-tailed Skimmer (a recent invader from the south), Yellow-winged Darter, Broad-bodied, Blue and Four-spotted Chasers. Such sites are also the places to search for Banded Darter and Dark Whiteface. Banded Darter is quite common in such pioneer habitats all over the Biebrza, but Dark Whiteface, in contrast, is extremely rare. It is found much more

Dragonflies

Lakes general Brown Hawker *(Aeshna grandis)*, Blue Hawker *(Aeshna cyanea)*, Blue Emperor *(Anax imperator)*, Lesser Emperor (Anax parthenope; local), Downy Emerald *(Cordulia aenea)*, Four-spotted Chaser *(Libellula quadrimaculata)*, Broad-bodied Chaser *(Libellula depressa)*

Oxbows and shallow waters Large Redeye *(Erythromma najas)*, Small Redeye *(Erythromma viridulum)*, Shallow waters, pits: Small Bluetail *(Ishnura pumilio)*, Green-eyed Hawker *(Aeshna isosceles)*, Green Hawker *(Aeshna viridis)*, Hairy Hawker *(Brachytron pratense)*, Eurasian Baskettail *(Epitheca bimaculata*, rare), White-tailed Skimmer *(Orthetrum albistylum*, rare), Yellow-spotted Whiteface *(Leucorrhinia pectoralis)*, Lilypad Whiteface *(Leucorrhinia caudalis*, rare), Banded Darter *(Sympetrum pedemontanum)*

Raised Bogs Sedgeling *(Nehallenia speciosa)*, Moorland Hawker *(Aeshna juncea;* rare), Bog Hawker *(Aeshna subarctica*, rare), Brilliant Emerald *(Somatochlora metallica)* Northern Emerald *(Somatochlora arctica*, rare), Four-spotted Chaser *(Libellula quadrimaculata)*, Small Whiteface *(Leucorrhinia dubia)*, Ruby Whiteface *(Leucorrhinia rubicunda)*, Yellow-spotted Whiteface *(Leucorrhinia pectoralis)*, Dark Whiteface *(Leucorrhinia albifrons)*, Black Darter *(Sympetrum danae)*

Rivers Blue Featherleg *(Platycnemis pennipes)*, River Clubtail *(Gomphus flavipes)* Green Snaketail *(Ophiogomphus cecilia)*, Small Pincertail *(Onychogomphus forcipatus)*, Blue Chaser *(Libellula fulva)*, Banded Darter *(Sympetrum pedemontanum)*

Fen Mires Yellow-spotted Emerald *(Somatochlora flavomaculata)*, Yellow-winged Darter *(Sympetrum flaveolum)*

The Banded Darter is an eastern specialty which occurs locally in the region. The dark wing patches make them unmistakable, even in flight.

frequently in another habitat, namely that of the *suchary* or peat bog lakes in the north.

Bog lakes have an interesting dragonfly fauna consisting of several species which are restricted to these habitats, such as Small and Ruby Whitefaces and Brilliant Emerald. Four species of whitefaces (Small, Ruby, Dark and Yellow-spotted Whitefaces),can be present in impressive numbers. They are joined by Ruddy and Moustached Darters which appear in equally large numbers. Walking along a trail on the border of a peatland, they fly off from the vegetation in the hundreds.

The Dark Whiteface
is an eastern specialty
that is most frequent
in the northern
Suchary.

Northern Emerald is a rare species of small peatlands surrounded by
forest. Its exact status is not clear, but its habitat is present in the Wigry
area. Another favourite is the Sedgeling, a tiny damselfly with a distinct
eastern European range that lives a hidden life between an open vegetation
of grasses and sedges. It is most easily found by crossing such terrain and
looking for a small feeble flying damselfly lifting off from the vegetation.
Sedgelings are not exclusive to raised bogs. They also occur in the more
open sedge marshes in the Biebrza, such as those on the Długu Łuka trail
(route 8). Otherwise, the fen mires support few typical species of their own.
Perhaps the Yellow-spotted Emerald is most confined to the mires. Most
large dragonflies patrolling over a patch of mire are likely to be this species.
The final habitat to visit for its dragonflies are the rivers. Banded
Demoiselles are abundant on the larger rivers while Beautiful Demoiselles
tend to seek out the smaller, more shaded rivers. Many rivers hold both
species. The Blue Featherleg is the most frequent damselfly. The Narew
river, with its sandy stream bed, is the place to seek River Clubtail and
Green Snaketail, while the fast-flowing, stony streams in Wigry are the
favourite haunt of Small Pincertail.

Other insects and invertebrates

The number of insects, spiders, centipedes, millipedes, snails and other
invertebrates in the region is dazzling. Walking over a dry grassland, you'll

Spruce Engraver

A fiercely debated 'plague insect' (whether the term 'plague' is applicable depends on your take on the function of a forest) is the Spruce Engraver or Bark Beetle, which produces a 'plague year' every 5 to 15 years. This beetle lives on and in spruce trees and is able to kill the entire tree. Male beetles sense weakened spruce trees and infest them. They produce pheromones, which attract other males and females. It is the beetle's tactic to team up in order to kill the tree. This is important, because otherwise the tree will kill them and their larvae by means of a self-produced insecticide. Only a swift and massive attack 'by surprise' leaves the tree too little time to put up its defence.

The beetles dig tunnels just under the bark in which they lay eggs. The particular, rune-like pattern of these tunnels gave the animal the name 'engraver' and its scientific name *Ips typographus*. The tunnels cut horizontally through the bark, thereby cutting off the tree's food supply and killing it. The Spruce Engraver's secretive tunnel-digging is likely to be more effective as a forest manager than the munching of the European Bison.

Spruce trees are shallow rooters and trees quickly tip over when they lose their grip on the forest floor. By falling over, these trees create new clearings, which promotes rejuvenation of the forest. The enormous root systems provide shelter for numerous insects and other animals. The larvae of the Spruce Engraver are the main food source for the one of the region's most attractive birds: the Three-toed Woodpecker. Hence the Spruce Engraver plays an important role in natural, mixed forests. But in a monoculture of spruce, its effect can be devastating.

≈ 1 mm

Leaves are the prime food source for caterpillars. By periodic outbreaks of plagues they allow sunlight to reach the forest floor, profitable for large herbs, which in turn provides shelter for prey animals. This is one of the complex ecological cycles that drive the old-growth forest ecosystem.

encounter many grasshoppers (particularly the conspicuous Blue-winged Grasshopper), moths and other insects. In particular the invertebrate fauna that is associated with primeval forests is very special.

The invertebrate fauna of Białowieża National Park is exceptionally well researched. Currently, over 11,000 species of invertebrates have been found within the forest complex! To put this in perspective: this is greater than all the world's bird species!

The buglife of Białowieża has received such attention because invertebrates play a key role in the ecosystem of primeval forests. Typical of old-growth is the central role of wood decay – a process that is largely absent from forestry-managed forests where wood is removed before it is able to decay. The sturdy wood fibres are resistent to rot – hence the process of decay is slow and involves many steps. In each of them a whole array of invertebrates play a significant role. Białowieża, being one of the most important (near-)primeval forests left in Europe, is home to a series of invertebrate species that are rare in, or even absent from, other forest reserves in Europe. Most of them are obscure critters whose scientific names are only known to a few specialists, but their role in the forest ecosystem makes them fascinating. Some species are so specialised that they only live under the bark of a specific tree species at a specific stage of decay (e.g. *Mycetome suturale*, which depends on the fungus *Ischoderma benzoinum*. Elsewhere, entire invertebrate communities occur in specific habitats related to old-growth forests. For instance, there is a specific group of invertebrates that live only in the humus and dead wood mass that accumulates in tree holes in forest giants! Some of them are unique to the Białowieża primeval forest.

Another reason for the interest in the invertebrates of Białowieża is that several insects are known as plague insects in the monocultures of intensive forestry. Białowieża forms the best showcase to research how these insects function in the species rich old-growth forests where they evolved. The role of these insects are a focal point of fierce debate among the foresters who want to manage, and the conservationists, who want natural processes to run the forest (see box on page 113).

Apart from boosting the biodiversity in the forest, dead wood also provides one of the forest's most important reserves of moisture and nutrients, which are released slowly over a long time. Decaying wood thus represents a long-term stabilising force within the forest ecosystem. The forest you are enjoying today thrives on centuries of dead wood of long-forgotten trees.

The forest is dead – long live the forest!

The expression that death is a part of life couldn't be more applicable to the Białowieża. The number of dead tree trunks and woody debris is enormous, especially in the strict reserve.

The process of decay is generally somewhat underappreciated. Decay is often smelly and alive with creeping and crawling animals. While all those bugs, centipedes, cockroaches, worms and snails disgust many people, many biologists don't care for them either as they lead a secret life and are far too hard to tell apart.

Nonetheless breakdown and death are valuable processes in ecosystems and they are an absolute necessity in creating all the beautiful things we do like to look at. From the first signs of decay to the complete disappearance of a tree, decades can pass. During the process, species come and go in a parade of invertebrates. It is just like the process of succession, but in reverse. Biologists discern no less than six stages of breakdown, each with its own set of invertebrate and fungus species.

In the pioneering stage, insects eat their way between bark and wood, leaving wounds for fungi and other, smaller invertebrates to colonise. Although the bark is often still quite intact, the soft layer of wood just underneath (the so-called sapwood) becomes mushy when fungi, bacteria, yeasts and the rest of the seamy side of life work through it.

Over time the centre or hardwood of the tree, which decays much slower than the surrounding sapwood, gets infected too. Now the diversity of 'inner-trunk life' is at its richest. Not only invertebrates, but also mice, shrews, voles, toads, frogs and salamanders take advantage of the moist, sheltered environment of the dead tree. Once the heartwood starts to rot, the trunk easily breaks down into fragments. Slowly, these pieces of wood get incorporated into the soil.

After reading the previous sections and looking at the photographs, you may well have arrived at the conclusion that North-east Poland is 'top-of-the-pops' naturewise. No argument here. Nevertheless, there are clear regional differences in habitats and species within the area covered by the book.

The area can be divided into three different regions, each with its own attractions. In the following section of this book, we briefly describe those regions and the various detailed routes which, combined, show you the best these regions have to offer. At the end of each of these sections we offer a number of extra sites and routes for further exploration.

In the northern part of the region, hugging the Russian and Lithuanian border, lies the Suwałki – Augustów region (routes 1 to 5). This is the Polish 'Siberia' – a region with a cold climate and distinct boreal influences which you will readily appreciate in the many lakes, bogs and coniferous forest. The hilly terrain, a result from the glacial period, gives this far corner of Poland a pleasant and beautiful landscape. As a consequence, it is a popular summer retreat among the Polish and Lithuanians.

South of Augustów, the landscape is flatter, and dominated by two elaborate river systems – that of the Biebrza (routes 6 to 13) and of the Narew (route 14). Both river valleys are such unspoilt gems of nature that they are often considered the benchmark by which the environmental status of other European river systems must be judged. Both rivers, but the Biebrza in particular, are famous for their many species of rare birds and largest population of Elk in Poland. It's an excellent idea to explore these rivers by canoe as well. For details on canoeing, see page 216.

East and south-east of the large city of Białystok, temperate old-growth forests dominate the landscape. The famous forest complex of Białowieża (routes 15 to 19) and the almost unexplored, but very rich, Knyszyn forest (page 208) are the great attractions here. Białowieża is famous for its vast primeval forest stands, for being the place where wild Bison survived (see box on page 86) and for its fascinating forest ecology and rich birdlife.

Cycling is the ideal way to explore Białowieża forest.

Augustów region

When driving up from Warsaw, you'll find that the landscape suddenly becomes hilly just before you arrive in Augustów. This was the southern border of the ice sheet in the last ice age, between 15–115,000 years ago. From Augustów to the borders in the north and east, this ice sheet has left a stunning, rolling landscape that today is dotted with lakes and covered in old forests interspersed with small-scale agricultural plots.

The main forest complex is that of Augustów forest, which is Poland's largest forest (much bigger in fact, than the more famous Białowieża). Augustów forest is largely under commercial management, but there are many smaller and larger forest reserves within the complex. There are small agricultural enclaves, peatlands and natural lakes. Unspoilt rivers like the Czarna Hańza and Rospuda dissect the forest.

Few people explore Augustów forest, which makes a visit a great adventure. But getting to grips with this forest is not as easy as the other reserves. The best sections are either small, nearly impenetrable or lie deep within the complex. Hence we chose to link some of the best and most accessible sites in a single, long car route (route 5).

The easy-to-visit part of the Augustów forest lies in the northwest and is protected in the Wigry National Park. Large forests, small scale agricultural plots, completely untouched rivers and the stunning lake Wigry (according to some, Poland's most beautiful lake) are all combined in a

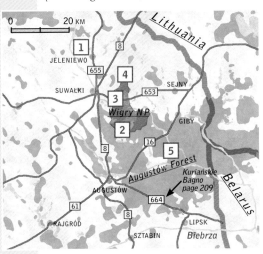

single, fairly small and easily accessible National Park (routes 2 to 4). The National Park takes particular pride in its stunning collection of bog-fringed fen lakes (routes 2 and 3), which are locally named *suchary*. They are a truly northern habitat which is, within Poland, pretty much confined to Wigry.

Further north, between Suwałki and the Russian border, lies the Suwałki Landscape Park (route 1), which stands out as the

Sunset at one of Augustów forest's many glacial lakes.

most hilly and stony area here. The whole park is a geological museum of the ice ages. Within a small area, there are boulder fields, an esker, glacial lakes (including the deepest lake in lowland Europe), *kames* and a hanging valley – all features associated with ice age. On top of this, the park's attractive scenery boasts the most flowery and butterfly-rich slopes in the entire region.

PRACTICAL PART

Route 1: Suwałki Landscape Park

FULL DAY
35 KM

Landscape created by the ice age,
with many geologically interesting features
Dry meadows with lots of wildflowers and
butterflies

Habitats Meadows, lakes, streams, alder carr woods, Oak-linden-Hornbeam
Forest, Coniferous Forest
Selected species Hobby, Goosander, Sand Lizard, Swallowtail, Long-tailed
Blue, Small Blue, Niobe's Fritillary, Pannonian Knapweed

This car route, with short walks, takes you through the Suwalski landscape park – a very picturesque, hilly area with many traces of the last glacial period. The 'recent' glacial history is evident in the many lakes, the remains of an esker, a hanging valley and several boulder fields. Do not expect the dramatic landscape of steep mountains and deep valleys; Suwalski's glacial relics are much more modest. If you are up for a pleasant day driving through an attractive landscape with some interesting flora, fauna and geological features then Suwalski is an excellent choice. This route can also be done by bicycle which may be rented at the Turtul information centre.

Departure point Jeleniewo, north of Suwałki.

At the conspicuous wooden church of Jeleniewo, which is home to one of only two colonies of Pond Bat in Poland, take the road to Kruszki. After 7.5 km, turn right to the information centre, signposted *Malesowizna-Turtul 500 m.*

1 Cross the bridge over the Czarna Hańcza, if you look to your left you will see the Turtul lake dotted with several islands. These islands and nearby hills, including the one on which the information centre is built, are part of an esker, an 'under-ice' river of the glacial period (see page 17). The remains of this esker run through the Czarna Hańcza valley for almost 3 km.

Follow the trail along the lake. The dry, flowery grasslands on this hill at-
tract Swallowtail, Long-tailed and Little Blues and no less than six species
of fritillaries. Look for Spreading Bellflower among the many wildflowers
and mind the basking Sand Lizards on the trail.
After 2 km the 'hanging valley' is visible as it comes down towards the
Czarna Hańcza Valley. This is the only valley of its kind in Poland, and
therefore quite interesting for geologists, but the casual observer might
not really notice it.

Return to the information centre and follow the route by car to Kruszki.
Here, take the turn to Bachanowo. After 1,4 km, a small car park to the
right marks the beginning of the trail down to the Bachanowo Reserve.

2 The Bachanowo reserve contains an attractive small boulder field
(rounded rocks that were brought down by the ice sheet). This field
has the highest density of glacial boulders in Poland. We, however, were
more impressed by the small platform down at the river's edge. The river
is fast flowing and gives the impression of one in the mountains rather
than in north-east Poland. Common Spotted-orchid and Beech Fern grow
close to the platform, while Small Pincertail and Beautiful Demoiselle
hunt over the river.

v = visitors centre

At a junction, turn left (sign-
posted Hancza) and then right to
Wizajny. Where the road bends
left, a dirt track signposted Stara
Hancza branches off to the right.
Take it and park beyond the
bridge over the Czarna Hańcza.
Follow the blue trail along the
river to lake Hancza, and further
along the lake.

3 Lake Hancza is, with a
depth of 108 metres, low-
land Europe's deepest lake. Its
dark depths are home to rare, rel-
ict invertebrates and fish. Where
there's an open view, scan the
water for Goosander, Goldeneye

and White-tailed Eagle (which visits the lake to hunt). Broad-leaved Sermountain and Spiked Rampion grow along the trail.

Follow this trail as far as you like, but the picnic spot on the shore of one of the small bays is as good a finishing point as any. Return by the same track.

Continue along the broad dirt track to Smolniki. At the second dirt track to the right, park, and follow the yellow educational trail named Jezioro Jaczno.

4 This trail circles lake Jaczno. The first section descends through a youngish, but not unattractive, oak-linden-hornbeam forest. The rich undergrowth includes Woodruff, Asarabacca, Spring Pea and a few Greater Butterfly Orchids An old water mill marks the lowest point of the trail after which you start climbing up to Smolniki on the other side of the lake. On this side of the lake conifer plantations dominate the landscape. Before arriving in Smolniki, a small alder-carr forest to the right has been flooded by an enormous beaver dam. In Smolniki the trail turns left and takes you back to the car.

The boulders of the Rutka reserve were left here by the retreating glaciers after the last ice age. It is one of the many geological ice age features on this route.

Take the car back to Smolniki and continue to the 655 and turn right, towards Suwałki. Shortly after the turn to Udziejek, a track turns right, signposted Gora Cisowa. Park here and follow the trail to a conspicuous hill.

5 Shortly after the car park, a small pool contains Fire-bellied Toads. The Gora Cisowa hill is the main attraction though. It is a big kame (see page 17) which rises high above the other hills. From the top of the hill you have splendid views over the hilly Park and its surroundings. In the evening the setting sun adds to the atmosphere.

At the main road, go back and left to Udziejek. In the hamlet a derelict old shed flanked by a big tree marks the place where you turn left onto an unmarked dirt track. Where the main track turns left (at a grey concrete shed) go straight. When this

track ends go left and immediately left again. The Rutka reserve is signposted on the left. Park your car and continue on foot.

6 Rutka is another reserve known for its high concentration of large boulders strewn about the landscape. These boulderfields are extensively grazed and abound in wildflowers. A small educational trail cuts through the area to a viewing platform and back. A small lake is visible from the viewpoint. This lake holds a population of Noble Crayfish, a species that has been wiped out in many parts in Europe since the introduction of American Signal Crayfish and the diseases it carries. Another interesting point is a shallow pond where cattle come to drink. The muddy fringes are visited by butterflies searching for minerals. Fire-bellied Toads can be seen, and heard, calling from the water. In early spring, you might want to check the edges of the pine forest, where Eastern Pasqueflower is reported to grow. Frog Orchid is also listed for the Rutka reserve.

The landscape of Suwałki Landscape Park is pleasantly undulating – another heritage of the ice age. Long-tailed Blue is one of the butterfly species that frequent the flowery grasslands.

Return to Jeleniewo to complete the circuit.

Additional remark
The restaurant in Jeleniewo serves the traditional food of North-east Poland.

Route 2: Loop around Wigry lake

**FULL DAY
60 KM**

Car route with short walks ideal for
an initial exploration of Wigry
Best locations for birdwatching in the Park

Habitats mixed and coniferous woodland,
lakes, suchary, reed beds, small-scale agricultural land
Selected species Creeping Lady's-tresses, Bog Arum, Bird's-nest Orchid, Red
Deer, White-tailed Eagle, Hazel Grouse, Goldeneye, Crane, Goosander, Ruby
Whiteface, Lesser Emperor

The loop around Wigry lake connects some of the easier-to-access sites
and is an excellent way to get a first impression of the National Park. Along
the way, you cross small farm plots (in its hilly post-glacial variety that is so
typical of this region), some excellent woodlands and, of course, the reed-
fringed lake Wigry itself.
The loop around Wigry lake runs along minor roads with several small
walks en route.

v = visitors centre
w = watchtower

Departure point National Park visitor's centre

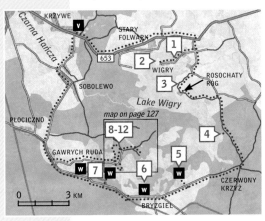

Follow the main road (653) east-
ward in the direction of Stary
Folwark and Krasnopol. Two km
beyond Stary Folwark, turn right
towards Wigry. After 700 m go
right signposted to Wigry.

1 This little stretch of road
offers good birdwatching.
Shrubs along the road are suit-
able for Common Rosefinch. The
shallow waters to the right har-
bour waterfowl (Crested Grebe,
Goldeneye, Garganey, Goosander,

The monastery as seen from the shores of the lake Wigry. The monastry of Wigry is the icon of the National Park.

Cormorant and Common Tern). The reed beds teem with Great Reed Warbler and echo to the 'booming' of Bitterns. In early spring, listen for the 'bubbling' of Moor Frogs.

2 Park your car at the end of the road and walk up to the beautiful monastery that is the centrepiece of Wigry National Park. Walk along the southern wall of the complex and look for thrushes (including breeding Redwing) and Thrush Nightingale. Scan lake Wigry carefully, for this part is often hunted over by White-tailed Eagle which breeds in the forest on the opposite side. Goosander may also be seen.

Go back and at the junction, turn right. Follow the road until you reach a dirt road signposted Rosochaty Róg.

3 Hilly meadows, patches of carr woodland, pools and, to the right, mighty Lake Wigry with its thin belt of reeds are home to Common Rosefinch, Red-backed Shrike and Thrush Nightingale. Fishermen's piers offer open views of Lake Wigry. Late winter and early spring is the time to see many ducks and grebes, and sometimes Black-throated Diver (we saw one here in April 2012). Bitterns boom from the reedbeds. The forest beyond the opposite bank is home to three pairs of White-tailed Eagle so keep an eye on the sky.

PRACTICAL PART

No less than three pairs of White-tailed Eagles breed along lake Wigry's shore.

At the T-junction, turn right here. After 500 metres, just before arriving at the tarmac road, take the dirt track that branches off to the right.

4 The track enters an old commercial forest, now unmanaged, which is gradually transforming into a more natural state. This is an excellent place to look for Hazel Grouse and Red-breasted Flycatcher. Stop at Piaski car park and walk down the trail towards the edge of the lake. There is a very boggy forest here which sometimes holds Hazel Grouse. At the lake, again look for eagles and ducks.

Continue and at the edge of the small clearing, turn right towards the small hamlet of Czerwony Krzyz. At the forest edge on the left, Red Deer or Elk may be seen, especially at dawn or dusk.

5 Beyond the Mułezyska Lake, turn right onto a dirt track to a lookout tower (signposted, but the text faces away from you as you approach). The tower usually does not offer much, but Cranes and White-tailed Eagle are quite possible.

6 Continue through the village of Bryzgiel. At the end of the village, there is a car park on the left in front of a wooden ranger's house. Left of the house, there is a path to another tower. The tower overlooks two small islands and reedbeds in a shallow part of Lake Wigry. This is one of the better places to observe waterfowl. Look for Goosander, Goldeneye, Tufted Duck, Pochard and, in winter, Smew. Furthermore, it is a good area to observe White-tailed Eagle, Marsh Harrier and Red Kite, a rare raptor in this part of Europe, which breeds nearby.

7 Continue along the road, towards two other viewpoints from which you can observe this shallow part of the lake. They are signposted from the road.

The first of these (Bartny Dol) is also interesting for its population of Bird's-nest Orchid. The next viewpoint, Binduga, is historically interesting as the viewpoint is a disused timber ramp built by the Germans during WWI when they were harvesting enormous tracts of primeval forest for the war machine. The narrow gauge railway next to the ramp was used to transport the timber out of the area. Siberian Iris grows along the trail.

Enter Gawrych Ruda and turn right after the church. Continue for about 4km until, once back in the woods, there is a small car park on your right where the road bends to the left. A 3 km circular walk, which we highly recommend, departs from here (see map).

8 Proceed on foot along the road until you see a small boardwalk on the left. It leads into a pine-fringed bog. Look here for typical bog plants like Cranberry, Round-leaved Sundew, Bogbean and Rannoch-rush.

w = watchtower
p = car park

9 On the righthand side of the road a viewing platform overlooking lake Wigry offers, apart from the usual wildfowl, an interesting view of the glacial features of the landscape. You are standing near what was once the edge of the giant ice sheet that covered a part of Europe during the last ice age. The two hills to the extreme right and left are kames while the far-away hills in between are part of the frontal moraine that marks the edge of the glacier during the last glacial maximum. Ecologically, it is interesting to note that the reed-fringed lake has a vegetation entirely different from the small lakes you are about to encounter. Lake Wigry is moderately rich in nutrients (mesotrophic, an ecologist would say), while the lakes-to-come are nutrient poor (dystrophic).

Creeping Ladies'-tresses (top) and Bog Arum (bottom) are plants of Europe's cooler regions.

10 At the crossing, go right. In this part of the forest Creeping Lady's-tresses is fairly common. Pied Flycatchers breed in some of the nest boxes here.

11 Further on, the trail leads to two beautiful nutrient-poor peat lakes *(Suchary)*. Both have a small boardwalk and a viewing platform so you can have a closer look at the mats of quaking bog with their typical vegetation. Labrador Tea, Cranberry, Round-leaved Sundew, Bog Arum, Bogbean, Rannoch-rush and Bog Rosemary can all

Lake Wielki, is one of the *suchary* or peat lakes that give Wigry its northern atmosphere.

be seen here. With some luck Goldeneye and Crane may be spotted in the peaty lakeside. In (early) summer, look for dragonflies such as Small, Dark and Ruby Whitefaces, Brilliant Emerald, and perhaps, the rare Northern Emerald. All in all the forest and the isolated lakes gives the feeling of being deep in Scandinavia.

Goosander is among the few birds that breed only in the northern part of the province of Podlasia.

12 Return and at the junction, go straight on, following the educational trail to a viewpoint over a mesotrophic lake. There's a stark contrast between the reedy edges of this fairly nutrient rich lake in comparison to the peat moss dominated *suchary* you visited earlier. Lesser Emperor was common here when we visited.

From this point, it is not far back to the car park.

Return to Gawrych Ruda and turn right. This road takes you through the village of Płociczno. In the village, take the road to the right signposted to Sobolewo. Follow the main road as it bends to the left. The flowery verges with lots of thyme attract many butterflies. Go straight on at the next crossing to a bridge on the Czarna Hańcza (a scenic old watermill to the right of the bridge may warrant a short stop). This road takes you back to Krzywe and the National Park visitor's centre where the route ends.

Route 3: The suchary of Wigry

2 HOURS
EASY

Splendid peat lakes and bog forests
Peatland flora and dragonflies galore

Habitats Suchary, raised bog, spruce bogs,
mixed forest, coniferous forest, alder carr wood,
oak-linden-hornbeam forest
Selected species Round-leaved Sundew, Great Sundew, Bog Arum, Bogbean,
Labrador Tea, Martagon Lily, Goldeneye, Bullfinch, Black Woodpecker, Moor
Frog, Dark Whiteface, Small Whiteface

!
Mosquitoes can be
a nuisance.

The *suchary*, or peat lakes, are the pride of Wigry National Park. Lack of
nutrients characterise this northern vegetation type of bogs and lakes. The
suchary on this walk, four in total, lie isolated amidst old coniferous wood-
land, but are connected by a pleasant educational trail.

Departure point Wigry NP visitor's
centre

Exit the car park and turn left through the
barrier onto the dirt track. After the first
two wooden houses the educational trail
(named *Las*) branches off to the right.
Follow this trail.

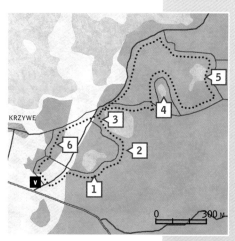

1 The first Suchar is just a short walk.
From the viewpoint you overlook
the lake, which is fringed with quaking
bog. The flora is particularly attractive,
with Round-leaved Sundew, Labrador
Tea, Cranberry, Bog Bilberry, Bog Arum,
Rannoch-rush and Bogbean growing
close to the platform. Dark Whiteface, a dragonfly which is typical for this
habitat, can be found here and on all other *suchary* along the route.

v = visitors centre

Continue along the trail.

2 The woodland, dominated by coniferous trees, has an undergrowth typical of oak-linden-hornbeam forest. Liverleaf and Martagon Lily for example, are fairly common. They reveal that the forest, although the trees are quite old, is actually a plantation, and that the original vegetation was a deciduous forest. Only the boggy forests close to the suchary are natural coniferous stands.

During the mating season, scores of Moor Frogs (bottom) can be found in the *suchary* (top).

The trail comes to the central track. Turn right and continue until you find the second *suchar* on the right. Follow the educational trail that branches off to the right.

3 The second *suchar* is less rich in bog plants, but sports a fine population of the rare, eastern dragonfly species Dark Whiteface. The south facing slope of the hill to the left harbours some warmth-loving plants like Bloody Crane's-bill and White Cinquefoil.

4 As you approach the third *suchar*, a coniferous forest can be seen on the right. It is, in contrast to the earlier patches of forest, original vegetation type. It is a spruce bog, a distinctly Northern type of forest that develops on hydrologically isolated depressions (see page 32). The enormous root plate of a windblown spruce is typical of this forest type, as the shallow rooting spruces are easily tipped over on the unstable peaty soil. A short boardwalk takes you to the heart of a quaking bog, a mat of sphagnum peat that floats on the water. The usual bog plants are joined by the rare Great Sundew and White Beak-sedge. The third *suchar* is perhaps the prettiest.

5 A small hide overlooks the fourth and last *suchar*. You can look down on the mat of quaking bog to scan the vegetation for interesting plants. In early spring, this is easily the best place to look for Moor Frog in the short period of time they are bright blue. They swarm around the edge of the sphagnum mat, producing their typical 'bubbling' call. Look out for Goldeneye, which breeds here in some years.

The trail ends on the main track again. Note how different in character the lake near the track is compared to the *suchary*. This lake is rich in nutrients.

Turn left to return to the visitor's centre. Close to the visitor's centre, follow the trail to the right. After the turnstile the trail leads onto a boardwalk.

6 This boardwalk traverses a small patch of alder-carr wood and, on the higher ground, an even smaller patch of old oak-linden-hornbeam forest. It is interesting to note the difference between these forest types and those encountered earlier. Access to ground water and subsequently higher levels of nutrients in the soil are the source of this difference.

The boardwalk forks in two directions but both lead back to the visitor's centre.

In many places, Liverleaf carpets the forest floor.

Route 4: Wigry by bicycle

5-8 HOURS
MODERATE TO STRENUOUS

A closer encounter with some of Wigry's typical landscapes
Scenic view of the park's many small rivers and the small-scale agricultural land

Habitats streams, alder carr woods, mixed forests, coniferous forests, fields
Selected species Ruthe's Marsh Orchid* (Dactylorhiza ruthei), Dark-red Helleborine, Yellow Bird's-nest, Yellow Foxglove, Forking Larkspur, Hazel Grouse, Small Pincertail, Beautiful Demoiselle, Pallas' Fritillary, Purple Emperor, White Admiral

This bicycle route explores the northern part of the National Park. Small rivers and agricultural land form the background for this scenic route. The hilly character of this area allows for some fast-flowing rivers which are distinctly unlike the rivers you encounter further south, giving rise to a different flora and fauna. Furthermore, this pleasant tour leads you through forest and the small-scale agricultural land, with typical Wigry inhabitants like Hazel Grouse and Black Woodpecker occurring throughout.

Departure point Wigry NP visitor's centre

Leaving the headquarters, go left on the 653 and subsequently turn right, following the well-signposted blue bicycle route to Sobolewo. Follow the track to where a bicycle trail signposted *Kładka* appears (on the way check the narrow flowery glades for White Admirals, Nettle-leaved Bellflower and Yellow Foxglove). Follow this track to a picnic area where a boardwalk begins. Leave your bicycle here and take the boardwalk.

1 This boardwalk takes you to the Czarna Hańcza. The first stream you cross is a minor arm of the river and is surrounded by well-developed peatland. The Wild Angelica that grows here in abundance attracts large numbers of butterflies (mainly Silver-washed Fritillary). The river is very narrow here, the substrate is peaty and the water flows gently. The next stream you cross is the main arm of the Czarna Hańcza. It is distinctly different from the previous arm in that it is broad, fast flowing and with sandy substrate. Look for both demoiselles and Small Pincertail here. With luck, even a Kingfisher may appear to grace the scene. Continue through the lush spruce bog and return to the bike where the boardwalk ends.

Retrace your steps to the Kładka sign and follow the blue route (see map). Upon leaving the forest, a beautiful meadow can be found to the left.

2 This warm meadow harbours some interesting plants, such as Northern Bedstraw, Snowdrop Anemone, Bristly Bellflower, Common Rockrose, Bloody Cranesbill, Cowslip, Branched St. Bernard's-lily, Eastern Bastard-toadflax* (*Thesium ebracteatum*) and Betony.

v = visitors centre

Continue, and beyond the bridge over the Czarna Hańcza, leave the blue route and take a right onto the tarmac road. On this road, take the first right (signposted Krzywe). Cross the Czarna Hańcza again (an old-watermill to the right makes for a picturesque view) and continue until you arrive at the 653 and at the visitor's centre.

Pass the centre following the yellow bicycle trail signposted *Kaletnik*. You pass through a pleasant landscape of woodland, agricultural land and over the beautiful Kamionka river. After a while you arrive at a small cluster of lakes and a flowery forest meadow. This point is again interesting for further exploration.

3 The hill on the edge of lake Galeziste is dry and open. The flowers that grow here attract many butterflies. On our visit we even found Pallas' Fritillary here! You can also swim here in the summer. On the trail further south, the forest on the left hand side harbours a significant number of

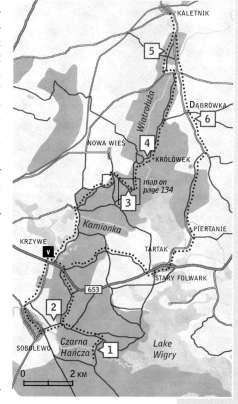

Yellow Bird's-nest, while the meadow a little further on is a good place to look for butterflies. The area as a whole is good for Viviparous and Sand Lizard.

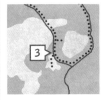

Continue on the yellow trail until it crosses another small river.

4 This is the Wiatrołuza, the river that feeds Wigry's lakes from the north. The stream itself is again good for both demoiselles and Small Pincertail. The peaty meadows on the far side of the bridge have a special flora, which include Marsh Helleborine and the rare and localised Ruthe's Marsh-orchid* *(Dactylorhiza ruthei)*. These peatlands are strictly protected and off-limits to hikers so bring binoculars along to look for the specialties.

Continue on the yellow route (the route may be cut short here by turning right to Krówólek (see map). This section of the trail traverses a forest with a distinctly more northern feel to it due to the dominance of coniferous trees. Cross the Wiatrołuza and on the tarmac, scan the roadsides for Dark-red Helleborine. Enter the forest again for the last section to Kaletnik.

Pallas' Fritillary is one of the eastern butterflies that may turn up here.

5 When the trail enters the forest again, keep an eye out for Narrow-leaved Everlasting-pea. On our own exploration of the route we spotted a pair of Hazel Grouse here.

As you approach the tarmac road, you leave the yellow route, and turn right (or if you are in need of refreshments you can take a left here to the shop in Kaletnik).

After roughly 1.5 km, turn left, signposted Piotrowa D. Here, follow the signposted route to Stary Folwark.

The fast-flowing Kamionka river. The Yellow bird's-nest (middle) is a parasitic plant. It lacks chlorophyll and is therefore entirely dependant on its host for nutrients. Dark Red Helleborine (bottom) is frequent along parts of the trail.

6 The glacial history of this area is visible in the form of small hills that stretch from horizon to horizon. This and the small-scale agriculture make for a very pleasant, picturesque landscape. Forking Larkspur still grows abundantly here, both in the verges and fields themselves. Typical farmland birds such as Yellowhammer, Whinchat, Red-backed Shrike and, with luck, Hoopoe occur. Small marshes have developed in the depressions between hills so marsh birds may be encountered as well.

The route traverses a stretch of coniferous forest with small patches of alder-carr wood before emerging onto the open agricultural land again. After the hamlet of Tartak you arrive at the 653 again. The signposted route to Stary Folwark turns left. Leave this route and turn right onto the 653 until a red bicycle route to Krzywe branches off to the right. Follow this route through another area of beautiful agricultural land and some forests until you hit the 653 again where you turn right to return to the National Park visitor's centre.

Route 5: Augustów forest

1-2 DAYS
75 KM

Excellent exploration of Poland's largest forest
A series of short walks through all habitat types of Augustów forest

Habitats dry pine forest, alder forest, spruce bog forest, rivers, small scale agricultural land, lakes, raised bog
Selected species Wolf, Three-toed Woodpecker, Hazel Grouse, Crane, Goldeneye, Hobby, Creeping Lady's-tresses, Pink Frog Orchid, Bog Arum, Round-leaved Wintergreen, Eastern Pasqueflower, Camberwell Beauty, Small Pincertail

In contrast to popular belief, Augustów forest, not Białowieża, is Poland's largest forest. Vast Puszcza Augustówska consists mostly of planted pine forest, but within the complex are various nature reserves that preserve large

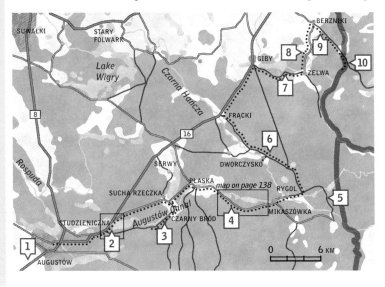

alder swamp forests, dim spruce bog forests, crystal-clear lakes and rivers, raised bogs and other treasures. Due to the dominance of coniferous trees and the presence of many lakes, the atmosphere is much more northern than in Białowieża. Augustów forest is full of surprises – ranging from wilderness species such as Wolf and Capercaillie to specialist wildflowers of bogs and on to the insects and plants of dry, open terrain. You will also find that Augustów's villages are picturesque, and that the many lakes and the famous Augustów Canal (see page 55) are perfect for canoeing and swimming. This attracts, particularly in the summer months, many Polish tourists.

This route offers a good first introduction to Augustów forest, by crossing it over its entire length from south-west to the north-east. Along the way, there are various short walking circuits through which to explore the forest. If this route gives you an appetite for more, we advise to visit the various forest reserves, which you can find on any map available in the tourist information centres.

Departure point Augustów

1 For those interested in nature conservation history – this is where the Via Baltica motorway suddenly ends at the roundabout on the south side of Augustów (see page 63).

Leave Augustów on the 16, signposted Sejny and Ogrodniki. After crossing the first bridge, turn right toward Sanktuarium Studzieniczna. In this small hamlet you will find a church, some tourist kiosks, a bar and a small information centre from which a short marked trail departs.

2 This trail is a short loop offering a first taste of Augustów forest, in which pine forest, marsh and alder swamp appear in rapid succession. You can rent canoes and rowing boats (5 Zł per hour in 2012) from the little café. It is worth renting one, particularly on a fine day, to row around Rezerwat Brzozowy grąd, a small island in the lake. The island is covered in natural forest, which is predominantly deciduous – a sharp contrast with the conifer-dominated Augustów forest. While on the lake, look out for Goldeneye, Hobby, Goosander, Common Tern and White-tailed Eagle.

Hobbies hunt for dragonflies over the lakes of Augustów Forest

Return to the 16, after the Augustów channel, turn right, signposted Płaska. After Sucha Rzeczka, the main road bends to the left. Go straight on along minor road (with a sign saying 10T). Immediately after the bridge over the channel, turn right towards the hamlet of Czarny Bród. After the hamlet, continue on foot and take the dirt track that follows the canal.

3 The Augustów Canal is unique not only in a historic sense (see page 55), but also ecologically. There are not many canals with pine and spruce trees growing down to water level. And it is precisely this 'natural' channel slope that has a unique hydrology which is perfect for the star wildflower of Augustów, the Pink Frog Orchid. This essentially Siberian orchid, has its westernmost population along the Augustów Canal. The population is said to be quite large, but we found only one plant, so if you are determined to find it, prepare for a thorough search. A great botanical support cast consists of thousands of Creeping Lady's-tresses, Dark-red Helleborine, Umbellate, Round-leaved, Serrated and Chickweed Wintergreens and Yellow-bird's-nest. Early July is the season for the wintergreens, late July-early August for the rest. While walking along the track, don't be surprised to find a Camberwell Beauty. This beautiful Butterfly is quite frequent on Augustów's forest roads.

Return to the road and continue to Płaska. In the village, turn right. Beyond Płaska, turn left (sign-posted Sluza) and park at the small camp

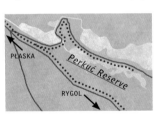

site at the lakeside. Continue on foot until you arrive at a small bridge. On the other side a trail follows a ridge between two lakes (see inset map).

4 This is the Perkuć reserve. It has a beautiful scenery, with lakes dotted with White and Yellow Water Lily and fringed with Bog Arum. Look for Goldeneye on the lakes near to which you can enjoy the masses of Liverleaf in spring and the many Creeping Lady's-tresses in summer. The old spruce-pine forest on the ridge is open, enabling you to look for birds along the tree tops. Lesser-spotted and Black Woodpecker are certainly present, but this also looks like an excellent place for Nutcracker and Three-toed Woodpecker. Don't forget to look at the trail though, for Hazel Grouse is frequent here. The trail continues for quite a while, so remember that you have to return the same way.

Continue (by car) further east to Mikaszówka, follow 'Rygol' across the river and turn right just before Mikaszówka's beautiful wooden church. After crossing the Czarna Hańcza and a channel, turn left onto a trail marked in yellow, follow this trail all the way to Dworczysko.

5 You now cut through the forest on a quiet track, leading through plantations of pine. Along this stretch, expect nothing in particular, but be prepared for any kind of wildlife crossing the track.

6 Where the track reaches Dworczysko, there is a very beautiful patch of alder forest, flooded by a beaver dam close to the road. Signs of Beavers are everywhere, and in early morning or evening you may see one. In spring, the area is alive with birds. Spotted and Pied Flycatchers are common. Green Sandpiper and Goldeneye also breed, the latter in the baskets placed on the trees. The area can be overlooked from the road, but if you are in for a little adventure, you can follow the ridge on the south side of the flooded forest, where fishermen have created small boardwalks into the swamp (be careful, they are very slippery and waterlogged early in the season).
At Dworczysko, walk down to the bridge over the Czarna Hańza for more birds. Cranes are common in the area, Hobby may pass, and all

Dworczysko's inundated alder carr wood. Many nest boxes have been put up for the Goldeneyes that breed here.

sorts of birds of small-scale agricultural land are present. Small Pincertail and both Demoiselles can be seen from the bridge.

Follow the track to Fracki and turn right on the 16, direction Ogrodniki. Just before Giby, turn right, following the direction Rygol. Soon afterwards, turn left towards Zelwa, keep heading for Zelwa until a sign *Reservat Tobolinka* appears. This sign indicates the beginning of a trail to a peatland reserve. Park (minding the Stag's-horn Clubmoss that grows here) and follow the trail on foot.

7 Tobolinka consists of two beautiful suchar-style peat lakes that sit like craters in the hilly landscape. A small trail encircles both of them. When walking the trail, make sure not to forget which trail takes you back to the car park.

The flora of Tobolinka is interesting. A strip of pine bog forest is dominated by Labrador Tea. This is followed by a floating mat of peat moss, on which you can discover Round-leaved Sundew, White Beak-sedge, Cranberry, Bog Bilberry, Bog Rosemary, Bogbean and Rannoch-rush (a few). Summer is the best season for Tobolinka.

The Pink Frog Orchid is right at the western limit of its range in Augustów Forest.

Continue to Zelwa. After the village turn left onto the main road to Wigrance. In Wigrance, turn right after the bus stop, onto a dirt track that ends at the forest edge, where you encounter a big sign marking the edge of the Lempis reserve. Continue on foot here. The trail is marked red-white, and runs between a series of lakes to your left, and a slope (and beyond, the road) to your right. There are a few side trails, but as long as the lakes and swamp is still on the left, and the hillside on the right, you cannot get lost.

8 Lempis' lakes vary from moderately rich to nutrient poor, and are fringed by beautiful spruce bog. The lake vegetation is very special, but remains largely hidden, as do the rare dragonflies Dark Whiteface and Northern Emerald. Keep your eye out for Hazel Grouse, which is

frequent. Note the swathes of Interrupted Clubmoss, perhaps the densest vegetation of this plant we've seen in the region. In Summer, Creeping Lady's-tresses is common.

Continue through Wigrance to Berzniki (keeping an eye out for Montagu's Harrier and Great Grey Shrike in the fields), marvel at Berzniki's wooden church, and turn right (signposted Przejscie Gr. Berzniki). At the end of the village, turn right again (at the cross; ignoring the track with a 10T sign that heads straight on). At a small cemetery, turn left. Follow this track to the Lithuanian border.

Round-leaved Sundew is common in raised bogs.

9 Where the forest begins on the right, again indicated by a big cross, the left side of the road boasts a splendid flora. In late April, this is one of the richest localities of the beautiful Eastern Pasqueflower and Suffolk Lungwort. Later in season, here and further along the track, look for Common Rockrose, Snowdrop Anemone, Branched St. Bernard's Lily, Bloody Crane's-bill and Angular Salomon's-seal. Viviparous Lizard is also common.

10 The last stop is just a little further, at the border. A broad strip of forest is cleared all along the border. Judging from the animal tracks, Elk, Wild Boar and Wolf frequently use this area. An early morning or late evening visit may very well be productive.
Being a Schengen country (nations without border controls), there is no tension between Lithuania and Poland and you may cross the border if you wish. However, the Belarussian border is not far away, so expect border patrols, especially when out and about at odd hours. Bring your passport.

Camberwell Beauties frequently drift over forest glades, such as the strip of heathland between Poland and Lithuania.

Biebrza and Narew region

The Biebrza National Park is the largest National Park of Poland. Together with the nearby Narew National Park it forms a huge area of near-natural river floodplain which is, above all, famed for its superb birdlife. This is one of Europe's top bird-watching sites, with breeding Cranes, Black Storks, White-tailed and Lesser Spotted Eagles, rarities like Great Snipe, Aquatic Warbler and Spotted Eagle, and much, much more. The park is also one of the best places to find Elk and is home to one of the larger populations of Wolf in Poland. And then there are rare dragonflies, butterflies and wildflowers galore in the marshes.

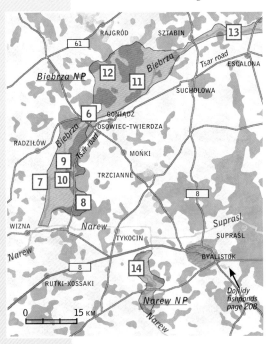

But the Biebrza and Narew is much more than a collection of rare flora and fauna. Within Europe, a floodplain of this size in such an unscathed state, is simply unique. As such, this is a must-see site for any European naturalist.

The variety of ecosystems, each of which in its own natural place in the riverine landscape, is extraordinary. There are extensive reedbeds (routes 6 and 14), countless secluded oxbows (routes 6, 7 and 14), wet meadows (routes 7, 8, 11 and 13), vast swamp forests (routes 7, 8, 10 and 12) and fen mires (routes 8, 9 and 10). There are small patches with special habitats, like calcareous spring mires (routes 10, 13), acidic bogs (route 8), dry sand dunes and grasslands (routes 8, 9 and 12). These latter account for the presence of wildflowers, such as Fen Orchid and Lady's-slipper and butterflies like Scarce Fritillary and Clouded Apollo – species you'd not generally associate with rivers.

Perhaps it comes as a surprise, but both Biebrza and Narew are rather narrow rivers. Their floodplains however, are huge. The spring floods inundate thousands of hectares. In Biebrza's southern basin the distance from the river channel to firm ground is easily 10 km – a stretch of impenetrable fen mires, alder swamps, old river arms and reeds. Forested 'islands' of dry sand dunes amidst these vast marshes act as retreats for Elks and Wolves, and are home for warmth-loving plants and butterflies.

Most of both Biebrza and Narew is simply impenetrable, but there are sufficient trails and tracks to get a good taste of all the habitats of these splendid parks, and to find most of its unique flora and fauna. An entry permit is required to visit the Biebrza, which can be purchased for 5 Złoty per day (€ 1.20) at the visitor's centre in Osowiec Twierdza, as well as at foresters' lodges, B&B's shops and restaurants.

The vast marshes of the Biebrza – Europe's most intact large river valley.

144

Route 6: The Biebrza at Osowiec Twierdza

3 HOURS
EASY

The perfect first introduction to the Biebrza National Park
A rich birdlife of reedbeds, oxbows and flood forest

Habitats reedbeds, oxbows, flood forest, oak-linden-hornbeam forest
Species Martagon Lily, Liverleaf, Beaver, Red-breasted Flycatcher, Penduline Tit, Bluethroat, Savi's Warbler, Garganey, Grass Snake, Hairy Hawker, Green-eyed Hawker, Yellow-spotted Whiteface

This short loop is situated at the narrow 'waist' of the Biebrza River, separating the lower from the middle basin. It is the place where, in the past, battles were fought and where today cars and trains cross the river. Nevertheless, this area offers some splendid opportunities, especially for birdwatchers. This is one of the few places where you can conveniently overlook the river, and have good views into the oxbows, without having to crawl into a canoe.

v = visitors centre
w = watchtower

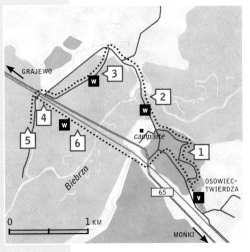

Departure point Visitor's centre at Osowiec Twierdza.

The visitor's centre is signposted on the 65 between Monki and Grajewo, on the east bank of the river.

Walk the tarmac road back in the direction of the 65, following the red marks. Just beyond the last building block (nr. 58), follow the red signs to the right onto a trail into the forest.

1 The trail leads over a steep hill on the banks of the Biebrza. This strategic position made it an

From the railroad bridge you have good views over the Biebrza river.

important military site, as witnessed by the ruins of many trenches and bunkers. The woodland (a youngish oak-linden-hornbeam forest) has an interesting spring flora, with masses of Bird-in-a-bush, Liverleaf, and, later in the year, Martagon Lily. In early spring, when the trees have no leaves, you have good views over the flooded river. Later in spring, listen for the song of the Red-breasted Flycatcher.

The trail ends at a road, where you turn right. On the left hand side, a platform gives a good view over an oxbow.

2 From the wooden bridge you have excellent views over the river and adjacent oxbow lakes. This is a good place to watch ducks, herons, Marsh Harriers, reed-dwelling warblers and marsh terns. On passage, many migratory birds that follow the river, pass through this narrow bottleneck.

Continue along the road (climb up the dikes on both sides of the road to overlook the marshes). Pass the turn to Osowiec and, in the bend of the road, turn left onto a trail (marked green) towards a watchtower.

3 This stretch runs over a boardwalk through the marsh. Look out for the many signs of Beaver (from the watchtower you have a fair chance on seeing the animal itself in the evening). In spring, look for Penduline and Willow Tits, Bluethroat, Savi's Warbler, and, with luck, Little Crake.

Bitterns 'boom' from within the reedbeds, while closer at hand, Viviparous Lizards use the boardwalk to bask in the morning sun. In May and June, dragonflies are numerous. Look for Yellow-spotted Whiteface, Hairy and Green-eyed Hawkers.

Towards the end of the trail, you cross a small patch of willow flood forest – one of the few patches of this woodland type in the Biebrza.

The flashy Martagon Lily occurs on the hill overlooking the Biebrza valley.

At the end of the trail, cross the busy 65 road and the railroad and then turn right.

4 The bridge is a spectacular place to watch the White-winged Terns in spring. They hunt here for insects and, if you sit still, they wheel right over your head.

After the bridge on the left hand side, a soggy trail, mostly used by fishermen, runs along the Rudzki channel. Follow this trail for a while.

5 The willow scrub here is a good place to look for Common Rosefinch. This is also an excellent, if not the best place to look for Beavers around dusk and dawn. The almost continuous presence of fisherman has made the Beavers here a lot less shy than most of their relatives elsewhere.

Beavers are present throughout the region, but the Rudzki Channel may be the best place to actually observe them.

Return and follow the narrow trail along the railroad.

6 The watchtower adjacent to the ruins of a bunker, and the subsequent bridge over the Biebrza, offers a text book example of a cross-section of a natural river valley. The meandering river, oxbows, flood forest and alder carr are all neatly visible. Because you look over the marsh from above, this is also an excellent place to watch birds. All the aforementioned marsh birds can be present here. Check the sky for Black Stork, Crane and White-tailed Eagle. The sun-warmed slope of the railroad dike is a favourite haunt for Grass Snakes, and spring wildflowers.

At the railroad crossing, turn left to return to the visitors'centre.

Route 7: The west bank

**FULL DAY
95 KM**

Excellent birdwatching at various points along
the Biebrza
Traditional agricultural land and picturesque
villages

Habitats rivers, oxbows, sedge marshes, reedbeds, meadows, alder-carr woods
Selected species Hoopoe, Ortolan Bunting, Black Tern, White-winged
Tern, Whiskered Tern, Black Stork, Ruff, Aquatic Warbler, Citrine Wagtail,
Bluethroat

v = visitors centre
w = watchtower

This car route takes you from Osowiec-Twierdza
to Gora Strekowa along the Western bank of the
river. Together with the next route which runs
along the east bank of the southern basin, this
is the most comprehensive route of the Biebrza,
visiting numerous good sites for flora, fauna and
landscape. In contrast to the east bank, this route
has good views of the Biebrza river and the tra-
ditional countryside with its small hamlets. It
is also one of the the best route for birds, such
as terns, Ruff, Black-tailed Godwits and the rare
Citrine Wagtail.

Departure point visitor's centre at Osowiec
Twierdza.

Take the 65 in the direction of Grajewo and after
the bridge, turn left onto the 668 towards Lomza.
After 2 km, turn left towards Sośnia.

1   From Sośnia, a pretty hamlet, a short trail
leads through alder carr woods to a low hill
with a beautiful view over the sedge marshes. In
early spring this is a good site for ducks and, a

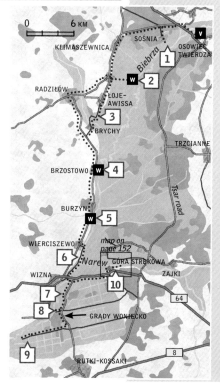

little later, waders. If you rise early, you'll witness a beautiful sunrise here. Come a little later in the morning, you look into the light, which is not very helpful for birdwatching so a late afternoon or evening visit may be better.

Continue down the 668. In Mscichy turn left (signposted Okrasin) and left again at the T-junction. Park at the end of the village and continue on foot (Wearing wellies is advised in spring on this wet track).

!

Wear wellies for the walk to the watchtower.

2 The area of Biały Grąd is the location for a big sedge marsh restoration project. The first part of the trail leads through meadows, home to the likes of Black-tailed Godwit, Redshank, Common Snipe and Lapwing. It is also one of the places where Citrine Wagtail is regularly seen. As it gets wetter the meadows give way to patches of alder carr wood and eventually, sedge marshes. The endangered Aquatic Warbler, a sedge marsh specialist and the reason for the restoration project, can be seen and heard here around dusk and dawn. Keep an eye out for Great Snipe as well. At the end of the trail you will find a watchtower. Scan the river with a telescope for Black Stork among the commoner White Storks. Ruff are numerous in the marshes east of the tower in spring. There are waterfowl and waders such as Wood Sandpiper, and there is a chance of spotting White-tailed or Spotted Eagle. The marshes of Biały Grąd is where Night Herons started to breed recently.

Return and drive on to Okrasin. In Okrasin go straight onto the dirt track.

The Biały Grad watchtower is an excellent place to observe the gracious White-winged Terns.

The view from the
Burzyn viewpoint

3 This track leads through a beautiful landscape of traditional agriculture and through hamlets of traditional farms made of wood and local boulders that were brought down by the glacier. Hoopoes fly around in the flowery meadows, herds of cattle graze on the small pastures and pollarded willows line the dirt tracks. Where the trail skirts a small patch of pine forest to the right, turn left. This is an excellent place to look (and listen!) for Ortolan Bunting.

!

Impossible to cross by car during periods of flooding or rain.

Where the track turns into a cobbled road, turn right to cross the bridge. After the bridge take the first left and after the small bridge just before Loje-Awissa, turn right. At the church, turn left onto the main road again. (If the dirt track is too wet, take the alternative route over Radzilow which takes you over tarmac roads at the expense of missing the beautiful farmlands).

Turn left at the Brzostowo sign post.

4 In Brzostowo you will find several watchtowers overlooking the river. They are on private land but you can use one for only two Złoty (€ 0.50). Brzostowo is one of the better sites of the Biebrza for birdwatching. The watchtower offers good views of Common, White-winged, Black

The Biebrza near
Wierciszewo

and Whiskered Terns, waders and waterfowl. White-tailed Eagle frequent-
ly soars by, as does Black Stork and groups of Cranes.

Brzostowo is also a spot where droves of cattle cross the river to graze in
the meadows on the other side. These 'happy cows of Brzostowo' as they
are called locally, maintain an area of grazed meadows which hold some
of the highest concentrations of breeding Black-tailed Godwit, Snipe and
Redshank in entire Poland. Look for Ruff on migration as well.

Continue southwards. Directly after Burzyn a viewpoint is signposted to
the left.

5 On one of the highest points of the moraine is a watchtower which
offers the most spectacular panorama over the Biebrza valley which
is at its widest here. Come here to watch the sun set, to see the early morn-
ing mist over the river, or, in early spring the spectacular flooding of the
river valley. For birdwatching, the marshes are rather far away, although
with a telescope you might be able to pick out waterfowl, Bittern, Crane
and Elk.

Continue onwards and take the road left signposted Wierciszewo. At the
base of the hill (house number 13) turn right onto a dirt track (on foot when
the track is very wet).

6 This track takes you to an old rampart overlooking the confluence of the Narew and Biebrza and a small area where seepage water comes to the surface on the other side of the track. Look for spring flora on the rampart. Fingered Speedwell is one of the attractions, while, a little further, masses of Yellow Star-of-Bethlehem grow alongside a small stream.

The road ends just after the hamlet of Rus. Take a left onto the 64 and cross the Narew. After the bridge turn right, signposted towards Rutki.

7 To your right you see the magnificent Pulwy meadows. In early spring, when water levels are high, this is an absolute hotspot for grebes, waterfowl, waders and all three marsh terns. Take your time scanning the wetlands, surprises occasionally turn up here. On the left, the meadows and wetlands frequently offer views of raptors (e.g. Lesser Spotted Eagle), while Common Rosefinch and Penduline Tit may be seen in the willow bushes.

Proceed south until you find a sign towards a picnic area (900 metres), take this trail.

8 The trail leads to a small complex of sand dunes. Strolling around here you will see some species typical for high and dry grounds like Iceland Moss, Tree Pipit and Woodlark. Whinchat and Hoopoe are other possibilities here. Also keep an eye out for lizards here, and, on spring evenings, this a very good place to find Spadefoots, a rare species of frog (pack a flash light).

Go back and continue to Grądy-Woniecko. After the village (actually an old communist collective farm and now a prison), take the first right onto a dirt track.

9 The first part of this dirt track leads through alder carr woods and willow scrub. Keep an eye out for Penduline Tit and their nests. After the forest you enter an open area

The Black Tern is one of five species of tern that breed in the Biebrza valley.

Courting Ruff engage each other in ritual battle.

with wet meadows on both sides of the road. Early in spring this is the place to head for if you want to see the endless fields of Marsh Marigold (see cover photo). Like in the Pulwy meadows, just about anything can turn up here, but the place is especially famous for its Ruff leks. Sometimes you can see them courting in the middle of the road!

Return to the 64 and turn right. After 5 km, turn left towards Gora Strekowa. Park your car in the village.

10 This picturesque little village is situated on the shore of an old oxbow. Explore its banks at will as many dragonflies (White-tailed Skimmer and others) may be found here. The hill overlooking the village is also worth climbing. The hill's sandy ridge is home to a Sand Martin colony and the dry grasslands on its crown sports Forking Larkspur, Carthusian Pink and Large Orpine which attract butterflies like Swallowtail. The hill was also the site of a tragic WWII battle.

If you continue on the main track through the village turn left after the

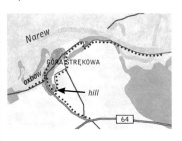

last farmhouse. Walk through the meadow to the edge of the Narew and turn right. This trail takes you along the meanders of the Narew and its oxbows. It is best known for its rich variety of dragonflies like Green Snaketail, River Clubtail and both demoiselles. If you wish you can follow it as far as Strekowa Gora where the trail ends.

You can then return by the way you came, or along the Tsar road, in which case you follow route 8 in opposite direction.

Route 8: The east bank

FULL DAY
65 KM

Day trip connecting some of the best
sites of the Biebrza
Rich bird and wildlife against back-
drop of beautiful, pristine landscape

Habitats River Dunes, Sedge Marshes, reedbeds, alder-carr wood, birch bog,
pine forest
Selected species Aquatic Warbler, Great Snipe, Tawny Pipit, Lesser Spotted
Eagle, Elk, Adder, Grass Snake, Sand Pink, Small Pasqueflower, Clouded
Apollo, Sedgeling, Yellow-spotted Whiteface, Banded Darter

This car route takes you along the historical 'Carska Droga' (Tsar's Road)
to some of the Biebrza's most famous sites. Along the way, you cross vast
alder swamps, endless fen mires (some of the
best in the Biebrza), wet meadows and sandy
moraines covered in dry pine forest. Several
stops and short walks allow you to explore this
otherwise impenetrable terrain, and offer good
possibilities of finding rare birds (e.g. Aquatic
Warbler, Great Snipe) and mammals such as Elk.

v = visitors centre
w = watchtower

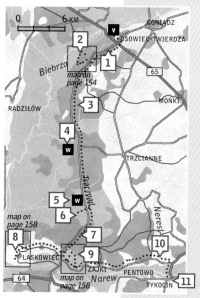

Departure point Visitor's centre at
Osowiec-Twierdza

Go east on the 65 in the direction of Monki and
take the first road to the right signposted for
Mezenin. Here you enter the Tsar Road.
After about 2 km, stop just before two traffic
signs that warn of crossing wildlife, park and fol-
low a small trail to the right.

1 This is one of the few raised bogs in the
area. In May and June, the masses of
Hare's-tail Cotton-grass and Labrador Tea make

this a beautiful site. Bog Bilberry is also abundant. The site supports a wonderful dragonfly fauna. Small, Ruby and Yellow-spotted Whitefaces are frequent among the overwhelming numbers of Ruddy Darters. Search carefully for the Sedgeling, a diminutive and very local damselfly, which can be found between the blades of loose stands of sedge and grass. Also keep your eyes on the trail, especially on sunny mornings, as Adders may bask on the path.

Be careful in this area, though, as left and right of the trail, there are square 'man holes' covered with Sphagnum moss which betray the activity of peat-cutters. So called because it takes a man one day to dig a hole this size, these hidden 1.5 metre deep pits, means that you can't safely step off the trail.

Take the car and proceed on the Tsar's road, until you come across a small car park with an information panel on the left side of the road. Park your car and take the trail that starts on the opposite side of the road (marked in green and white).

Hare's-tail Cotton-grass in the raised bog along the Tsar's road.

p = car park

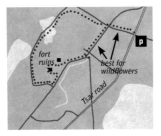

2 This short walk follows a section of an educational trail. Follow the green markings. The trail takes you to the remains of Fort IV, one of the enormous fortifications the Russians erected along the Biebrza prior to WWI to defend the western border of the empire which then included Poland. Demolished bunkers, overgrown trenches, defensive moats and ramparts are visible reminders of the fierce battles that were fought here in the past. Apart from the rich history the trail also has a lot of botanical treasures. It is especially good for wildflowers of warm pine forests and sand dunes such as Small Pasqueflower, Swallowtail, Broad-leaved Sermountain, Soapwort, Sand Pink, Branched St. Bernard's Lily, Goldenrod, Umbellate Wintergreen, Chickweed Wintergreen, Creeping Lady's-tresses and Large Orpine. The first 2 km (up to the fort) are the best, with most species growing close to the track. Coal and Crested Tits are frequent birds. The educational trail has a small detour marked with a green triangle that takes you to an old moat and blasted bunker. This is an impressive site and another excellent place for wildflowers. From here you can return to the car although you can, of course, also complete this circular trail.

Sand Pink (top) and Small Pasqueflower (bottom) are plants of open forests' sandy soils.

Continue down the Tsar road.

3 If wildflowers are your interest, keep a sharp eye out in the road verges for interesting flora (e.g. Creeping Lady's-tresses, Sand Pink, Stag's-horn Clubmoss and Small Pasqueflower).

4 Those keen on butterflies will want to stop at the crossing to Trzcianne and check out the exposed patches of thyme here, which attract a score of fritillaries in summer. Just beyond the crossing there is a large alder carr wood, flooded by Beavers.

Walk or drive to Gugny, which lies opposite the turn to Trzcianne.
This trail leads to a watchtower just west of the hamlet (wear wellies!) The watchtower provides a panoramic view over the sedge marshes dotted with

Early Marsh-orchids in spring.Cranes are often seen too as are Elk around dawn and dusk. At these times the atmosphere is heightened by sewing-machine like chunter of River Warblers, the comb-rasping of Corncrakes and the throbbing 'bleat' of displaying Common Snipe overhead as they plunge to earth. From various little ponds Fire-bellied Toads add their chorus to the general cacophony.

Continue through beautiful alder-carr woods, past the track to the Honczarówska embankment (route 10) and as you come to another clearing, you will find a watchtower on the right.

5 The flowery glade close to the tower is alive with Early Marsh-orchids and is a very good place to look for Clouded Apollo among other butterflies (The Tsar road from here to where you enter the forest again, is also good for Clouded Apollo). From the tower, Elk may be seen in the early morning and late evening.

6 The next stop is a short boardwalk, known as the Długu Łuka boardwalk. It is only 400 metres long, but it is a true gem and worth spending some time on. This is the single best place in the world to see the rare and localised Aquatic Warbler. Hidden in the sedges during the day, look for it in the early morning and, especially, in the evening when it perches up, singing a laid-back Sedge Warbler like song. Other birds here include Snipe, Montagu's Harrier, Spotted and Corncrakes, and in some years, Short-eared Owl. The sedge marsh consists of a loose mat of vegetation – among the most intact of its kind in the Biebrza. Look carefully for Sedgelings, a small damselfly that in distribution and rarity can well

The Neresl river is known for its population of Banded Darter.

be seen as the damselfly equivalent of the Aquatic Warbler. Look also for Yellow-spotted Whiteface, which often rests on the boardwalk. Botanists may be interested to look for the Downy Willow, a northern species at the edge of its range, and for Early Marsh-orchids, including the cream-coloured *ochranta* variant. The small population of Snake's-head Fritillary at the start of the boardwalk (flowering in April), is not native, but seems to persist quite well.

Return to your car and continue south. After the clearing you enter a vast alder-carr forest.

7 The sheer acreage of this alder carr forest is impressive. If you would like to see Elk in woodland scenery in early spring, look for them in these forests. The spring flora in the forest is quite amazing. Wood and Yellow Anemones, Bird-in-a-bush, Liverleaf, Moschatel and Alternate-leaved Golden Saxifrage literally carpet the forest floor. The forest is protected as a strict reserve, because of its breeding population of Black Stork, Spotted Eagle and Eagle Owl.

The little ponds beyond the forest near Laskowiec harbour Fire-bellied Toads and Tree Frog.

The wet meadows of Zajki are among the most reliable sites to see Whiskered Tern (top). The star of the sedge marshes, the Aquatic Warbler (bottom). The Biebrza holds the largest and only thriving population in the world of this rare bird.

Turn right into the village of Laskowiec. In Laskowiec, take the road signposted for Gielczyn. On this road, take the road signposted for Kolodzieje.

8 Scenic hedgerows separate several small plots with lots of wildflowers. Take the first dirt track to the left. On a crossing this dirt track turns into a tarmac road, follow it into Gielczyn. From here, walk the little circuit depicted on the small map below.

PRACTICAL PART

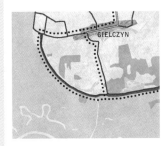

This short circuit is, above all, scenic. Woodlands, meadows and oxbows and a pretty hamlet are an agricultural idyll. And surely, there are plenty of birds to be seen (e.g. Black Stork, Crane, Lesser Spotted Eagle, Corncrake, etc.).

Return to the Tsar road, turn right and then left to Zajki. At the left side of this road an information panel marks the start of a walking trail into the meadows of Zajki.

Head out on warm evenings on the minor road between Zajki and Tykocin. Nightjars are quite common in this area.

 = watchtower
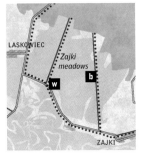 = bird hide

!

Wear Wellingtons when going into the Zajki meadows.

9 These wet meadows are an excellent spot to watch birds (depending on water levels). All three marsh terns may breed and hunt here. With some luck a White-tailed, Lesser Spotted or Spotted Eagle may be seen soaring above. Spotted and Little Crakes are common here although rarely seen. The hedgerows are good for passerines. In the ditches and ponds, look for Fire-bellied Toad.

Continue towards Zajki to find the watchtower overlooking the meadows left of the road and, just before the village of Zajki, another information panel marks the beginning of a similar trail, this time to a hide.

Continue along the pleasant country road until you approach the village of Piaski. Just before the village, park at the small bridge.

10 Just before the small Neresl stream lies a large area of dry sandy dunes, which is one of our personal favourite areas. It seems to be a neglected area, but there is much to discover. On the open sands, Tawny Pipit breeds. The area is regularly hunted over by Lesser Spotted Eagle. Great Grey and Red-backed Shrikes are frequent as are Woodlarks. Sand Pink and Small Pasqueflower are among the wildflowers, while Glanville Fritillary, Eastern Bath White and Brown Argus are frequent butterflies (but there is bound to be more here). The Neresl, especially towards the north, supports a large population of Banded Darter, which can be seen at the bridge.

!
Be careful not to damage the lichen vegetation.

11 Continue to Tykocin to end the day. This small town is famous for its architecture, its (Jewish) restaurants, and we'd like to add to this the massive numbers of House Martins and Swifts that breed in the old synagogue. If you have time, continue to Pentowo, the White Stork village.

The Tawny Pipit feels at home in open sand dunes with Junipers.

Route 9: The Sedge Marshes of Barwik

4 HOURS
EASY-MODERATE

An adventurous walk through the vast sedge marshes of the Biebrza
The classic site for watching Great Snipe

Habitats sedge marshes, reed beds, alder-carr wood, dry grassland
Selected species Elk, Great Snipe, Bluethroat, Common Rosefinch, Chequered Skipper, Large Copper, Banded Darter, Yellow-spotted Whiteface

!
Be be very careful not to get lost when venturing beyond the watchtower.

Wear wellies on this route.

The trail that ventures into the marshes at Barwik is both famous and infamous. It is rightly famed for its excellent sedge marshes where a lek (display site) of Great Snipe can be viewed (although in recent years, the birds have not always been present). The birdlife in general is rich, and there are a number of interesting butterflies and dragonflies to be seen here. However, the trail also has a bad name, because beyond a certain point, it becomes extremely wet and occasionally difficult to find. Recently, some visitors had to be rescued because they got lost in the marshes. Here, only the relatively dry, and highly-visible, part of the trail is described. Still, rubber boots are handy. Since the trail is drier than the surrounding marshes, small predators like Foxes and Polecats may be seen trotting along the track.

w = watchtower

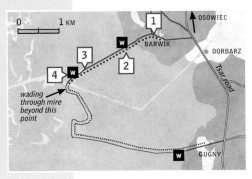

Departure point Barwik

Getting there From Osowiec, take the 65, direction Monki and take the first right onto the Tsars' road. Just before the forest clearing of Dobarz (with the restaurant) turn right and park at the car park.

1 In the summer time, the area around the car park attracts large numbers of butterflies.

The sedge Marshes of Barwik. Large Copper is possible along the embankment.

(Marbled White, Silver-washed Fritillary, etc.). In spring, look for Black Woodpecker, Hoopoe and Woodcock here.

Follow the trail into the marshes, marked by red signs. You swiftly pass from pine forest through carr wood to the open sedge marshes.

2 In spring, the sedge marshes are alive with birds. Savi's Warbler sings from the patches of reed while Thrush Nightingale sings from within the shrubs. Look for Common Rosefinch, River Warbler and Bluethroat in and around the willow bushes and note the Snipes 'bleating' overhead. On your right-hand side, you will find a viewing platform, which used to be *the* place to watch Great Snipe. The lek was deserted, but in recent years, some birds returned (usually some 400 metres to the west of the original lek), so if you visit at dusk you might get lucky. This is also a good time to see Elk. Keep a low profile for the sake of the birds!

The majestic Elk can often be seen (and heard!) splashing through the sedge marshes.

Along the trail in late spring, Yellow-spotted Whiteface and Large Copper may be found. In summer, look for Banded Darter and the large numbers of Yellow-spotted Emerald.

After the platform, the path crosses a small dike towards a 'mineral island' – a dry sand dune in the middle of the marshes.

3 As soon as the ground becomes drier, you find yourself in a flowery field. Among the wildflowers, Spreading Bellflower stands out, but this site's pride lies in the dwindling population of Frog Orchid. Being greenish and small it is difficult to find, but in your search you may stumble on Grass Snake or Adder, both of which using the dry hill to bask. Butterflies include Glanville Fritillary and Chestnut Heath.

4 Climbing up to the watchtower, notice the bomb craters from the Second World War when the Germans bombed the partisans who hid on this island.

The watchtower is the end of the 'easy' part of the trail. From here on, the red poles continue to the mark the route to Gugny (see map). Continuing from here means you will not emerge from the mire until you are in Gugny. Read the section safety in the sedge marsh on page 220 before continuing. Butterfly enthusiast may want to proceed some 100 m. into the wet zone, to look for Chequered Skipper.

Route 10: The Honczarówska Dike

5 HOURS
EASY

Walk through Biebrza's finest sedge marshes
Stunning birdlife, flora and some rare butterflies

Habitats river dunes, sedge marshes, reed beds,
alder-carr wood, birch bog, pine forest
Selected species Polecat, Elk, Aquatic Warbler, Thrush Nightingale, Jacob's-ladder, Lady's-slipper, Red Helleborine, Scarce Fritillary, Scarce Heath, Clouded Apollo

The Honczarówska Dike or embankment is a must-see area in Biebrza. This 5 km long embankment runs straight through alder carr forest, sedge marsh and ends at a raised dry area in the marsh – hence it is a unique opportunity to see these impenetrable habitats without getting your feet wet (well, not seriously wet). It was created by the Russian officer Honczarow, who had his men build a grange on the island in the middle of the marsh, connected by the dike. The villa was destroyed, but the dike remains for all of us to enjoy.

Added bonus is the fact that the dike runs through a part of the sedge marsh that is very well-developed. It is an excellent place to see Aquatic Warbler and several elusive butterflies. The presence of many mineral-rich swells make the dam botanically outstanding. In particular orchids are well represented. The dike, being a dry 'island' in itself, is often used by small predators, like Polecat, Fox and even Wolf.

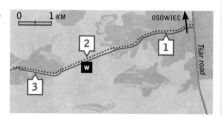

w = watchtower

Getting there From Osowiec, follow the Tsar road down south. 4 km beyond the turn to Gugny-Trzcianne, until you see a information panel on your right. This marks the start of the trail.

1 The first 3 km you cross a youngish alder carr forest and willow shrubs. River and Grasshopper Warblers sing, and in the evening Woodcocks fly over, producing their odd, somewhat eerie croaking and sneezing calls. At a small car park (for personnel only!) on the right side of the embankment, start looking for Lady's-slipper, which grows a little behind this car park. Poland's largest population of this flashy orchid is found in the Biebrza, but this is the only place where you can actually see it close to the path. Red and Marsh Helleborines grow a little further along the dike. In the small open patches in the swamp forest, look for butterflies. This is one of the better spots in the National Park, with rarities such as Scarce Fritillary and Scarce Heath.

Red Helleborine (top) and Lady's Slipper (bottom) are orchids of the calcium-rich marshlands along the Honczarowska track.

2 The vast area of open sedge marshes is, first and foremost, the terrain of the Aquatic Warbler, which can be seen at dusk and dawn. They are most active in May and June. Other frequent birds are Snipe, Spotted Crake, Corncrake and Marsh Harrier. In June, search for Scarce Fritillary and Scarce Heath on this section. Signs of Beaver activity are everywhere. Gnawed branches and trunks and even a lodge partially on the trail indicate the presence of Europe's largest rodent.

Pay special attention to the vegetation. Looking down into the sedge marsh, notice how open the vegetation is, and how many Marsh Fern, Marsh Cinquefoil and Water Horsetail is present. Near the watch tower, search for Early Marsh-orchid, and its rare and local cream-coloured variant *ochranta*.

Polecat may be seen running up and down the dike hunting for frogs. Like yourself, many mammals take advantage of the dry passage the embank-ment provides. Look for Scarce Heath along the first part of the trail.

This is one of the last places in the Biebrza valley where the mires are still mown traditionally. In August and September, people come with scythes to cut the hay and collect it on big haystacks. In the course of win-ter, when the ice is strong enough to hold tractors, the hay is brought to the farms to feed the cattle.

3 Upon reaching the hillock where once Honczarow's grange stood, a drier grassland and alder woods appear. This is a good place to look for Clouded Apollo, a beautiful but rare butterfly. Siberian Iris and Jacob's-ladder grow left and right of the ridge.

Return by the same way.

Route 11: Hamlets in the middle of the marsh

!

Route not possible during times of flooding.

5 HOURS-FULL DAY
EASY-STRENUOUS

A drive into the heartland of the middle basin. An optional adventurous crossing to the most attractive river dune of the Biebrza.

Habitats river, reedbeds, sedge marshes, meadows, hamlets
Selected species Elk, Common Rosefinch, Black-tailed Godwit, Redshank, Lapwing, Spotted Eagle, Corncrake, Spotted Eagle, Banded Darter, Dark Whiteface

The middle basin is dotted with small mounds that rise subtly above the surrounding marshes. Settlements have been built on most of them and small-scale agriculture has created a beautiful mosaic of habitats. Wet and dry meadows around the hamlets are strongholds for birds like Lapwing, Black-tailed Godwit, Redshank and Skylark. This general area is also the stronghold of the rare Spotted Eagle in Poland.

w = watchtower

This lovely route follows minor roads that connect several of these agricultural 'islands'. But at the end, you are challenged to experience such a crossing from island to island on foot, and discover how impenetrable these marshes really are!

Departure point Osowiec Twierdza

Take the 670 north-east in the direction of Goniądz. Drive past Goniądz in the direction of Sucholwola and Dabrowa Bialostocka along the east section of the Tsar road.

1 For a view over the Biebrza you can drive into Wrocen. The campsite in this hamlet has a viewing tower which can be climbed for a small fee.

Continue along the 670 and go left when Dolistowo is signposted. In Dolistowo, go right and take the road signposted Bialobrzegi. Cross the wooden bridge and follow the river.

2 This part of the trail runs right beside the main river bed. The vegetation flanking the road is good for Common Rosefinch. Fishermen have created gaps in the vegetation and in these places you can easily park and look over the river. Check the river for dragonflies and Kingfisher and scan the sky for raptors. Spotted Eagle may fly by, but be aware of Lesser Spotted Eagle too, which remains the commoner of the two. In the evening the wet meadows left of the road are alive with the rasping of Corncrakes, and, in some years, White-winged Terns.

!
The road is flooded when water levels are high. If so, don't attempt to cross!

In Jasionowo take the road signposted Bialobrzegi. The road forks at a sluice (this sluice is actually the beginning of the famous Augustów Canal), turn right towards Jagłowo.

3 On this section of the route you will find many different water habitats. Some waters flow, others are standing. Some are well vegetated, others more open. This is good for finding a wide range of dragonfly species.

The Biebrza was Jaglowo's 'main street' in a time when there were no roads to connect the isolated hamlet with other villages 'on shore'.

In Jagłowo village, park your car at the first dirt track that leads to the river and walk to the edge of the water.

4 Jagłowo is mainly of cultural interest. The village was, not so long ago, an island in the marsh that could only be visited by boat. Therefore all houses face the river as it used to be the 'main street' of the village. Enjoy the scenic stroll with the traditional village on one side and the Biebrza river on the other. Banded Darter is common here in summer. Just beyond Jagłowo, the road ends at a large sandpit, which is interesting for its dragonflies. In summer, Banded Darter is frequent, Dark Whiteface has also been seen.

The Black-tailed Godwit breeds in the meadows around Jasionowo and Kopytkowo.

Return to Jasionowo and continue further to Kopytkowo.

5 The meadows around Jasionowo and Kopytkowo are good places to look for breeding waders. In spring, Redshank and Black-tailed Godwit are not hard to find here and Lapwing and Skylark are everywhere.

In Kopytkowo, a small gate to the right gives access to a small car park and a watchtower. The watchtower is privately owned and the admission fee is 3 Złoty. The tower gives excellent views over the sedge marshes and the Czerwone Bagno/Grzedy forest complex on the other side of the valley. A pair of Spotted Eagle breeds in the forest of Grzedy across the marsh, and it can sometimes be seen from here. It is also a good place to spot Elk in the early morning or around dusk, while Black Grouse are heard and sometimes seen here displaying in early April.

6 After the small gate a green barrier marks the beginning of the yellow trail which leads all the way from Kopytkowo to the sand dunes of Grzedy. These dunes are in the middle of the marshes and are an important retreat for Elks and Wolves. From the watchtower on the dunes, Elks are often seen in the marsh, while Wolf tracks are frequent in the sand dunes. Spotted, Lesser Spotted and White-tailed Eagles are all frequently seen. In short, the Nowy Swiat sand dunes are superb.

However, the trail over is beyond soggy: it requires wading through the marsh. The crossing is a true adventure as the peat layer is like a quaking bog. In some places, the peat layer is broken and, unless you are very careful, you may suddenly find yourself up to the belly in black mud. Great fun, but be aware: this walk is not without danger and should be undertaken only if you are physically fit and in a group (see also page 220).

For this trail, the Czerwone Bagno–Grzedy admission ticket is required, which you can purchase at the camp site in Kopytkowo.

Route 12: The Red Swamp

FULL DAY
EASY-MODERATE

Diverse walk through old-growth forest, marshes and over sunny sand dunes.

Habitats Alder carr wood, oak-linden-hornbeam forest, pine bog, sedge marshes, reedbeds, sand dunes
Selected species Lynx, Wolf, Elk, Red-breasted Flycatcher, White-backed Woodpecker, Green Sandpiper, Spotted Eagle, White-tailed Eagle, Sand Lizard, Carthusian Pink, Large Orpine

!
Entry tickets are required. Purchase them at the information centre in Osowiec Twierdza or in Grzedy forester's lodge.

Although this place is almost universally known as Czerwone Bagno, meaning the Red Swamp, this is actually in Grzedy, a forest complex just south of Czerwone Bagno (which is strictly protected and off-limits to tourists). Grzedy is a beautiful, well-developed forest of considerable age. In a way, Grzedy is, together with Czerwone Bagno, Biebrza's heartland.

v = visitors centre
w = watchtower

It was the last retreat of wild Elk in Poland after WWII, and hosts a healthy population of Wolf. On your walk through Grzedy you'll encounter various types of forest, ranging from lush oak-linden-hornbeam forest to swampy alder carr and 'nordic' pine bogs. Species such as Red-breasted Flycatcher and Spotted Eagle breed here and even Lynx are occasionally seen.

Departure point Grzedy forester's lodge

Getting there From Grajewo. Follow the 61 to Augustów. Upon entering Tama, turn right,

Wolf prints can often be found in the sand of Grzedy's dunes.

signposted Woznawies, and subsequently take a right onto a dirt track signposted Kuligi. When the road forks in Kuligi, turn left, when that track end, turn right (signposted Grzedy) and park at the forester's lodge.

1 The area around the centre itself is interesting with Icterine Warbler and Common Rosefinch present in spring and Hawfinch year round. Walk the track into the forest that starts at the green barrier. After a while you pass a small animal rehabilitation centre on your right. Some very tame Wild Boar, Elk and Wolf live here. At an information panel the blue trail branches off to the left, follow this trail.

2 Some impressive, old oaks grow here. Red-breasted and Pied Flycatchers breed in this area, and are easiest to find in spring when in song. The trail leads to the edge of the forest through lush alder-carr woods. Two Pine Martens crossed our path here, but they could turn up anywhere. The path leads over an old sand dune offering a good ecological insight in the various forest habitats. The forests on both sides of this dune are wet, but on the left, the groundwater-fed alder-carr woods exhibit an entirely different flora than the pine bog on the right which grows on an hydrologically isolated depression fed solely by rainwater. Green Sandpiper breeds in the trees here.

Facing page:
An ancient oak in a stand of oak-linden-hornbeam forest.

3 When the blue trail goes right, the black educational trail begins. Follow it but don't forget to check the viewing platform on the left! Common Rosefinch is common in the scrubs. The educational trail leads over a boardwalk through the enormous pine bog and explains the existence of this habitat type through information panels. Interesting to note is that the pines here reach great heights despite the poorness of the soil. This is because the layer of peat is thin enough for the pines' roots to extend to reach more nutrient-rich soil, enabling them to grow much larger than the small, crooked pines that grow on thicker layers of peat.

At the end of the educational trail the blue trail crosses the red trail, follow the blue one.

4 The forest here is less uniform due to the presence of old overgrown sand dunes. Wetter parts and dry sandy parts with Bilberry, Heather and Lichens follow each other in rapid succession. Keep an eye out for Hazel Grouse here. White-backed Woodpecker is also possible.

Labrador Tea is a typical plant of dry bogs. It's name betrays both its range (North America as well as Europe) and its former use as an infusion to flavour hot water. This custom is now abandoned because of the (mild) toxins in the leaves.

When the blue trail reunites with the red trail, turn right.

5 Soon you arrive at the sand dune complex of Nowy Swiat, one of the remotest places of the Biebrza. The open sandy patches here and further ahead are excellent for finding tracks of large mammals. Elk, Red Deer, Roe Deer, Fox, Wolf, Lynx and Badger all occur here. Especially the big paws of the Wolves are fairly easy to find here. Sand Lizard also frequents these dunes. The open dunes are dry with small patches of open sand and a lot of Pannonian Knapweed, that attract butterflies like Glanville Fritillary, Sooty and Scarce Coppers and Swallowtail. Wildflowers include Forking Larkspur, Carthusian Pink, Large Orpine, Spiked Speedwell and Goldenrod.

6 In the centre of Nowy Swiat dune complex is a watch tower from which you have unimpeded views to the south over the middle basin, all the way down to Goniądz. This is an excellent place to take a break and scan the marshes. Elk is usually present in the marshes. When the vegetation is high you need to scan patiently though, before you discern a pair of ears or a big nose from the high vegetation. Look carefully

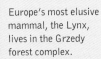
Europe's most elusive mammal, the Lynx, lives in the Grzedy forest complex.

for eagles as well. White-tailed and Lesser Spotted Eagle are possibilities here, but the big attraction is Spotted Eagle, of which various pairs breed in the wider area.

Return as you came and straight on over the main track (marked red).

7 This red trail is the main track through Grzedy. It is also the place where Lynx has been seen on several occasions (even with cubs). Spring Pea is common on the track, as is Wood Cow-wheat and various other forest plants.

Follow the green trail as it branches off to the left.

8 The first part of this trail crosses an oak-linden-hornbeam forest, some very old oaks can be found here. Towards the edge of the forest the soil gradually get wetter. Near the edge of the forest some majestic old oaks can be seen as well as very old Spruce, Maple and Hornbeam. The trail leaves the forest and runs over an open sand dune. The dunes are fringed by alder carr woods. Look for Hoopoe and Woodlark here. This dune complex used to be inhabited, but in the Second World War the Germans burned down the houses and killed most inhabitants.

Currently, this is where the public track ends. Return by the same track.

Routete 13: The upper basin

FULL DAY
60 KM

Diverse tour through a little visited part of the Biebrza
An agricultural idyll with a rich flora and insect life

Habitats Traditional agricultural land, wet meadows, sedge marsh, oak-linden-hornbeam forest, river
Selected species Jacob's-ladder, Early Marsh-orchid, Marsh Helleborine, Grass-of-Parnassus, Elk, White Stork, Common Rosefinch, Barred Warbler, Middle Spotted Woodpecker, Banded Darter, Violet Copper

The northern part of the Biebrza National Park is not so frequently visited. The riverbed, though narrower than in the south, is no less attractive. Seemingly forgotten, small-scale agricultural land is as much a part of this region as the fen mires, reedbeds and swamp forests. This route, which can be completed by car, but is much more attractive by bicycle, leads through this quiet and off-the-beaten-track part of Biebrza. It is perhaps not as rich in bird species as the lower basin sites, but the flora and butterfly and dragonfly life is very attractive. There is a bicycle hire at Lipsk at Silencium agro-tourism: **www.silencium.pl** (+48 876421258).

w = watchtower

Departure point Lipsk

Leave Lipsk towards Sztabin.

A White Stork strolls through Hruskie's colourful meadows.

1 This quiet road immediately sets the tone for this route. Mires and thickets of Willow alternate with woodlands (which are in fact southern protrusions of the Augustów forest). Signs of Beaver are frequent, with several lodges and large dams in the channels. The vivid blue Jacob's-ladder flowers in spring, when River, Grasshopper and Savi's Warbler, Thrush Nightingale, Bluethroat and Common Rosefinch sing from the marsh. Keep an eye out for Barred Warbler. From Nowy Lipsk onwards, the road crosses drier terrain.

For an interesting detour, turn right to Hruskie, beyond Jastrzebna II.

2 The meadows around Hruskie seem to come from a old romantic painting. They are very beautiful in May, when assorted flowers turn them into seas of pink, yellow, red and white. Corncrake and Corn Bunting are plentiful, and the shrubs flanking the road are good for Common Rosefinch, Barred Warbler and Red-backed Shrike.

Return to the main road, turn left and then right, towards Jastrzebna/Ostrowie. Pass the village of Jastrzebna I over the cobblestone road. Cross the railroad twice, after the second crossing, turn right.

3 At the bridge, you have a good views over the Biebrza, with its many Demoiselle Damselflies, Reed and Great Reed Warblers. Park the car, walk on and at the first option, turn left. The dry grassy patches between willow bushes are a favoured haunt for the splendid Violet Copper and for Banded Darters. This short track ends at some wet meadows with Bistort, the host plant of the Violet Copper.

Return to the car and continue on the road. At the first option, turn right, crossing the railroad (a site with many wildflowers, attracting the same butterflies as above) and leading into Las Trzyrzeczki forest. This woodland is part of an ecological corridor from the Białowieża forest, via Knyszyn forest to the Augustów Forest – and an important route for large mammals (see also page 63).

4 If you fancy a walk or bicycle ride through a fairly well-developed oak-linden-hornbeam forest, follow the blue signs into the forest. The route turns left and where an information sign is present on a grassy glade on the left (the sign is a little away from the main track), follow this educational trail (see map above). Hawfinches are common and Red-breasted Flycatcher, Black and Middle Spotted Woodpeckers breed here.

Return to the main track where you entered the forest, turn right, and right again, towards the railroad. Cross the railroad and at the tar-mac road, turn left, crossing the railroad again. Before the village of Kamienna Stara, follow the main road as it crosses the small stream. In Kamienna Stara, turn left to the wooden church. When in a car, park here. Continue following the blue route. Beyond the last house, there is a fork which is not marked. Take the branch that goes straight on and you'll see the blue markings reappear. The blue trail ends at a complex of meadows.

The Violet Copper (top) is the star butterfly of the meadows near Las Trzyrzeczki. The Early Marsh Orchid (bottom) is the most frequent orchid of the marshes. It is very abundant on the edge of the marsh east of Szuszalewo.

Middle-Spotted Woodpecker breeds in Las Trzyrzeczki.

5 These beautiful meadows are filled with Marsh Marigold, Brook Thistle and, in summer, Bistort. This is a good area to look for butterflies with, among the many fritillaries, Violet Copper. Banded Darter is frequent in summer.

Return and continue to Dabrowa Bialostocka. Turn left onto the 673. At the roundabout, head for Lipsk. After 4.5 km on this road, turn left to Szuszalewo. In the village turn left.

6 From the Szuszalewo watchtower you have excellent views over the marshes and, in the background, Puszcza Augustówska. The tower is good for watching Cranes and Lesser Spotted Eagle with chances on Elk in the evening. Instead of returning the same way, take the road to the left at the end of the cobblestone road. This track follows the edge of the marshes.

7 The last few metres of this route has a splendid surprise in store. The sedge marsh close to the edge of the road is influenced by calcium-rich seepage water and sports an excellent flora. Hundreds of very stout Early Marsh-orchids bloom here in May, including the rare white *ochranta* variant. Later in the season, enjoy the flowers of Brook Thistle, Marsh Helleborine and Grass-of-Parnassus. Don't enter the mire here – the vegetation is fragile.

Jacob's ladder grows along the road from Lipsk to Nowy Lipsk

The track ends on the 673. Turn left to return to Lipsk.

Route 14: Narew National Park

FULL DAY
EASY

A daytrip around the Narew National Park with its reedbeds and riverside nature

Habitats Rivers and oxbows, reedbeds, flood forest, sedge meadows, willow scrub
Selected species Aquatic Warbler, Bluethroat, Bittern, Ortolan Bunting, Yellow-spotted Whiteface, Green Hawker

The Narew National Park is a small park West of Białystok. It is known for its myriad of small river channels and several rare species of insects. Although it is significantly smaller than the Biebrza National Park, it boasts many of the same species but is a lot less touristic. Instead it oozes a laid-back atmosphere of forgotten countryside and vast marshes.

This route through the National Park does not add species you would not be able to find in the Biebrza, but with its large reedbeds and countless river channels, it has a different focus than the Biebrza routes.

v = visitors centre
w = watchtower

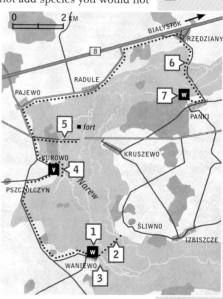

Departure point Waniewo

As you approach Waniewo from the South, turn right into the village. Just before the road bends to the right towards the church, two dirt tracks run towards the watchtower on the edge of the river. Park your car here and climb the watchtower.

1 Here you have an excellent view over the Narew river valley, its many river channels, sedge marshes and reed beds. The structure of many parallel river channels, known as an *anastomising* river

178

The view over Waniewo from the boardwalk to Sliwno.

The elaborate nest of the Penduline Tit is a fairly frequent sight in the willow thickets of the Narew valley.

(see page 18). The Narew is the only of its kind in Poland and one of the few known examples in the world.

2 From the watchtower, go left along the edge of the water. A trail leads to a small, manually operated 'floating bridge' linked to each bank by a tethered rope. On the other side a boardwalk takes you all the way to Śliwno on the other side of the valley. This trip through the otherwise inaccessible sedge marshes and reedbeds gives you a unique chance to explore this ecosystem, and to come close to Bluethroat, Savi's Warbler, Little Crake, Spotted Crake and Water Rail. Marsh Harriers are regularly seen hunting over the valley and Cranes are often seen and heard here. In Śliwno the trail ends so you'll have to return the way you came.

3 Around dusk and dawn the sedge marsh south of the church is a good place to look for Aquatic Warbler as several pairs nest here.

Return to Waniewo, turn right on the crossing just beyond the village. Take the dirt track to the right just before Pszczolczyn and go right at the next crossing. This track takes you to Kurowo, where the headquarters of the National Park is located. It has a little museum, good maps of the area and several English speaking guides.

4 There is a short boardwalk around the visitor's centre that takes you through the extensive reedbeds that fringe one of the river channels. Scan the reed stems for Bluethroat and Savi's Warbler. Marsh Harriers glide back and forth further out on the marsh. Look for White-tailed and Lesser Spotted Eagles above, here and the remainder of this route. In summer this is an excellent place to look for dragonflies. Twenty-seven species have been recorded, including Green Hawker and Yellow-spotted Whiteface.

Follow the unpaved track in the direction of Pajewo until you come to a junction with a massive pollarded willow to the right with markings of

The mystery of the disappeared bridge

The reason why the bridge (see point 5) is a ruin is simple – it's haunted! There is a beautiful local tale about this bridge.

Construction of a bridge across the Narew began in 1903, but technical problems hindered progress. One day a mysterious man stepped up and offered to help, but in return he demanded the soul of whoever would be the first to cross the bridge. The villagers agreed and construction was resumed. When the bridge was completed the villagers were reluctant to keep their end of the bargain so instead of a person, they sent a blind horse across the bridge. This so enraged the mysterious helper that he cursed the bridge. For several years people crossed the Narew here, but when WWI broke out, the bridge was destroyed by the Russians. After  the war, the bridge was rebuilt, but come WWII, it was destroyed again, this time by the Poles to slow down the advancing German army. Believing all this had to do with the curse, the locals refused to rebuild the bridge. Even today when the NP directors announced plans to construct a footbridge here as part of a tourist trail, local villagers alarmed the media and rose up in protest and the plan was put on hold.

Cranes in flight

bicycle routes attached to it. Turn right. Park at a small bridge crossing one of the Narew's channels and continue on foot.

5 This nondescript dirt track used to be the main road from Białystok to Warsaw. However, the bridge crossing the river is gone and the road has been abandoned (see box on the previous page). Search the willows along the track for Penduline Tits and their pouch-shaped nests. From the end of track you have a good view over the river marshes.

Adventurous visitors may try to proceed along the river bank to north. After 350 m you arrive at the fundaments of an old fort, where an interesting flora is found.

Return and continue to Pajewo and take the first right towards Radule. The new motorway that was being constructed here at the time of writing, makes it difficult to give instructions on how to proceed. Check a local map and proceed towards Rzedziany. Here, continue to the crossing over the river. The road across the river is a bumpy stretch of concrete blocks and driving it is a tedious experience. We advise you to proceed on foot.

6 Along the track, reedbeds and willows support the usual cast of Bittern, Bluethroat, Common Rosefinch and Penduline Tit. This area is little watched by birdwatchers, and may possibly have more in store for you.

At the far end, you arrive in the village of Pańki. Continue, still of foot, to the right and on the other side of the village, a dirt track to the right brings you to a viewing tower.

7 This tower offers good views over willow scrub and marsh. It was newly erected on our visit so not much is yet known about what can be seen here. The terrain is likely to produce the same species as at point 6.

Return the same way.

Białowieża

Białowieża is the most famous National Park of Poland, and is known Europe-wide as THE last primeval forest of the continent. Strictly speaking, this isn't true, since Białowieża is neither an entirely primeval forest (as in: untouched by human hands), nor is it the only more-or-less primeval forests in Europe: there are more in the far corners of the eastern European mountains and the Scandinavian boreal forests. What makes Białowieża unique is that it is the nearest thing we have to a primeval forest in Europe's temperate lowlands (for more information on primeval forests and Białowieża, see page 26). As such it gives the most evocative image we are ever likely to find of the forests our ancient ancestors encountered when they arrived in lowland Europe.

A visit to Białowieża is to submerge oneself in a vast deciduous forest, to search for wild Bison, to look for rare forest birds and to become mesmerised in the fascinating history of the near-primeval landscape of temperate Europe (including all its controversies – see page 29). However, the many glades, marshes, meadows and hamlets within the forest will likely prove to be equally attractive and scarcely less productive for birds and wildlife.

When heading to this wonderful region, don't confuse the Białowieża forest complex with the Białowieża National Park. The Białowieża complex is a huge forested area on the border with Belarus. Just under 50% of this forest lies in Poland, the rest lies in Belarus. Most of the complex on either side of the border is commercial forest, used for timber extraction. Within it, there are various reserves, some of which are part of the National Park, and others are not. Białowieża National Park consists of three different parts, of which the Strict Reserve is the largest and most important. Of this 10,000 ha forest reserve, 5,000 ha is strictly off-limits to visitors, except for two trails which you can walk with a guide (see page 207). Only in the northern part are you allowed to enter freely (route 18). A guided visit to the strict reserve is highly recommended, see page 207.

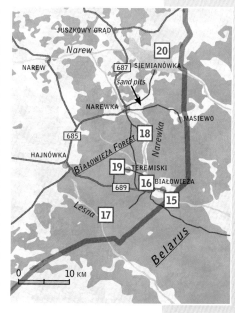

The other two parts of the National Park are the forest along the Hajnowka-Białowieża village road, the Bison breeding station and the Palace Park (route 15). The latter is a beautiful park around the old hunting estate in Białowieża forest, which currently houses the National Park headquarters and visitor's centre.

All the flora and fauna that occurs within the National Park boundaries are also present in the surrounding forest complex. And since the strict visitor regulations do not apply here, it is likely that this is where you will be spending most of your time. The vast oak-linden-hornbeam forests will provide the backdrop on routes 15, 16, 17 and 18. Stunning, jungle-like alder swamps are present on routes 16, 17, 18 and 19. The rarer forest types like spruce and pine bogs are to be found on routes 15, 17 and 18. The open clearings – which are usually best for finding mammals and most birds – are also found outside the strict reserve (routes 15 and 19). Białowieża is also the best base for a visit to the bird-rich reservoir of Siemianowka (route 20). For accommodation, see page 213.

The alder carr forest occupies the wet valleys within the Białowieża forest complex. Because of the swampy soil, lush undergrowth and large amount of rotting wood, this is the most jungle-like forest type.

Route 15: Białowieża and surroundings

8 HOURS-FULL DAY
EASY

A good introduction to the forests
and marshes of Białowieża, including its wildlife
A breath of the rich history and culture of a unique reserve

Habitats hamlets, meadows, alder carr woods, oak-lin-
den-hornbeam forest, mixed forest, coniferous forest, streams, reed beds.
Selected species Collared Flycatcher, Lesser spotted Eagle, Wryneck, Middle
Spotted Woodpecker, River Warbler, Barred Warbler, Bison

This easy cycling route through the Białowieża Village and its immedi-
ate surroundings is a perfect introduction to this area. You'll get to know
the area and the habitats and have a good chance of seeing some of the
region's excellent birdlife. Patches of old-growth forest and the bird-rich

v = visitors centre

marshes along the Narewka River
rival for attention with the beauti-
ful Palace Park, and old buildings
of the royal village of Białowieża.

Departure point The Palace
Ponds car park

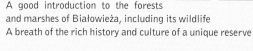

1 Explore the park on foot,
starting at the Palace Ponds'
gate (Icterine Warbler and Serin
are among the possibilities here).
Cross the bridge on foot. The reed-
beds here are alive with the 'chog-
ging' of Great Reed Warblers. A
stroll around the ponds is also possible. In front of the museum's entrance
you will find some magnificent ancient oaks. A walk around this park
and its stands of old trees and flowery meadows is highly recommended,
not only for the splendid scenery, but also for encounters with Collared
Flycatcher, Wryneck, Green and Middle Spotted Woodpecker and passing
Black Stork and Lesser Spotted Eagle.

PRACTICAL PART

Białowieża village and its direct surroundings is often just as attractive for naturalists as the interior of the old-growth forest. You might see Barred Warbler from the bridge over the Narewka (point 5).

Return to the car park and continue towards the village centre. Cross the Narewka, turn right and after the Orthodox church, turn left and immediately right again to cycle along a street that runs parallel to the main road.

2 In this quiet street you'll be able to enjoy Białowieża village and its gardens. Some traditional wooden houses and sheds may be seen here and the gardens are full with 'garden' birds like Wryneck, Hawfinch and both redstarts.

At the end of the street take the small trail into the park. On the other side, turn left onto on Browska Street.

3 This road leads to the edge of the strict reserve. Here you will be able to see the difference between stands of even-aged production forest and the old-growth forest for which Białowieża is famous. The first type consists of dense patches of trees, all planted at regular intervals and of the same age. Undergrowth is meagre or non-existent and the ecological value of such stands is very limited. The old-growth patches (oak-linden-hornbeam here) consist of a spacious forest with ancient giants, young saplings and everything in between. The undergrowth is lush and diverse and the ecological value is tremendous. These are the places to look for Collared and Red-breasted Flycatcher and, with some luck, a White-backed Woodpecker may show up. The Strict Reserve to the left is off-limits so don't be tempted to go in for a brief exploration. The fines are heavy!

The trail leads all the way to the Belarusian border where it ends. Feel free to follow it as far as is allowed (don't go further; you don't want trouble with the border patrol here!), but to return to your bike you'll have to retrace your steps.

Lesser Spotted Eagles hunt over the meadows of the Białowieża village clearing.

Follow Browska Street to the main road and turn left. As the road leaves the village and bends further towards the south, turn left onto a dirt track into the forest. At the sign that says you are not allowed to follow this track any further, turn right.

4 This trail slowly descends towards the Narewka through patches of spruce bog and alder carr wood (keep an eye out for Three-toed Woodpecker, Pied Flycatcher and Pygmy Owl).
Further ahead, pause on the bridge over the Narewka, where sedge marsh and reed beds are home to Grasshopper Warbler and Thrush Nightingale.

At the next crossing, take the little trail that runs between the outhouse and the picnic table. When it ends on a track, turn right, back towards the Narewka. When you leave the forest you will be able to see the old trains that are part of the Carska tourist complex. Turn right towards the bridge over the Narewka.

5 This bridge provides some excellent views over the Narewka, the willow scrub here is good for Barred Warbler, Red-backed Shrike, Thrush Nightingale and River Warbler. From the reed beds Savi's Warblers may be heard. Little pools in the valley are teeming with Tree Frogs.

Continue in the direction of the village and take the dirt track left that runs past hotel Bialowieski. Beyond the hotel, turn right.

6 This dirt track follows a dike that runs through some beautiful small meadows. In the evening, this is an excellent place to enjoy a choir of Corncrakes. Look for Red-backed and Great Grey Shrikes. This general area is also a place where Lesser Spotted Eagles are known to hunt.

Where the track ends on a road of concrete plates, turn left towards the river.

7 The bridge here is a good place to look for Beautiful Demoiselle hunting over the water and Common Rosefinch singing from the willow shrubs. The reed beds are alive with the songs of Savi's and Great Reed Warblers.

Cross the railroad and go right onto Graniczna street. At the T-junction, turn left onto Kolejowa street to return to the Palace Ponds car park.

The mig hty oaks of the Palace Park. Note the impressive girths and big, low lateral branches – features typical of a tree that grew up in open, park-like conditions.

Route 16: Zebra-Zubra

4 HOURS
EASY-MEDIUM

Impressive old alder carr woods and
oak-linden-hornbeam forest
Rich bird and plant life

Habitats alder carr forest, oak-linden-hornbeam, meadows
Selected species Three-toed Woodpecker, White-backed Woodpecker, Hazel
Grouse, Red-backed Shrike, River Warbler, Greater Spearwort, Spring Pea,
Alpine Enchanter's-nightshade, Early Marsh-orchid, Common Spotted-orchid

!
Mosquitoes can be a
nuisance. Don't enter
during storms. In
2012, the boardwalk
was in a state of
disrepair.

The Zebra-Zubra boardwalk runs through a majestic alder carr wood and
an equally impressive oak-linden-hornbeam forest. This is an easy route,
right outside Białowieża village, for finding a good share of Białowieża's
special birdlife, plus a large number of wildflowers.
Note that at the time of writing, the Zebra-Zubra trail was closed due to
the bad condition of the boardwalk. It will be restored and reopened in the
near future.

Departure point Zebra-Zubra car park

Getting there From Białowieża, take the minor road towards Pogorzelce
and Budy. The car park is situated on the left.

1 The trail crosses a typical alder
carr wood. There are some mas-
sive forest giants and metres-high
root plates of old Spruces that toppled
down. In this jungle, look carefully for
woodpeckers (especially White-backed,
Three-toed, Lesser Spotted and Grey-
headed), Golden Oriole, Collared
Flycatcher and Hazel Grouse. There
is a rich undergrowth, with a lot of
Isopyrum in spring. Later in the sea-
son, look for Common Spotted-orchid,

v = visitors centre

Touch-me-not Balsam, Greater Spearwort and both enchanter's-nightshades.

The trail ends at a track. Turn left, and pass the Zoo.

The Zebra-Zubra area boasts well-developed alder carr woods. The Three-toed Woodpecker is one of the rare attractions of this trail.

At the next crossing (which doubles as a parking facility for the zoo), a trail departs towards the southeast into forest parcel 450. It is marked yellow, and signposted Białowieża 3 km.

2 This trail runs through an old oak-linden-hornbeam forest, with some giant trees that match those on the Zebra-Zubra trail in impressiveness. The forest is typically open and park-like, as most old oak-linden-hornbeam forests. This is another good place for woodpeckers, most notably Black, White-backed and Middle Spotted Woodpeckers.

At the road, turn left, into Białowieża. At the first track left (recognisable by a worn plan of the village), turn left. Then at the T-juntion left again to return to the Pogozelce-Budy road.

3 This section follows the edge of the wet meadows of Pogorzelce. The tall herbs, willow and alder bushes are home to Whinchat, Common Rosefinch, Thrush Nightingale, Red-backed Shrike and, less commonly, Barred Warbler. Check the sky for passing raptors and Black Stork. The meadows support the Early Marsh-orchid, Marsh Helleborine, Brook Thistle and Long-leaved Speedwell.

Route 17: To the Lesna by bicycle

FULL DAY
STRENUOUS

A bicycle route through all of the forest's habitats

Good opportunities to observe the forests special wildlife

!
Mosquitoes can be
a nuisance.

Habitats Coniferous forest, mixed forest, spruce bog, alder carr wood, streams, reedbeds, hamlets, meadows.
Selected species Red Helleborine, Red-breasted Flycatcher, White-backed Woodpecker, Hoopoe, Crested Newt, Adder, Poplar Admiral.

This cycle route through the forest complex south of Białowieża village offers an excellent opportunity to explore the various forest habitats. Differences in elevation and hydrology make for visibly different forest types, each with its own set of associated species. But it is not only a scholarly trip. The forest in this generally quiet corner is beautiful, birds are plentiful, and the bicycle allows for an excellent opportunity to explore Białowieża thoroughly.

Departure point Białowieża village

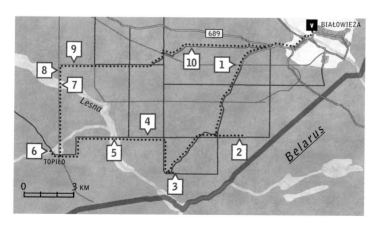

V = visitors centre

Leave Białowieża in direction Hajnowka. After 1 km, turn left towards Miejsce Mocy. After 2.5 km you arrive at a railroad, which is worth exploring on foot.

1 The dry and sun-soaked railway supports warmth-loving species which are quite rare in Białowieża. Reptiles like Sand Lizard and Adder warm up here, while butterflies frequent the many flowers, which in turn consist of southern species like Wild Gladiole.

The Podcerkowka catchment is covered in a lush alder-carr wood. The Red-breasted Flycatcher is hard to find unless you know its call. It prefers old oak-linden-hornbeam forests.

Continue down the track, crossing a patch of well-developed mixed forest. After 4.5 km you reach a fork in the road, go left here and, soon after, at plot 607B, go left again (east) towards the Podcerkowka catchment.

2 The Podcerkowka catchment is one of the lushest and best developed alder carr woods Białowieża has to offer. In the first part the vegetation is dense and jungle-like, but after 1 km, the forest on the left is much thinner, because most of the trees are dead. This is the work of Beavers who have flooded the terrain by damming the outflow channel – a superb example of the profound effect Beavers have on their environment. The enormous quantity of dead wood works like a magnet on woodpeckers, including the sought-after White-backed Woodpecker. The lack of foliage in this place gives you a good chance of spotting them. Other interesting birds include Green Sandpiper and Swift, both breeding here in the cavities of trees.

Return to the main track and continue in a westerly direction. Shortly, you arrive at a small signpost on the left side of the road, which marks the beginning of an educational trail (signposted przewloka). Follow this track (look for Hazel Grouse here) until it leads onto a small forest clearing. Go left and soon you arrive at a small sand pit.

3 At the bottom of the pit is a shallow pond with Edible Frog, Spadefoot and Crested Newt. The sun-soaked slopes of the pond harbour some long, mature specimens of Grass Snake.

Return to the forest clearing, cross it and follow the black trail as it bends to the right. At the crossing where the black trail ends, turn left.

4 After a while the track crosses a spruce bog, where rare butterflies like Moorland Clouded Yellow and the Cranberry Fritillary are said to occur.

5 Beyond the spruce bog the track enters the valley of the Lesna, which is one of the highlights of Białowieża. This fully natural river snakes its way through the forest, and is difficult to explore, except from two points, this being one of them. The scrub around the dam supports Common Rosefinch and Thrush Nightingale. Savi's Warbler and Great Reed Warbler can be heard singing in the vast reedbeds. The river itself is fringed by sedges where, with some luck, you may even see a Little or Spotted Crake rummaging about. Look for Hoopoe along the dam itself and don't forget to scan the sky for raptors and Black Storks.

The Lesna bridge is also the point to decide whether to continue or return. Continuing will offer similar

Lake Topiło

habitat, much of which in excellent state, although the cycling conditions are a bit more challenging.

Continue until you arrive at a T-Junction. Go left, following the yellow markings into Topiło.

The first building is a little shop where you can buy some refreshments. Take the road that turns left in the direction of Hajnowka until the bridge over the lake.

Grass Snakes love to bask in the sun on exposed shores. Look for them at the sand pit near point 3.

6 From this bridge you have a good view over lake Topiło, where Goldeneye occurs. Return to the shop and turn left. Here you will find a railway bridge over the lake which is another good point to scan the water. At the little car park just right of the bridge, a small trail starts which leads around the upper part of the lake. Take this trail for some more views over the lake. Where it ends at the narrow-gauged railroad, turn right.

The trail left of the railway is solid enough to cycle. Follow it to arrive on another bridge over the Lesna.

7 With a similar outlook and range of species as the previous spot, this is another excellent place to overlook the Lesna.

Keep following the railway until you find a short boardwalk on the right. Explore it on foot.

8 You cross a lush and picturesque alder carr wood. Look here for White-backed Woodpecker and Collared Flycatcher.

Return to your bicycle and continue to a crossing with a wooden Orthodox cross on the left. Turn right and follow this overgrown track. It is actually another narrow gauge railway but the rails are hardly visible here – the track is in a good enough state to cycle.

9 The alder carr woods you cross are of sublime quality. They are lush, old and the amount of dead wood is enormous. All the birds of old-growth forests can be seen here. The track is hardly visible, which adds to

The Lesna valley, here seen at point 7, is a ribbon of open marsh in the dense forest. It is of huge importance for birds and large mammals.

the 'jungle-experience' of this section of the route – yet the fact that you follow an embankment that takes you above the swamp makes it is impossible to get lost. The same species as at point 8 can be seen here, perhaps even with more ease.

Go through the forest clearing of Czerlonka L. and follow the main track as it bends to the left. Cross the railroad and turn right into Czerlonka. After the last house there is a fork in the road, where you turn right into the forest.

10 These drier coniferous, mixed and oak-linden-hornbeam forests are exploited for timber. What is interesting to note here is how varying forestry methods produce great differences in the ecological value of the forest. The patches where 'clear-cut' methods were used can be recognised by the equally old, evenly spaced trees and an almost complete lack of undergrowth. The patches which have been selectively cut are in some places almost as impressive and species-rich as the old-growth forests. The only drawback is the lesser quantity of dead wood which betrays their commercial nature. Red-breasted Flychatcher breeds in the older deciduous stands.

The track comes to a junction with many dirt tracks branching off in all directions. Take the one that is marked with the symbol of a Nordic walker. At the yellow route, turn left to return to Białowieża.

Route 18: Kosy Most

5-6 HOURS
EASY

! Mosquitoes can be a nuisance.

Splendid forest river and very old alder forest
Some of Białowieża's best places for mammals, birds, plants and butterflies

Habitats oak-linden-hornbeam forest, alder carr forest, mixed forest, spruce bog, pine bog, river meadows
Selected Species Yellow Star-of-Bethlehem, Heath Fritillary, Wolf, Bison, Red Deer, White-backed Woodpecker, Black Woodpecker, Collared Flycatcher, Crossbill, Common Rosefinch, River warbler, Black Stork, Nutcracker

Kosy Most is a must. It is one of the most intact forest sections in Białowieża outside the strict reserve. Strictly speaking, Kosy Most refers to the nearby bridge over the Narewka. Both sides of the Narewka sport excellent old-growth forest, separated by the river that is a natural jewel in itself. Also of interest at Kosy Most is the large variation of forest types, making this an excellent showcase of the forest diversity of Białowieża. The birdlife and flora is equally rich, and along the narrow-gauge railroad, there are many butterflies.

w = watchtower

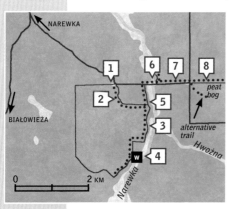

Departure point Kosy Most car park

Getting there Kosy Most is signposted on the road between Narewka village and Białowieża, some 2.5 km from Narewka. Follow this track until it ends at a big forest clearing (drive very carefully: it is an excellent place to see Wild Boar and there is more than just a theoretical chance on seeing Wolf. There is a pack in this general area, and we have actually seen one crossing this track).

1 The forest clearing, with its disused railway track in the middle, is worth an exploration. Nutcracker and Crossbill may be seen here, and wildflowers include Wood Cow-wheat, Martagon Lily, Slender St. John's-wort in the forest edge, and Carthusian Pink, Dark-red Helleborine and Wild Basil close to the railway track. In summer, this is also an excellent area for butterflies, with Dark Green and Heath Fritillaries, and Scarce and Sooty Coppers. Blue-winged Grasshoppers are common on the driest and most open areas.

Follow the track left of the picnic place, indicated Carska Tropina.

2 The first bit of the walk runs through a pine plantation which is a little dull. But soon, you go up a low, sandy ridge with a more natural coniferous forest dominated by spruce and pine.

The Carska Tropina trail, one of the better trails to watch birds in the Białowieża. The Kosy Most car park is one of the best places to observe Nutcrackers.

PRACTICAL PART

The birch bog near the Kosy Most bridge. Bog forests are the least frequent of the forest types in Białowieża.

At the crossing, follow the sign to the right, indicated Carska Tropina.

3 The trail runs through an old-growth oak-linden-hornbeam woodland, and subsequently through a splendid alder carr forest. This stretch is excellent for birdwatching. Look for White-backed, Three-toed and Black Woodpeckers, and Pied, Collared and Red-breasted Flycatchers. There is a number of interesting plants here, including Wood Horsetail, Beech Fern and Oak Fern. The wet trail is also used by mammals and, particularly in spring, it is easy to find the tracks of Roe and Red Deer, Elk, Bison and even Wolf and Lynx.

The track makes a sharp turn around an enclosure, crosses a small forest river (very picturesque) and comes to an observation platform overlooking another part of the Narewka river.

4 This next section runs through another excellent old-growth alder carr forest, which is worth exploring not only for its birds and plants, but also its general scenery. It is similar to 3.

Return all the way to the beginning of the Carska Tropina and turn right to a picnic place and, a little left of it, a hillock with the remains of a watchtower.

An alder carr forest
flooded by Beavers.

9 This stretch of track runs through a mixed forest of moderate age, where Black and Three-toed Woodpeckers, Hazel Grouse and Pygmy Owl are regularly seen.

Follow the Nordic walking trail until it arrives at the road to Narewka. Turn right, cross the Lutownia once more and stop at the Stara Białowieża car park to your right. Follow the short circuit.

10 Stara Białowieża means old Białowieża and for centuries this was the site of the hunting palace. In those days it was the centre of human activity in the Białowieża forest (see box on page 64). The boardwalk takes you to some of the ancient oaks that grace the site. Most of them are named after prominent members of the Polish and Lithuanian royal families that once used the palace as a hunting lodge.

Pygmy Owl

A little further on (note the Yellow Foxglove here in summer), you arrive at the road that took you from Pogorzelce to Teremiski earlier. Turn left here (signposted Białowieża) to return to Białowieża.

PRACTICAL PART

Route 20: Siemianowka Reservoir

UP TO FULL DAY
50 KM

Car route with short walks around the
famous Siemianowka reservoir
Excellent birding with many rare species

Habitats reservoir, reedbeds, sedge marshes, meadows, agricultural land
Selected species Yellow Scabious, Purple Mullein, Citrine Wagtail, Lesser
Spotted Eagle, White-Tailed Eagle, Black Stork, Whiskered, Black and White-
winged Terns, Marsh Sandpiper, Roller, Fire-bellied Toad

Siemianowka Reservoir and its surroundings is famous among bird-
watchers. It is a large, shallow reservoir with, in the east, a broad strip of
marshland. Towards the south and north, meadows and fields dominate
the landscape.

For some reason, Siemianowka has a distinct eastern character, with steppe
plants like Purple Mullein and the essentially Asian Citrine Wagtail. For
years, the reservoir was its westernmost breeding site and it is still the
best place to see this beautiful species in the area. During migration, east-
ern rarities often turn up, such as Red-footed Falcon, Marsh and Terek
Sandpipers and Pallid Harrier.

The Siemianowka
Reservoir as seen from
the embankment.

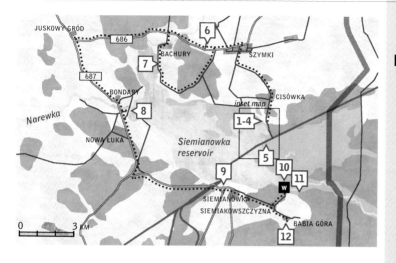

w = watchtower

Departure point Juszkowy Gród

Take the 686 to Szymki and turn a right onto the road to Cisowka. In Cisowka turn right. Park at the pumping station to your right.

1 The area around the pumping station and the meadow on the other side of the road are favourite haunts for Citrine Wagtail. Hoopoe is also possible here. Check the wires here (and later on the railway embankment) for Great Grey Shrike, which is fairly common here.

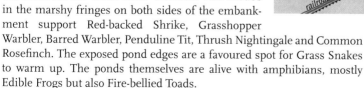

Turn right on the embankment behind the pumping station.

2 This track leads to several small ponds. Follow the dike, keeping the ponds to your right. Check the reedbeds for Great Reed Warblers. The shrubs in the marshy fringes on both sides of the embankment support Red-backed Shrike, Grasshopper Warbler, Barred Warbler, Penduline Tit, Thrush Nightingale and Common Rosefinch. The exposed pond edges are a favoured spot for Grass Snakes to warm up. The ponds themselves are alive with amphibians, mostly Edible Frogs but also Fire-bellied Toads.

204

Purple Mullein (top) and Yellow Scabiose (bottom) are representatives of the Pontic flora in the region.

3 After 100 metres a dirt track appears to the left. If you choose to go left here, you cross the marshes to the reservoir's edge. Explore this area for more scrublands and good views over the reservoir. Return to the main track (see inset map) and follow the trail behind the pines.

4 The trail on this side of the pond is drier and sandy. Look for Viviparous Lizard and, on warm and rainy nights, this may be a good place to look for Common Spadefoot and Natterjack Toad. Northern Wheatear also breeds here, and Purple Mullein and Yellow Scabious are common wildflowers in summer.

Follow the trail back to the pumping station.

5 Follow the dam in the direction of the railroad. The extensive reedbeds on the reservoir side house Savi's Warbler, Great Reed Warbler, Reed Bunting and Bittern. You can follow the trail on either side of the railway tracks for some time (there are only very slow freight trains heading back and from Belarus, but obviously, be careful if you decide to cross the tracks). The height makes it a good vantage point to scan the sky for soaring raptors. White-tailed and Lesser Spotted Eagles are often seen hunting here but other eagles are also possible. Also keep an eye out for Common, Whiskered, Black and White-winged Terns. The embankment itself is good for basking Viviparous Lizards. In summer, cream-coloured Yellow Scabious and Red Hemp-nettle are frequent wildflowers on the railroad dam. On one side of the embankment you can scan the vast reedbeds while on the other side you can overlook the sedge marshes where you can hear various crakes rummaging about.

Return to the car and drive back to Cisowka. In Cisowka take the first track to the left (after house number 26). Follow this track through Szymki and after the village, then take a left back onto the 686. To your right, a road signposted Luplanka branches off. Take it.

6 The tall trees near this crossing are favourite perches for Ortolan Buntings. Listen for their ringing peal of fluty notes, or scan the branches.

Continue and take the track to the left that is signposted Budy. Follow this track through the forest (ignoring the second Budy sign) until the Bachury fishponds turn up on the right.

7 The fish ponds are all private property and fenced off, but can be overlooked from the track. Some islets in the ponds support colonies of Common Tern and Blackheaded Gull. Various terns can be seen hunting over the water, and in the more quiet ponds, Goldeneye and other wildfowl can turn up.

In Bachury, take the first tarmac road to the left. It takes you back to the 686, where you turn left. In Juszkowy Gród, turn left towards Bondary. After crossing the Narew, take the first dirt track left towards the reservoir dam. Park there.

8 From here you can walk onto the dam. This is an excellent place to scan for raptors and storks. It is also the deepest part of the lake and therefore favoured by the various grebes and in wintertime it is also the place to look for Whooper Swan, Red-throated and Black-throated divers.

Continue South on the 687 and take the road signposted Siemianowka and Tarnopol. After crossing the railroad, immediately turn left onto a dirt track, park your car at the end of the track and climb the embankment.

205

The village of Szymki is a good place to see Ortolan Buntings.

With some luck you might see a Little Crake or another rail along the embankment (point 5).

The essentially Asian Citrine Wagtail is one of the highlights of the Siemianowka Reservoir.

9 Here you have a good view over the widest part of the reservoir. It is again a good place to scan the sky for eagles and storks, and the reservoir for waterfowl.

Return and take a left onto the road that leads through Siemianowka village. In Siemianiakowszczyzna, turn left onto a dirt track signposted Maruszka. On this dirt track the watchtower is signposted Wieza Widokowa.

10 The watchtower and surroundings forms the best site on the south shore of the reservoir. The shallow water is fringed by large reedbeds and marshes. Black, White-winged and Whiskered Terns may be observed here as well as significant numbers of waterfowl. Gadwall, Common Teal, Garganey, Shoveler and Whooper Swan are among the possibilities, although a telescope is needed here to get a good view of them, Marsh Harrier is seen regularly and in the small ponds below, the continuous *pjuups* betray the presence of large numbers of Fire-bellied Toads.

Walk onto the embankment that runs past the water pumping station.

11 As with the other side of the reservoir, the water pumping station and the surrounding meadows are the place to search for Citrine Wagtail. Scan possible perches for this bright yellow bird. The ditch that runs parallel to the dike on the right hand side is a place where Whiskered Terns like to hunt.

Take the car back to Siemianiakowszczyzna and after the village, turn left to Babia Gora.

12 This small and traditional hamlet is surrounded by scenic, extensively used meadows. The track to the right before the first house takes you to a viewing platform south of the village overlooking a Bison feeding station. In wintertime this is an excellent place to observe the large herds that often gather here to feed. Another option is to park your car east of the village and proceed on the track on foot to explore the forest around Babia Gora a bit.

Visiting the strict reserve

Giant Oaks, rotting snags and dead trees everywhere, jungle-like alder carr woods, a lush undergrowth and all the mysterious forest species Białowieża is famous for; this is the Strict Reserve. When scientists, alarmed by the massive destruction caused by World War I, visited Białowieża to determine what was left of the forest, they found that this area was in the most pristine condition of the entire forest complex and therefore warranted immediate protection. A reserve was created and the result is that this is the most intact patch of primeval lowland forest anywhere in Europe today (see page 64). A visit to Białowieża is not complete without a tour through the strict reserve. It is without a doubt one of the best places to observe the ecological features of the old-growth forest, as well as its inhabitants Collared Flycatcher, Red-breasted Flycatcher, White-backed Woodpecker, Three-toed Woodpecker and many others.

The Strict Reserve is off-limits without buying admission tickets and using a guide. The regular guides can be booked in the small tourist office near the Palace Pond car

The strict reserve – the oldest and most unscathed part of the forest – can only be visited with a certified guide.

park (see map on page 183). To make the most of your trip, make sure to book a guide who can cater to your wishes. Some guides know more about the history of the forest while others have more expertise in the field of birds, wildlife and flora. For some outstanding independent guide services, see page 218. The standard tour is a short loop of approximately 2 or 3 hours. A trip deep into the forest off the beaten track is also possible, but you will have to ask for it specifically.

Additional sites in North-east Poland

Dojlidy Fishponds

The large reed-fringed Dojlidy fishponds are a delight for birdwatchers. Here you can find, with ease and in an accessible site, lots of waterfowl, including Red-necked, Black-necked and Little Grebes, Great Reed Warbler, Bluethroat and Penduline Tit.

The Dojlidy fishponds are just east of Białystok (see map on page 142) and make for an easy short stop on your transfer between Biebrza and Białowieża.

Approaching Białystok on the 19 (coming from Białowieża), take a right after the cemetery onto Plazowa street. On Plazowa, take the first right, Dojnowska street. After 280 meter, a gravel track branches off to the right. Follow it on foot as it leads through the fishponds, looking for birds as you go along.

Another part of the complex can be accessed by following Dojnowska street (it turns into Rybacka street later on). After 2,3 km turn right onto a dirt track after the last house on the right. This brings you to the ponds on the other side. The open water is less easily viewed from here, but there is more marsh and forest. This area is also quieter and we even had a close encounter with an Otter here!

Puszcza Romincka

Another old-growth forest North-east Poland has to offer is Puszcza Romincka, 30 km north-west of Suwałki. This forest has a distinctly boreal character, with large stands of taiga-like coniferous forest, pine and spruce bog, and the region's typical *suchar* bog lakes (see page 49). It is quite hilly, with height differences of up to 150 metres. The forest harbours a rich wildlife with Wolves, Lynx, Elk, Red Deer, Beaver and Otter. The birdlife is also worth mentioning with species like White-backed Woodpecker, Three-toed Woodpecker, Lesser Spotted Eagle, Osprey (one of very few breeding sites in our region), Black Stork, Pygmy and Tengmalm's Owl. There is an information centre in Dubeninki. The address is Ulica Szkolna 1 and it is open from Monday to Friday from 7:30 to 15:30.

Puszcza Knyszynska

Puszcza Knyszynska is a large forest complex north-east of Białystok. Knyszyn's forest has a more northern feel than Białowieża, with large stands of coniferous forest and well-developed spruce bogs in addition to oak-linden-hornbeam stands, lush alder carr woods and the beautiful Suprasl river. The forest is home to Wolf, Lynx, Elk, Beaver, Otter, Tengmalm's Owl, Pygmy Owl, Black Grouse, Black Stork, Three-toed Woodpecker and even Booted and Short-toed Eagle. Knyszynska is also the site of Podlasia's second herd of free ranging Bison (over 100 animals). There is a visitor's centre in Suprasl. The address is Abp. Gen. M. Chodakowskiego 6 and it's open year round from 7:30 to 15:30. Another place of interest just east of the forest is the area between Krynki and Kruszyniany. This is the best place in the region to see Black Grouse.

Kurianskie Bagno

Kurianskie Bagno is a big swamp in the southern part of Augustów forest, and is the largest of the forest reserves in Puszcza Augustówska. A large depression, partially filled up with peat, supports a large old-growth pine bog.

The sound of Cranes resonates in the forest, while in patches of clear-cut, it is worth scanning the tree tops for Pygmy Owl. Hazel Grouse is quite common and Three-toed Woodpecker occurs. This is also one of the last places in north-east Poland where Capercaillie still occurs. Puszcza Augustówska's remnant population of Capercaillie is declining rapidly in spite of extensive conservation efforts. The odds of running into one are negligible, but the mere idea that this bird is 'out there' adds to the excitement. If you do, however, see or hear one, enjoy the moment, but don't go chasing after it as they are very vulnerable and easily disturbed. Kurianskie Bagno is also home to a sizeable pack of Wolves (these elusive hunters are rarely seen, but their tracks are more easily found).

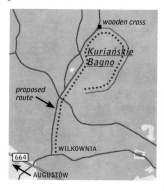

To visit Kurianskie Bagno, follow the 664 east of Augustów, and turn left to the hamlet of Wilkownia. Here you park and proceed on foot. A visit to Kurianskie Bagno is easily combined with route 13.

TOURIST INFORMATION & OBSERVATION TIPS

Travelling to North-east Poland

Most visitors to Podlasia will come from Warsaw and drive from there in the direction of Białystok. A new motorway is currently (2013) being built between Warsaw and Białystok, whilst the new motorway connecting Berlin and Warsaw was completed in 2012. These new connections greatly speed up the drive through Poland, which used to be a tedious experience. The nearest international airport is Warsaw, where one can rent a car or travel on by train or bus. Alternatively, there are good, fast international train connections to Warsaw and Białystok from Berlin and Amsterdam. Several bus services run from most European countries to Białystok, Augustów and Suwałki.

Travelling in North-east Poland

Travelling by car is by far the easiest method of transport in Podlasia, especially if you want to explore every corner of the province. Distances between some of the destinations can exceed 200 kilometres. The quality of the roads is usually good and is improving as roads are being repaired and constructed throughout the province. The Tsar's Road along the East bank of the Biebrza (route 8) is an exception. It is deliberately kept in a state of disrepair to keep traffic densities low and to keep people from speeding.

North-east Poland is ideal for cycle tourism. Both for day trips on rented bicycles in Białowieża and Wigry (see page 215), or for a complete cycling holiday, Podlasia province is perfect. Its terrain is gentle, traffic is generally light, services like shops, agrotourism B&B's and camp sites are frequent and people are helpful and friendly. Bring your bicycle on the train to Białystok and your holiday starts right away. Only word of warning: plan your itinerary so as to avoid provincial roads as much as possible – they are long, dull and straight, and drivers almost invariably drive too fast.

It is also possible to travel by public transportation but keep in mind that only the large cities (Białystok, Hajnowka, Augustów and Suwałki) can be reached by train. From these cities, almost all other settlements can be reached by bus, but most of the smaller settlements are only serviced twice a day, once early in the morning to pick up school children and commuters, and once late in the afternoon to bring them back home. Speaking rudimentary Polish is recommended if travelling by public transport because meeting people who speak any foreign language is a rare commodity in Poland (except for younger people who usually speak some English).

When to go

North-east Poland has something special to offer almost any time of the year. Which season would suit you best depends on what you would like to see. Early spring (April) is the time when early migrants arrive (in order of arrival: Crane, Ruff, Black Stork, Lesser Spotted Eagle, Hoopoe, Greater Spotted Eagle, Black Tern, Collared Flycatcher, Great Snipe, Whiskered Tern and White-winged Tern). It is the best season for finding woodpeckers as they are then busy calling or drumming while the lack of foliage makes them easier to see. Hazel Grouse is also most active and visible in early spring, as are most owls. Elk migrate from the moraines to the wetlands and are regularly seen close to the Tsar road in the Biebrza. At times Bison may be seen grazing in the meadows around Białowieża's hamlets. The beautiful fields of Marsh Marigold and the carpets of spring flowers make for spectacular views. The Eastern and, a bit later, Small Pasqueflowers also bloom fairly early in spring.

Late spring (May–early June), when nature is in full swing, is the most popular season among naturalists. Wildflowers colour the meadows, otherwise shy and elusive birds suddenly perch up and sing their hearts out in plain sight. On warm, sunny days, raptors and storks roam the skies, butterflies and dragonflies begin to fly, rapidly building up good numbers. The old-growth forests turn into green cathedrals. Wherever you are, you will not have enough eyes and ears to keep track of all the interesting animals, plants and landscapes around you. The closing of the canopy in the forest impairs visibility of the forest-dwelling animals so being familiar with the songs and calls of your target species increases chances of finding them.

In early summer (late June to mid July), birds become more elusive and limit their activity to dusk and dawn. This is, however, the best season for butterflies and dragonflies, while entire ranks of wildflowers take over from the spring species. Flowery meadows and dry grasslands are alive with butterflies. Habitats where butterflies are less abundant, like raised bogs, harbour some rare specialties that cannot be found anywhere else. Dragonflies haunt the wetlands.

In August, the proliferation of life has come to an end. A few late flowers (notably the sought-after Pink Frog Orchid and dragonflies peak in this season, but many breeding birds are already packing up for the journey south. July and August is also the time of a pleasant, but locally quite busy tourist season (especially in Białowieża, Wigry and Augustów).

Late August to early October has its own attractions. Tourists have left, leaving the region in a beautiful quietude. Migration brings birds (most notably waders) to the region's wetlands (especially the Biebrza basin and Siemianowka reservoir) which are important stop-overs on the east-European migration route. Autumn (September–October) is also the rutting season for Elk, Red Deer and Roe Deer. These species are especially visible (and vocal!) in this period as the males lose some of their prudence due to their temporary, hormone-induced bravado. With some luck you can see male

Red Deer or Elk males do battle with each other with their, by now fully developed, antlers. In October, head for Białowieża to look for fungi, and come home to your agro-tourism farm to enjoy the local mushrooms in a home-cooked traditional dinner. Winters (December–February) are often snowy and cold, which is why it is the best season to see some of the region's mammals. Beavers and Otters are especially easy to spot during harsh winters as they now depend on the few remaining ice-holes to enter and exit the water. Local guides usually know the best spots to get good views of these otherwise only rarely seen animals. Bison are also quite easy to see in this time of year. Large herds gather near the feeding stations where they may readily be observed. Snow also enables you to look for the tracks of Wolves and Lynx.

Accommodation

One of the great attractions of North-east Poland is the chance to stay in 'agro-tourism places' – small-scale countryside bed-and-breakfasts run by local people. Although there is some variation in quality, all these places have the basic facilities (often you have a small kitchen at your disposal, sometimes there is also internet access) and they are generally quiet and clean. Usually you literally rent a part of a farm. Sometimes people will cook for you when asked, and some even specialise in local cuisine. Sometimes people speak English and/or German and are in their normal life foresters or farmers – hence an evening chat over a beer or wodka is bound to give you insights into the local life that this or any other guidebook could never provide you.

In similar fashion, there are also many camp sites all over the region. Many of those are very basic (sometimes just a field behind a farm), while those in Wigry are, in summer, quite busy and some might even be a little noisy.

Big, luxury hotels are quite rare, except in Białowieża village itself. All along the Augustów-Suwałki road there are roadside truckers' hotels where you presumably do not want to spend your holiday.

There are two ways of arranging your stay in North-Poland. The adventurous way is to simply go there, follow one of the many signs saying 'agroturystyka', knock on the appropriate door, and arrange your stay. Local tourist information points are often very helpful, up to the point that they pick up the phone and call the farms that offer rooms to arrange them for you.

The second way is to contact agro-natura, a Dutch-Polish organisation which mediates between agro-tourism farms and visitors, and can arrange your stays up front. The great advantage of this is, apart from being certain of your accommodation, that Agro-natura knows the places which will cook traditional meals if asked, speak German or English, or are knowledgeable about birds, nature, or local history. See **www.agro-natura.eu**; phone: +31-85-7853820 (NL) and +48-87-7371172 (PL). (website is in Dutch, but you can contact them in English, German or Polish).

Accommodation in Wigry/Augustów Plenty in Stary Folwark and Tartak. In Augustów forest, there is a concentration of venues in the villages along the Augustów Canal.

Accommodation in Biebrza There are various locations quite widespread over the basin. For an overview, check **www.wildpoland.com** – resources by location.

Accommodation in Białowieża. There are plenty of hotels and guest rooms in Białowieża village, but there are also agro-tourism farms in the hamlets of Teremiski, Budy, Narewka village and the other villages in the north. For an overview, check **www.wildpoland.com** – resources by location.

Eating local and organic food

Straight from the land, local and organic food is good for land and people, usually healthy, frequently tasty, and always an adventure. In analogy with biodiversity, gastro-diversity is fascinating and worthy of your attention.

North-east Poland has, as in much of eastern Europe, a tradition of home cooking rather than dining out. The best way to experience it is by staying at agrotourism houses and ask the lady of the house (it usually is the lady) if dinner could be included. Ask for *nocleg z wyzywienie* (stay with meals), or more specifically: *obiado-kolacja* (dinner), *sniadania* (breakfast) or *suchy prowiant* (packed lunch). Speaking a little Polish, or giving it an honest attempt, opens doors that otherwise stay closed. You could also arrange your stays in advance through Agro Natura (see page 213), who can book guest houses where dinner may be included.

In recent years, more restaurants have opened their doors and serve local food. Here are a few ideas:

Biebrza area Restaurant Dobarz (on the Tsar road) and the restaurants in Tykocin.

Wigry area The restaurant in Jeleniewo (near Suwałki Landscape Park).

Białowieża There is a very good restaurant in a railway coach close to the eastern Narewka bridge in Białowieża.

The local cuisine is typical for a region where people do hard physical labour. It is honest, fairly basic food, from a time in which the word 'calorie', had a positive connotation. Much of the locally produced foods meet some of the criteria of organic food, since they either come straight from nature (berries, mushrooms, game) or from local vegetable gardens (vegetables, fruit). However, it will be hard to find them labelled as organic, and the dishes will be supplemented with 'regular' food from the supermarkets. Meat is an important, although not necessarily dominant part of the traditional Polish meal, and there are quite a few vegetarian dishes: *dania wegetariańskie*.

Some typical local dishes *(kuchnia regionalna)*

Kartacze Typical for Podlasia, Kartacze are large balls of potato-flour, filled with meat and spices. They are rather greasy, but, thankfully, a lot tastier than they look!

Pierogi Poland's National dish, Pierogi is a kind of dumpling, which can be filled with meat, cheese or, in a sweet variant, with berries. The sweet version is nevertheless eaten as a main course. In the urban parts of Poland, there are restaurants specialised on Pierogi.

Bigos Polish stew, usually with meat and coleslaw as main ingredients. There are 1001 versions, most of which are savoury and tasty.

Barszcz Beet-soup, typical of Slavic countries.

Babka ziemniaczana Kind of potato cake.

Kiszka ziemniaczana Kind of potato sausage.

Buckwheat In summer, you cannot miss the fields of Buckwheat in full flower. Buckwheat may be called 'the poor man's carbs' but it is actually very tasty and rich in proteins.

Berries The forests and raised bogs produce loads of berries in summertime and many local people harvest them to make jams or to stuff their Pierogi. Berries are often sold by the side of the road.

Mushrooms Like berries, mushrooms are picked straight from the forest and collecting them is a national hobby. Some conservationists frown upon this habit – we make no judgements.

Bison steak Very local, coming only from Białowieża, bison steak is a recent invention. It is a clever product in an area where tourism is booming, but has little to do with traditional food.

Zubr The beer with the bison (Zubr in Polish), is Białystok-brewed, and tastes, in our humble opinion, like a regular pilsner.

Zubrowka (little bison) Wodka The Wodka with a blade of Bison Grass – the favourite food of the bison, according to the firm. It is a successful export product whose success hinges in no small part on the association with bison (a good example of the indirect economic value of nature). It is a much celebrated Wodka, but the association of the Bison with the grass is a myth. This grass does not grow in forests but in marshlands, in places where no Bison would ever venture. In reality the grass was probably chosen because of its distinct sweet taste.

Riding and renting bicycles

The level or slightly sloping terrain and the small and quiet roads and tracks are just begging to be explored by bicycle. Białowieża and Wigry-Augustów in particular, with their long stretches of forests can be a little monotonous for a good walk, but by car you miss the feel of the wind, the smells, the sounds of the outdoors (and thereby many species). However, the bicycle is perfect for this, plus it is healthy and environmentally friendly. And to this we may add that if you are out and about early, the forest tracks are places to see the wild mammals. Explore them by bicycle so you are able to cover enough ground to have a good chance of finding Pine Marten, deer, Wild Boar, Bison, etc. A colleague of ours was even lucky enough to see a Lynx this way.

Białowieża and Wigry-Augustów are the areas most suitable for exploring by bicycle. In Białowieża village you can rent bicycles in various places – e.g. across the Zubrowka Hotel. Some hotels can arrange this for you. The cost is between 25 and 50 Złoty.

In Wigry, you can rent bicycles at the visitors centre in Krzywe (see departure point route 4). In Lipsk you can rent bicycles at the Silencium agro-tourism company. **www.silencium.pl** (markusjola@wp.pl; phone +48 876421258).

Canoe and Kayak rentals

A visit to North-east Poland simply isn't complete without at least one day of kayaking. The river ecosystem can only be explored in a limited way from land or from bridges. For a deeper exploration, you need to take the canoe. From the low position over the water and the lack of clear landmarks you are truly entering a wilderness world. It is perhaps not the best way to see many species (although for some dragonflies it is usually the only way), and photography is a bit of a hassle. But the quietude is amazing, as is the jungle of water plants and the close encounters with wildfowl.

Canoeing is popular, so in holiday periods, you need to seek out the quieter sections. Here are some options.

Narew National Park The multi-channelled river Narew allows for a circular route through river channels. A unique experience! Canoes can be rented at the visitor's centre in Kurowo (see map on page 177). Prices are 5 Złoty for half an hour (up to 30 Złoty for a full day) plus a 5 Złoty entrance fee.

Biebrza National Park Canoes are for rent at the campsite of Osowiec, see map on page 144. A superb but popular section is going downstream from there. You can also make a multiple day trip and arrange to be picked up at one of the villages downstream.

Wigry / Czarna Hańza Canoeing on Lake Wigry can be done from Stary Folwark and Gawrych Ruda. The Czarna Hańza river downstream from Lake Wigry is simply superb, although it can be quite busy in summer. The most beautiful stretch is the one from Fracki south (downstream), which goes straight through Augustów forest. Ask the visitors centre in Krzywe (see map on page 129) for details on how to arrange such a trip. They know companies who rent out canoes and can bring you and pick you up where you want.

Augustów Canal The famous Augustów Canal (see page 55) is actually a string of beautiful lakes connected by stretches of fairly narrow and natural-looking canals. In summer it is very popular among Polish tourists. Canoe rental is possible in, amongst others, Przewiez (point 2 on route 5).

Visitor's centres and museums

Wigry National Park Visitor's centre Nature exhibition, visitor information, book and map shop, bicycle rental.
Address: Krzywe 82
16-402 Suwałki
www.wigry.win.pl

Wigry Muzeum Excellent exhibition on the geology, ecology and nature of the Wigry area.
Address: Stary Folwark 50
16-402 Stary Folwark
www.wigry.win.pl/mw

Biebrza National Park visitor's centre Selling point of entrance tickets to the National Park (see permits chapter on page 218), shop with maps and books, small exhibition.
Address: Osowiec-Twierdza 8
19-110 Goniądz
www.biebrza.org.pl

Narew National Park visitor's centre Small exhibition and selling point of maps of the Narew River, visitor information and canoe rental.
Address: Kurowo 10
18-204 Kobylin Borzymy
www.npn.pl

Białowieża National Park museum and visitors centre Beautifully located on a hill in the Palace Park (route 15), the visitor's centre has a museum and book shop. There is a ticket office for tours in the Strict Reserve near the car park on the opposite side of the ponds, but most hotels can also arrange visits to the Strict reserve for you.
Address: Park Pałacowy 11
17-230 Białowieża
www.bpn.com.pl

Permits, entrance fees and private property issues

Permits are required to enter Biebrza National Park and a different one for the Grzedy (Czerwone Bagno – route 12) section of the National Park. Tickets are 5 Złoty per day (€ 1,25), and become a little cheaper when bought for a week or for groups. The tickets for Grzedy are about the same price.

The strict reserve in Białowieża National Park can only be entered when accompanied by a certified guide (see page 207).

Other reserves in the region can be entered if you stay on tracks and waymarked trails. The Poles are rather relaxed when it comes to private land (in comparison with some western European countries). Most land is not fenced off, and no one would object if you took a peek in the woods or in a meadow. Obviously there are exceptions, and of course you need to be careful not to damage other people's land (or the nature that is there).

One exception are the fishpond complexes, most of which are private (except Doylidi – see page 208). These cannot be entered, but some nature guides have received permission to enter these complexes – since some offer excellent birding and bird photography it may be worth booking a guide for this.

Hiring a bird or nature guide

If you are a keen birdwatcher, with the aid of this book you'll probably track down all or most of the flycatchers, woodpeckers, warblers (including Aquatic Warbler) and most other birds for yourself. However, if you contact a local guide, not only will your chances will be much increased, but also you'll probably add the rare owls, Great Snipe, and most of the mammals to your tally, especially in Białowieża.

Fortunately, there are several guides that are experienced in finding birds and mammals. Better still, they are able to show you them in a responsible way, without disturbance. Most guides know one another well and form a network in which they exchange information and cater for clients together. Many good guides work for or in close collaboration with Wild Poland, and we recommend you start your search for a guide there (Wildpoland has also contributed to the information presented in this guidebook). On **www.wildpoland.com** you can book an excursion, and you also find a list of other companies. Another excellent guide service is Sóweczka (Pygmy Owl) Tours. Visit **www.bialowiezaforest.eu** (online in the course of 2013) for more information. In the Biebrza area, Biebrza Eco-Travel is a renowned and reliable guide service (**www.biebrza.com/en**).

Be aware that if you book an excursion into the Strict Reserve of Białowieża, you have to be accompanied by a National Park certified guide, this certification does not mean that he or she knows how to find birds or mammals. Be sure to hire a guide who is specialised in your field of interest (birds, plants, ecology, etc.).

Recommended reading

Besides the usual field guides, the following books are recommended.

Wildflowers The online *Vascular plants of Poland photoflora*, **www.atlas-roslin.pl** is the best source of information. In the course of 2013, the information on it will be made available in various European languages. For English readers, there is not much to recommend other than general floras on wildflowers of Europe. A mountain flora such as the one from Marjory Blamey will go a long way though, and even a good, comprehensive flora of the British Isles will cover many of the wildflowers of Poland. If you read German, you are much better off. The Schmeil & Fitschen is, if a bit dry, excellent for naming the vast majority of the species. More colourful is the *Flora Helvetica*, which covers over 95% of the species present.

Birds and birdwatching The *Atlas Rozmieszcenia Ptaków Lęgowych Polski 1985–2004* (The Atlas of the Breeding Birds of Poland 1985–2004) gives an excellent account of the breeding birds in Poland. It is in Polish but with quite extensive summaries in English. Wild Poland, a local nature travel organisation led by excellent and highly experienced local birdwatchers (who have also collaborated in the production of this guidebook) has produced two excellent *site guides* with detailed information on where to watch birds and mammals in the Biebrza and Białowieża. They are for sale at **www.wildpoland.com**

Insects A good website on the butterflies of Poland is **www.lepidoptera.pl**. An atlas on the Polish butterflies is also availaible, *Fauna Polski Motyle Dzienne* (Polish fauna; butterflies). Unfortunately, it is entirely in Polish, but the Latin names and distribution maps still make this a useful title. It is not readily available. For dragonflies, the *Distribution Atlas of Dragonflies (Odonata) in Poland* is an excellent title. It is written in Polish and English.

Maps

There are excellent maps available on Białowieża, Biebrza, Wigry and Augustów in the local visitors centres (see page 217). They are highly detailed and, in case of Białowieża, even show the various forest vegetation types. If you don't want to wait until you arrive to buy your maps, the Biebrza and Białowieża maps are available through **www.wildpoland.com**. The Michelin 555 map (1:300.000) provides a useful overview of the whole of North-east Poland.

Annoyances and hazards

There is very little to worry about when travelling in North-east Poland. Crime is low and traffic light. As far as wildlife is concerned – as long as you don't aggravate wild animals you won't be hurt. For example, in spite of a good population of Wolves in the region, there have been no records of Wolf attacks on humans. Brushes with Bison have caused injury, but these cases always involve over-eager photographers or, in case of one particular youtube movie, drunken young men who were teasing a Bison bull. When you encounter a Bison grazing on the meadows around Białowieża's hamlets, it is wise not to approach them. Snorting, shaking the head and scraping the ground with its hooves are signals that the Bison is getting agitated.

Old-growth forests, with their many dead and dying trees, present a threat during storms when branches or even entire trees may come crashing to the ground. Białowieża's strict reserve is closed during storms, and we would advise strongly against an excursion into the rest of the forest complex during a storm.

This leaves only two other potential problems which we discuss in further detail: the bugs and getting lost in the marshes.

Mosquitoes and other bugs

The most ominous annoyance is that of mosquitoes, midges and horseflies. As spring progresses the mosquitoes become more and more numerous in the wetlands. In late spring and summer, when they are joined by horseflies, an otherwise pleasant walk can turn into a true ordeal.

The numbers of mosquitoes vary considerably depending on the amount of snow (and hence shelter) in the winter time. Summers following snowy winters are more 'challenging' than those following cold, snow-free winters.

Mosquitoes are fussy creatures. They don't like wind, drought and bright sunshine. Hence the worst places are damp forests such as those in Białowieża. Open marshes, like the fen mires or open water (when in a canoe) are usually mosquito-free. Using insect repellent (and use it frequently) helps, as does the 'Polish deterrent': gently chastising oneself with a leafy twig when walking around. Nevertheless, in the mosquito season (from mid-May to mid August) a certain attitude of stoic acceptance is needed to enjoy your stay here.

The latter also goes for the horseflies which are less easily deterred. Embrace it as part of the 'wilderness experience'!

Safety in the sedge marshes

Most trails in this book that cross the marshes are (largely) situated on embankments. In designated places however there are 'trails' that simply plunge into to mud (e.g. at Barwik and Kopytkowo – routes 9 and 11). Signposted with nothing more than, colour-barred poles you may try your luck in the marsh. Walking (wading may sometimes be a better description) can be great fun, but is not without danger.

The peat layer along these trails has been damaged by the many tramping boots that have come this way. In such places it is quite possible to sink waist-deep into the peat. Another problem presents itself in summertime when the reed stalks reach so high that they obscure the tall poles that mark the trail (especially as your lower half has disappeared in the mud), which makes it easy to get lost in this marshy jungle.

First off, head out on such trails only if you enjoy the struggle with the forces of nature, not simply as a means of getting from A to B. Because the risk of getting stuck or lost is very real, we strongly discourage walking such trails alone. Also, don't forget to bring a good walking stick (or get yourself a straight and strong stick from the forest), your mobile phone and gps (and keep it dry – so not in your trouser pockets). Make sure you have the phone number of someone on 'shore' who speaks your language. And finally, retrace your steps if you have lost the waymarked route. People have gotten lost and in need of rescue in the past!

Responsible tourism

'Take nothing but your photo, leave nothing but your footprint', is the well-known phrase that summarises the idea of responsible tourism. It goes without saying that, as you are a guest of nature here, you have a responsibility to leave your surroundings and everything in it undisturbed.

Increasing eco-tourism in the region can play an important part in how the situation will, for good or ill, develop in the future.

To maximise your positive impact make sure what you spend goes to local, nature-friendly organisations, tour guides and companies. Stay in the agro-tourism venues, eat local dishes and buy local produce. In this fashion, nature becomes a source of income which justifies conservation not just from an ecological, but also from an economic perspective. What's more, it offers a more authentic Polish experience than staying in a four-star hotel and having fastfood dinners. Make sure you have tickets for the Biebrza NP for your entire stay. Apart from the money, the registration of visits is one of the measuring tools that is used to demonstrate the importance of the National Park. While you are in the area, it doesn't harm to show people that it is nature that you have come to admire. So don't hide your bins.

To minimize your negative impacts, keep your distance from all animals, especially during the breeding season. Photographers are sometimes tempted to sneak up to a Great Snipe lek or a Ruff arena to get that pretty, low-angle, close-up shot, but as harmless as it may seem, the effects can be disastrous. Use your car or a prepared hide for photography.

The same goes for vulnerable landscapes. Sedge marshes for instance are easily damaged. Stay on the marked trails and boardwalks to enjoy this habitat type. Even more fragile is the raised bog, it takes centuries to develop but is easily damaged or destroyed. Again, stay on trails and boardwalks and resist the temptation to venture onto the mats of quaking bog.

Some trails may be off limits during certain periods due to the presence of rare breeding birds and most national parks, and landscape parks have within them nature reserves, which are off limits to tourists. Respect these regulations.

Finally, be careful when driving in winter and early spring, when mammals and (early spring) reptiles and amphibians often cross the roads. This goes for any road in natural areas, but especially the Tsar Road (route 8). This one has some long straight sections which may tempt you to speed up (fortunately they are rather pot-holed), but there are plenty of Elks, birds, frogs, toads, Grass Snakes and sometimes even Wolves, which may suddenly cross.

Nearby destinations worth a visit

Should you have time left to travel on to other destinations, there are various possibilities for further travel.

First, you can head west from Augustów, to explore the famous lake district of Masuria. Thousands of lakes, one even more picturesque than the other, make Masuria a famous travel destination for Poles and also for Germans. In spite of its scenic beauty, the Masurian Lake district is not nearly as attractive naturewise as the region described in this book. The best sites are at lake Łuknajno near Mikołajki.

Heading east into Lithuania or Latvia is, perhaps, a more attractive option. Generally speaking, nature here is similar to that of North-east Poland, with vast and wild forests, swamps, mires and bogs. The National Parks of and Aukštaitija and the Nemunas Delta in Lithuania and the Teiči reserve and the Nagli fishponds in Latvia can compare to the Biebrza and Białowieża in certain respects. They have a distinctly more boreal touch though, with taiga-like coniferous forests and large bogs.

For a completely different scenery, we advise you to head south. First you will come across the interesting Bug Landscape Park (near Siemmiatycze), a beautiful unspoilt river section, with, especially during migration, a rich birdlife. Further south you will find the Lublin uplands. The gentle landscape is roughly comparable to the hilly landscape of central Germany, with forests, fields and pretty brooks and rivers. Roztocze National Park, with its many orchids, is especially attractive. The marshes of Chelm are another highlight – this is a little visited wetland comparable to the Biebrza marshes, holding similar bird species.

From the Lublin uplands it isn't very far to Biesczcady National Park in the extreme southeast of Poland, on the border with Slovakia and the Ukraine. These rocky, low mountains, clad in thick wild beech forest mixed with rocky mountain pastures are part of the great Carpathian mountain chain and hold Poland's largest population of Wolf.

Watching mammals

North-east Poland is probably the best place to watch mammals in Europe. There are, of course, the spectacular species like European Bison, Elk, Wolf and Beaver, for which the region is deservedly famous. But the more widespread and familiar species like Fox, Polecat, Pine Marten and Badger are often relatively easy to find.

Bison The easiest season during which to find Bison is wintertime, when food is scarce and large herds gather around the well-stocked feeding stations. The Babia Gora feeding station (route 20) is known to attract dozens of animals, which are easy to observe. In early spring the herds break up into smaller groups which move around a lot more. At this time Bison are often present in the forest clearings of Białowieża village (15), Pogorzelce, Teremiski and Budy (19) and Olchowka, Nowe and Stare Masiewo (northern Białowieża). Early mornings offer the best chance. Later in the year, the animals tend to stay in the forest. To find them in this season you need to get up very early and visit small forest clearings. It is best, however, to hire a local guide who is more likely to get you more sightings (see page 218).

Elk Head to the Biebrza, where the odds of running into Elk are infinitely higher than in any other place in Poland. The Czarska Droga or Tsar's Road (8) south of the road to Trzcianne is the most accessible place to see them. Other good sites are basically all the watchtowers which overlook a good stretch of marshland (such as those on routes 7, 9, 10, 11 and 12). Although dusk and dawn in winter and spring up to roughly early May is the best time and season, Elk can be seen at any time of day and in any month. In the summer, check the marshes more carefully, as it is sometimes no more than a big nose or floppy ears that stick out of the reeds and sedges.

Beaver Beavers are very common in the region. Dams, lodges and gnawed trees are found in many places, but the most beautiful examples are readily found on routes 1, 5 and 13. In summer, forests flooded by Beavers are easily recognised, because the dead and dying trees bear little or no leaves. Seeing the animals themselves remains a matter of luck. The best place is at the Rudzki channel (route 6) where Beavers have gotten used to the fishermen, and are a lot less shy than they are elsewhere. Evenings and early mornings are the best times, and winter is the best season.

Otter Otters are quite common, but very hard to find, except in winter when they depend, like Beavers, on gaps in the ice to enter and exit the water. You have a good chance of stunning views when booking a guide in the winter time (see page 218).

Lynx and Wolf First, abandon any expectation of actually seeing Lynx or Wolf to avoid disappointment. Then visit the following sites for all the other great things that you may find there, but with an eye open for tracks of Wolf and Lynx. If you are lucky you may catch a glimpse of Wolves, or – vastly more improbable – Lynx. To give you an idea: most rangers, who spend a lot of time in the field, have seen

Wolves (some do so annually), but only a small minority of them ever saw a Lynx. Your best bet in Białowieża is to explore the Kosy Most area (18) and the Narewka – Białowieża road around dusk and at night. In the Biebrza, the forest of Grzędy harbours both Wolf and Lynx (12). The Southern part of the Puszcza Augustówska is home to several packs of Wolves (Kurianski Bagno reserve; page 209).

Roe Deer, Red Deer and Wild Boar These three animals occur throughout the region, and can be seen in many places. In our experience, the Białowieża forest clearings (Teremiski, Budy, Masiewo, Narewka, etc.), the Białowieża – Narewka road and the Narewka – Masiewo road are good places. Leave early for the forest by bicycle and you have the greatest chance (which also applies to other mammals). Scanning the forest edges or the riversides at dusk and dawn is often rewarding too. In Wigry, the meadows between Czerwony Krzyż and Bryzgiel are good around dusk and dawn (2).

Fox, Badger, Pine Marten, Raccoon Dog, Polecat etc. In our experience, all these animals are seen much more often in North-east Poland than in other parts of Europe. Just by spending time in the forest, keeping your eyes open on the tracks and forest glades, you are likely to encounter at least some of these species. Two very good areas in the Biebrza are the dams that run into the mires of the southern basin (routes 9 and 10), and the forest tracks of Grzędy (route 12). In Białowieża, rent a bicycle, get up at the crack of dawn and go down the long and straight tracks – they are used by wild mammals as well – especially in wet areas.

BIRD LIST

The species in the list below can be found in spring and summer, unless otherwise stated. The numbers between the brackets (...) refer to the routes from page 120 onwards.

Swans, geese and ducks Mute Swan is common. Whooper Swan breeds around lake Wigry, at the Dojlidy fishponds and various other places. It is increasing (2;Dojlidy fishponds, page 208). Bewick's Swan can be found in most wetlands during migration. Greylag Goose is present year round and common in the wetlands. White Fronted, Lesser White Fronted and both Bean Geese are possible during migration (7). Mallard, Gadwall, Teal, Garganey, Common Pochard and Tufted Duck all breed in the area and are most numerous in and around nutrient rich lakes and rivers (2, 5, 6, 7, 14, 20). Pintail, Shoveler and Wigeon are rare. Scaup is possible during migration. The only ducks typical of lakes are Goldeneye and Goosander (1, 2, 3, 5).

Partridges and grouse A small population of Capercaillie survives scattered across the Augustów forest. Black Grouse numbers have fallen but they breed locally in the Biebrza's sedge marshes (10) and Knyszyn Forest (page 208). Hazel Grouse is common in large forests with lush undergrowth (1, 4, 5, 12, 16, 17, 18, 19). Grey Partridge is frequent, and Quail fairly rare in the fields and meadows.

Divers Red-throated and Black-throated Divers can be found during migration and in winter on large and deep bodies of water (2, 20).

Grebes Great Crested Grebe is common on all lakes. Little Grebe is a quite rare bird of well vegetated lakes. It is best seen in the Dojlidy fishpond complex (page 208), where Black-necked, Red-necked and (occasionally) Slavonian Grebes can be found.

Cormorants, herons and egrets A small colony of Great Cormorant lives around lake Wigry (2). Bittern is very common (if elusive) in all reedbeds (1, 5, 6, 7, 8, 9, 10, 11, 13, 14, 15, 17, 20). Little Bittern occurs in roughly the same habitat but is very rare (7). In 2012, a pair of Night Herons bred near the Biały Grąd watchtower (7). Great White Egret breeds in the Biebrza Basin and on the shores of the Siemianowka reservoir (7, 20). Grey Heron is common in all wetland types.

Storks In summer White Stork is impossible to miss, breeding in nearly all villages. The Pentowo Stork Village just west of Tykocin has the highest numbers. Black Stork breeds in the forest but is most easily seen when foraging in the wetlands or soaring through the sky (7, 8, 15, 19, 20).

Birds of prey White-tailed Eagle can be spotted throughout the Biebrza, but two other sites are especially good: Wigry's strict reserve (2) and Siemianowka (20). Osprey can be found on the larger lakes and rivers, but only during migration.

Lesser Spotted Eagle is fairly common in the Biebrza, but most frequent in and around Białowieża (7, 8, 15, 19, 20). Spotted Eagle breeds in several locations in the Biebrza middle basin (6, 11, 12). Golden Eagle is occasionally seen here too. Short-toed and Booted Eagles breed in the Białowieża and Knyszyn forests in very small numbers – sightings are rare. Red and Black Kites are also very rare. Red Kite breeds near Bryzgiel (2). Marsh Harrier is very common in all wetland habitats with sufficient reeds. Hen Harrier is possible in the entire region thrghout the year, while Montagu's Harrier is present in spring and summer. It occurs throughout open fields and marshes (best 8). Buzzard is very common but check soaring birds carefully in winter as Rough-legged Buzzard is then common (e.g. 8, 9) and Honey Buzzard occurs in summer (best Białowieża). Sparrowhawk and Goshawk are present in all forests. Red-footed Falcon is seen in small numbers during migration (best 20). Hobby is most frequent in the north (e.g. 1, 2, 5).

Rails, crakes and coots Water Rail, Spotted Crake and Little Crake are present, if elusive, in most wetlands (6, 8, 10, 14, 17). Corncrake is very common. It prefers a bit drier ground (meadows and sedge marsh). Find it on 7, 11, 13, 15 and 19. With all these species, it is the call by which you locate them, as seeing them is tricky. Coot and Moorhen breed in most wetlands.

Common Crane Common Crane is indeed common in the region and can be seen almost anywhere. Highest numbers are in the Biebrza and lowest in Białowieża.

Waders Lapwing breeds in good numbers and Redshank, Curlew and Black-tailed Godwit in small numbers in small-scale agricultural land (7, 11). Green Sandpiper breeds in alder carr woods (12, 17). Woodcock is frequent in the forest and can be seen in display flight over clearings (e.g. 8, 12, 15, 19). Snipe is very common in sedge marshes (especially Biebrza), where Jack Snipe and Great Snipe are rare breeders too. The latter – now declining – breeds in inaccessible places in the marsh. Barwick (9) is the best place to find it yourself, but this bird is easiest seen by hiring a guide (page 218). The Biebrza's famous scores of courting Ruff in late April are best seen on routes 7 and 8. A variety of waders migrate through the region, and include uncommon migrants from the east like Marsh Sandpiper, Broad-billed Sandpiper, and Terek Sandpiper (best 20, and some fishponds – contact a local guide; page 218). Marsh Sandpiper and, in some years, Terek Sandpiper, breeds at Siemianowka (20).

Gulls and terns Of the gulls only Black-headed Gull is locally common. Little Gull is a rare breeding bird of the Biebrza and Siemianowka (20). Little Gull, Caspian Tern and skuas are occasionally seen on migration (20). Common Tern is frequent and Little Tern very rare over rivers and lakes (2, 5, 7, 20). Black, White-winged and Whiskered Tern breed in oxbows and often occur together (6, 7 and 20 are best). Whiskered is the rarest, Black on average the commonest. White-winged numbers fluctuate strongly.

Pigeons and doves Wood Pigeons and Collared Doves are common and Stock and Turtle Doves frequent throughout.

Cuckoos Cuckoo is common in the region and frequently heard in spring and summer.

Owls Tengmalm's and Pygmy Owls are fairly frequent in Białowieża (15, 17, 18, 19 but to find them, hire a guide; page 218) Numbers of Short-eared Owl, a rare bird of sedge marsh, fluctuate. If any, Długu Łuka Boardwalk (8) is the most reliable site. Tawny Owl is common in all forested areas, while Long-eared, Little Owl and Barn Owls can be found in villages – none of them really common though. Eagle Owl is a rare breeding bird of large forests. There is a population of Great Grey Owl in the Belarussian part of Białowieża. It is only occasionally seen in the Polish part of the forest.

Nightjars Nightjar occurs in sandy, semi-open areas. The campsite near Budy and the road from Stojka to Nowa Wies (8) are good sites.

Swift Swift breeds, apart from urban areas, (e.g. Tykocin's synagogue, 8) also in cavities in the old-growth forests (15–19).

Roller, Kingfisher and Hoopoe Roller has become rare breeding bird of agricultural land (most around Białowieża – e.g. 20 – but better still to ask a guide). Kingfisher is quite rare. Taking a canoe down the Czarna Hańcza, Biebrza, Narew or Rospuda may be the best way to find it. Hoopoe is relatively common in small-scale agricultural land (7, 8, 11, 12, 15, 19, 20) Bee-eaters bred in 2012 close to Cisowka (20).

Woodpeckers The region may be the only place in Europe where all European woodpeckers occur. Black Woodpecker, though never common, is frequent in all well-developed forests. Green and Grey-headed Woodpeckers are frequent in more open forests, forest edges and parks (e.g. 14, 15, 19). Great Spotted Woodpecker is by far the commonest species, occurring throughout in good numbers. Its close relative the Syrian Woodpecker has started to colonise the area recently. It has been found in Hajnowka park, Białystok and Tykocin (8). Middle Spotted Woodpecker is fairly common in deciduous old-growth forests and has a penchant for old oaks (its preference for horizontal oak branches leads to a preference for park-like landscapes). Lesser Spotted Woodpecker is uncommon but occurs throughout. White-backed Woodpecker is a true old-growth woodpecker which often feeds on fallen timber. Routes 12, 16, 18, 19 and the strict reserve offer the best chances. The Three-toed Woodpecker is locally frequent in coniferous and mixed stands with enough dead and dying trees. It also occurs in alder carr with sufficient Spruce (5, 16, 18, 19 and Knyszyn forest; page 208) Wryneck is common, with a clear preference for parks and villages with orchards (e.g. 7, 12, 13, 14, 15, 19).

Larks Skylark is very common in rural areas. Woodlark is locally common (7, 8, 12). Crested Lark is rare, if present at all (but common around petrol stations on the motorway between Berlin and Warsaw). Horned (Shore) Lark is possible during migration and in winter.

Swallows and martins Sand Martin is locally common (e.g. 7). House Martin and Barn Swallow are common.

Pipits and wagtails Tawny Pipit is a rare and localised bird of sand dunes (8), Tree Pipit prefers these sites too but is more common (7, 8, 12). Red-throated Pipit is rare on passage (20). White and Yellow Wagtails are both common in their habitats. Breeding 'Yellow' Wagtails here are of the Blue-headed race (*flava*) whilst darker headed northern Grey-headed (*thunbergi*) pass through on migration. The eastern speciality Citrine Wagtail is increasing (7 and 20 are reliable sites). Despite the presence of apparently good habitat, Grey Wagtail does not occur in this region.

Waxwing and accentors Waxwing is a regular visitor in wintertime. Dunnock is common in wooded areas.

Thrushes, chats, wheatears, redstarts and allies Thrush Nightingale is common in (willow) scrub, mostly in damp places (6, 7, 8, 9, 10, 13, 14, 15, 19, 20). Bluethroat is locally common in willow scrub (6, 7, 8, 9, 10, 14). Common Redstart is an uncommon and Black Redstart a fairly common bird of gardens and parks. Northern Wheatear occurs locally in dry, sandy areas (20). Whinchat is common in small-scale agricultural land. Song Thrush, Fieldfare and especially Blackbird are common throughout. Redwing breeds locally in forests, especially alder carr (e.g. 2, 15).

Warblers Barred Warbler is local in scrubland. (6, 7, 8, 9, 10, 14, 15, 19, 20). Garden Warbler Blackcap, Whitethroat and Lesser Whitethroat are common in their pre-ferred habitats. Sedge Warbler is very common in reed beds. Aquatic Warbler breeds in open sedge marshes (7, 8, 10, 14). Grasshopper and River Warblers are common in riverine scrubland (8, 9, 15, 16, 18, 19), the first prefers open, rough vegetation, whereas the latter seeks out willow bushes, young alder stands and edges of alder woods. Savi's, Reed Warbler and Great Reed Warblers all breed in extensive reed beds (6, 14, 20; Dojlidy Fishponds, page 208). Marsh Warbler in-habits the scrubs in the wetlands. Icterine Warbler occurs locally in open, park-like woodlands (12, 15). Willow Warbler and Chiffchaff are common, but Wood Warbler, whose distinctive call can be heard in all forested areas, is abundant. Greenish Warbler is a rare but possibly under-recorded breeding bird of parks (15, Goniądz).

Goldcrest, Firecrest Both Goldcrest and Firecrest breed in coniferous forests.

Flycatchers Spotted Flycatcher is common in villages and parks. Red-breasted Flycatcher is found in the better developed deciduous forests (6, 12, 13, 16, 17, 18, strict reserve, page 207). Pied Flycatcher is locally common in most woodlands while Collared Flycatcher favours open old-growth forests and lush parks (15, 16, 17, 18 and the strict reserve of Białowieża).

Tits and allies Great, Blue and, to a somewhat lesser extent, Long-tailed Tits are common throughout. Coal and Crested Tits can be found in all forests with enough coniferous trees. Marsh and Willow Tits are frequent throughout although most numerous in wetlands. Penduline Tit is common in reedy areas with willows (6, 7, 14, 20; Dojlidy fishponds, page 208). Bearded Tit is rare, but breeds in extensive reed beeds (best Dojlidy, page 208).

Nuthatch and treecreepers Nuthatch, Treecreeper and Short-toed Treecreeper are all fairly common in most woodlands.

Shrikes Great Grey Shrike is frequent in open terrain with shrubs, both wet and dry (7, 8, 9, 20). Red-backed Shrike is very common and can be encountered around most scrublands. Lesser Grey Shrike is used to breed near Siemianowka (20).

Crows and allies Magpie, Jay, Jackdaw and Hooded Crow are common throughout. Rook and Raven are locally common. Nutcracker is a rare and local breeding bird that occurs in spruce-dominated forests (2, 3, 4, 5, 16, and best 18).

Starling and Golden Oriole Starling is frequent in agricultural areas and villages. Golden Oriole is fairly common in deciduous forest.

Sparrows House Sparrow and Tree Sparrow are both locally common.

Finches and allies Chaffinch, Linnet, Goldfinch and Greenfinch are widespread. Siskin and Bullfinch are locally common in coniferous and mixed forests (e.g. 2, 4, 5). Serin is fairly common (e.g. 15). Hawfinch is common in Białowieża forest's deciduous stands (15, 16, 17, 18, 19) and again in Las Trzyrzecki (13). Crossbill is common in well-developed coniferous forests (4, 5, 18). Common Rosefinch is common in scrubland in wet meadows and river valleys (6, 7, 8, 9, 10, 11, 13, 14, 15, 17, 19, 20). Common Redpoll is possible in wintertime. Brambling passes through the region during migration.

Buntings Reed Bunting is common in reedbeds. Ortolan Bunting is local and declining but faithful to its sites (7, 14, 20). Yellowhammer is very common in all agricultural areas. Corn Bunting is uncommon (13). Lapland Bunting and Snow Bunting are possible during migration.

SPECIES LIST & TRANSLATION

The following list comprises all species mentioned in this guidebook and gives their scientific, German and Dutch names. It is not a complete checklist of the species of North-east Poland. Some names have an asterisk (*) behind them, indicating an unofficial name. See page 7 for more details.

PLANTS

English	Scientific	German	Dutch
Adder's-mouth, White	*Malaxis monophyllos*	Einblattorchis	Eenblad
Agrimony	*Agrimonia eupatoria*	Kleiner Odermennig	Gewone agrimonie
Alder	*Alnus glutinosa*	Schwarz-Erle	Zwarte els
Anemone, Snowdrop	*Anemone sylvestris*	Grosses Windröschen	Grote anemoon
Anemone, Wood	*Anemone nemorosa*	Busch-Windröschen	Bosanemoon
Anemone, Yellow	*Anemone ranunculoides*	Gelbes Windröschen	Gele anemoon
Angelica, Wild	*Angelica sylvestris*	Wilde Engelwurz	Gewone engelwortel
Archangel, Yellow	*Lamiastrum galeobdolon*	Gewöhnliche Goldnessel	Gele dovenetel
Arrowhead	*Sagittaria sagittifolia*	Gewöhnliches Pfeilkraut	Pijlkruid
Arum, Bog	*Calla palustris*	Drachenwurz	Slangenwortel
Asarabacca	*Asarum europaeum*	Haselwurz	Mansoor
Ash	*Fraxinus excelsior*	Gemeine Esche	Gewone es
Aspen, Trembling	*Populus tremula*	Espe	Ratelpopulier
Avens, Water	*Geum rivale*	Bach-Nelckenwurz	Knikkend nagelkruid
Balm, Bastard	*Melittis melissophyllum*	Immenblad	Bijenblad
Balsam, Touch-me-not	*Impatiens noli-tangere*	Grosses Springkraut	Groot springzaad
Baneberry	*Actaea spicata*	Christophskraut	Christoffelkruid
Basil, Wild	*Origanum vulgare*	Gewöhnlicher Dost	Wilde marjolein
Basterd-toadflax, Eastern*	*Thesium ebracteatum*	Vorblattloses Leinblatt	Oostelijk bergvlas*
Beak-sedge, White	*Rhynchospora alba*	Weisses Schnabelried	Witte snavelbies
Bearbery	*Arctostaphylos uva-ursi*	Echte Bärentraube	Berendruif
Bedstraw, Lady's	*Galium verum*	Echtes Labkraut	Geel walstro
Bedstraw, Northern	*Galium boreale*	Nordisches Labkraut	Noords walstro
Beech	*Fagus sylvatica*	Buche	Beuk
Bellflower, Bristly	*Campanula cervicaria*	Borstige Glockenblume	Ruw klokje
Bellflower, Clustered	*Campanula glomerata*	Geknäuelte Glockenblume	Kluwenklokje
Bellflower, Creeping	*Campanula rapunculoides*	Acker-Glockenblume	Akkerklokje
Bellflower, Nettle-leaved	*Campanula trachelium*	Nesselblättrige Glockeblume	Ruig klokje
Bellflower, Peach-leaved	*Campanula persicifolia*	Pfirschblättrige Glockenblume	Prachtklokje

Bellflower, Spreading	*Campanula patula*	Wiesen-Glockenblume	Weideklokje
Betony	*Stachys officinalis*	Echter Ziest	Betonie
Bilberry	*Vaccinium myrtillus*	Blaubeere	Blauwe bosbes
Bilberry, Bog	*Vaccinium uliginosum*	Rauschbeere	Rijsbes
Birch, Downy	*Betula pubescens*	Moor-Birke	Zachte berk
Birch, Silver	*Betula pendula*	Hänge-Birke	Ruwe berk
Bird's-nest, Yellow	*Monotropa hypopitys*	Fichtenspargel	Stofzaad
Bird-in-a-bush	*Corydalis solida*	Gefingerte Lerchensporn	Vingerhelmbloem
Bistort	*Persicaria bistorta*	Schlangen-Wiesenknöterich	Adderwortel
Bitter-cress, Large	*Cardamine amara*	Bitteres Schaumkraut	Bittere veldkers
Bladderwort, Greater	*Utricularia vulgaris*	Gewöhnlicher Wasserschlauch	Groot blaasjeskruid
Bogbean	*Menyanthes trifoliata*	Fieberklee	Waterdrieblad
Bugloss	*Anchusa arvensis*	Acker-Krummhals	Kromhals
Bulrush	*Typha latifolia*	Breitblättriger Rohrkolben	Grote lisdodde
Burnet-saxifrage	*Pimpinella saxifraga*	Kleine Bibernelle	Kleine bevernel
Buttercup, Goldilocks	*Ranunculus auricomus*	Gold-Hahnenfuss	Gulden boterbloem
Buttercup, Woolly	*Ranunculus lanuginosus*	Wolliger Hahnenfuss	Wollige boterbloem
Canary-grass, Reed	*Phalaris arundinacea*	Rohr-Glanzgras	Rietgras
Cinquefoil, Hoary	*Potentilla argentea*	Silber-Fingerkraut	Viltganzerik
Cinquefoil, Marsh	*Comarum palustre*	Sumpf-Blutauge	Wateraardbei
Cinquefoil, White	*Potentilla alba*	Weisses Fingerkraut	Witte ganzerik
Clover, Hare's-Foot	*Trifolium arvense*	Hasen-Klee	Hazenpootje
Clover, Mountain	*Trifolium montanum*	Berg-Klee	Bergklaver
Clubmoss, Interrupted	*Lycopodium annotinum*	Berg-Bärlap	Stekende wolfsklauw
Clubmoss, Stag's-horn	*Lycopodium clavatum*	Keulen-Bärlapp	Grote wolfsklauw
Coralroot	*Cardamine bulbifera*	Zwiebel-Zahnwurz	Bolletjeskers
Cottongrass, Hare's-tail	*Eriophorum vaginatum*	Scheiden-Wollgras	Eenarig wollegras
Cowbane	*Cicuta virosa*	Wasserschierling	Waterscheerling
Cowberry	*Vaccinium vitis-idaea*	Preiselbeere	Rode bosbes
Cowslip	*Primula veris*	Wiesen-Schlüsselblume	Gulden sleutelbloem
Cow-wheat, Common	*Melampyrum pratense*	Wiesen-Wachtelweizen	Hengel
Cow-wheat, Wood	*Melampyrum nemorosum*	Hain-Wachtelweizen	Schaduwhengel
Cranberry	*Vaccinium oxycoccus*	Gewöhnliche Moosbeere	Kleine veenbes
Crane's-bill, Bloody	*Geranium sanguineum*	Blutroter Storchschnabel	Bloedooievaarsbek
Crane's-bill, Wood	*Geranium sylvaticum*	Wald-Storchschnabel	Bosooievaarsbek
Cudweed, Heath	*Gnaphalium sylvaticum*	Wald-Ruhrkraut	Bosdroogbloem
Cudweed, Jersey	*Gnaphalium luteo-album*	Gelbweisses Ruhrkraut	Bleekgele droogbloem
Currant, Black	*Ribes nigrum*	Schwarze Johannisbeere	Zwarte bes
Currant, Downy	*Ribes spicatum*	Ährige Johannisbeere	Noordse aalbes
Currant, Mountain	*Ribes alpinum*	Alpen-Johannisbeere	Alpenbes
Dog-violet, Common	*Viola riviniana*	Hain-Veilchen	Bleeksporig bosviooltje
Dog-violet, Early	*Viola reichenbachiana*	Wald-Veilchen	Donkersporig bosviooltje
Dog-violet, Heath	*Viola canina*	Hunds-Veilchen	Hondsviooltje
Elm	*Ulmus sp.*	Ulme	Iep

SPECIES LIST & TRANSLATION

Enchanter's-nightshade	*Circaea lutetiana*	Gewöhnliches Hexenkraut	Groot heksenkruid
Enchanter's-nightshade, Alpine	*Circaea alpina*	Alpen-Hexenkraut	Alpenheksenkruid
Everlasting-pea, Narrow-leaved	*Lathyrus sylvestris*	Wald-Platterbse	Boslathyrus
Fern, Beech	*Phegopteris connectilis*	Gewöhnlicher Buchenfarn	Smalle beukvaren
Fern, Marsh	*Thelypteris palustris*	Sumpffarn	Moerasvaren
Fern, Oak	*Gymnocarpium dryopteris*	Eichenfarn	Gebogen driehoeksvaren
Flowering-rush	*Butomus umbellatus*	Schwanenblume	Zwanenbloem
Foxglove, Yellow	*Digitalis grandiflora*	Grossblütiger Fingerhut	Grootbloemig vingerhoedskruid
Fritillary, Snake's-head	*Fritillaria meleagris*	Schachbrettblume	Kievitsbloem
Frog-bit	*Hydrocharis morsus-ranae*	Froschbiss	Kikkerbeet
Gladiole, Wild	*Gladiolus imbricatus*	Dachziegelige Siegwurz	Wilde gladiool
Goldenrod	*Solidago virgaurea*	Gewöhnliche Goldrute	Echte guldenroede
Golden-saxifrage, Alternate-leaved	*Chrysosplenium alternifolium*	Wechselblättriges Milzkraut	Verspreidbladig goudveil
Grass-of-Parnassus	*Parnassia palustris*	Sumpf-Herzblatt	Parnassia
Hair-grass, Grey	*Corynephorus canescens*	Silbergras	Buntgras
Hawkweed, Mouse-ear	*Hieracium pilosella*	Mauseohr-Habichtskraut	Muizenoor
Hazel	*Corylus avellana*	Gemeine Hasel	Hazelaar
Heather	*Calluna vulgaris*	Heidekraut	Struikhei
Helleborine, Broad-leaved	*Epipactis helleborine*	Breitblättrige Stendelwürz	Brede wespenorchis
Helleborine, Dark-red	*Epipactis atrorubens*	Braunrote Stendelwürz	Bruinrode wespenorchis
Helleborine, Marsh	*Epipactis palustris*	Sumpf-Stendelwurz	Moeraswespenorchis
Helleborine, Red	*Cephalanthera rubra*	Rotes Waldvögelein	Rood bosvogeltje
Hemp-nettle, Large-flowered	*Galeopsis speciosa*	Bunter Hohlzahn	Dauwnetel
Hemp-nettle, Red	*Galeopsis angustifolia*	Schmalblättriger Hohlzahn	Smalle raai
Herb-paris	*Paris quadrifolia*	Einbeere	Eenbes
Hornbeam	*Carpinus betulus*	Hainbuche	Haagbeuk
Horsetail, Water	*Equisetum fluviatile*	Teich-Schachtelhalm	Holpijp
Horsetail, Wood	*Equisetum sylvaticum*	Wald-Schachtelhalm	Bospaardenstaart
Iris, Siberian	*Iris sibirica*	Siberische Schwertlilie	Siberische lis
Iris, Yellow	*Iris pseudacorus*	Sumpf-Schwertlilie	Gele lis
Isopyrum	*Isopyrum thalictroides*	Muschelblümchen	Valse ruit
Jacob's-ladder	*Polemonium caeruleum*	Himmelsleiter	Jakobsladder
Juniper	*Juniperus communis*	Gewöhnlicher Wacholder	Jeneverbes
Knapweed, Brown	*Centaurea jacea*	Wiesen-Flockenblume	Knoopkruid
Knapweed, Pannonian	*Centaurea pannonica*	Schmalblättrige Wiesen-Flockenblume	Pannonisch knoopkruid*
Lady's-slipper	*Cypripedium calceolus*	Frauenschuh	Vrouwenschoentje
Lady's-tresses, Creeping	*Goodyera repens*	Netzblatt	Dennenorchis
Larkspur, Forking	*Consolida regalis*	Acker-Rittersporn	Wilde ridderspoor

Lily, Branched St. Bernard's	Anthericum ramosum	Ästige Graslilie	Vertakte graslelie
Lily, Martagon	Lilium martagon	Türkenbund-Lilie	Turkse lelie
Lily, May	Maianthemum bifolium	Schattenblume	Dalkruid
Linden, Small-leaved	Tilia cordata	Winter-Linde	Winterlinde
Liverleaf	Hepatica nobilis	Leberblümchen	Leverbloempje
Loosestrife, Tufted	Lysimachia thyrsiflora	Straussblütiger Gilbweiderich	Moeraswederik
Loosestrife, Yellow	Lysimachia vulgaris	Gewöhnlicher Gilbweiderich	Grote wederik
Lousewort, Marsh	Pedicularis palustris	Sumpf-Läusekraut	Moeraskartelblad
Lungwort, Suffolk	Pulmonaria obscura	Dunkles Lungenkraut	Ongevlekt longkruid
Maple, Norway	Acer platanoides	Spitz-Ahorn	Noordse esdoorn
Marigold, Marsh	Caltha palustris	Sumpf-Dotterblume	Dotterbloem
Meadow-rue, Common	Thalictrum flavum	Gelbe Wiesenraute	Poelruit
Meadowsweet	Filipendula ulmaria	Echtes Mädesüss	Moerasspirea
Mezereon	Daphne mezereum	Gewöhnlicher Seidelbast	Rood peperboompje
Milkvetch, Purple	Astragalus danicus	Dänischer Tragant	Deense hokjespeul*
Moor-grass, Purple	Molinia caerulea	Blaues Pfeifengras	Pijpenstro
Moschatel	Adoxa moschatellina	Moschuskraut	Muskuskruid
Moss, Iceland	Cetraria islandica	Isländisch Moos	IJslands mos
Moss, Peat	Sphagnum sp.	Torfmoos	Veenmos
Mullein, Purple	Verbascum phoeniceum	Violette Königskerze	Paarse toorts
Oak, Pedunculate	Quercus robur	Stiel-Eiche	Zomereik
Oak, Sessile	Quercus petraea	Trauben-Eiche	Wintereik
Orchid, Baltic Marsh	Dactylorhiza baltica	Baltisches Knabenkraut	Baltische orchis*
Orchid, Bird's-nest	Neottia nidus-avis	Nestwurz	Vogelnestje
Orchid, Bog	Hammarbya paludosa	Sumpf-Weichorchis	Veenmosorchis
Orchid, Common Spotted	Dactylorhiza fuchsii	Fuchs' Knabenkraut	Bosorchis
Orchid, Coralroot	Corallorhiza trifida	Korallenwurz	Koraalwortel
Orchid, Early Marsh	Dactylorhiza incarnata	Fleischfarbenes Knabenkraut	Vleeskleurige orchis
Orchid, Early-purple	Orchis mascula	Mannliches Knabenkraut	Mannetjesorchis
Orchid, Fen	Liparis loeselii	Sumpf-Glanzkraut	Groenknolorchis
Orchid, Fragrant	Gymnadenia conopsea	Mücken-Händelwurz	Grote muggenorchis
Orchid, Frog	Dactylorhiza viride	Hohlzunge	Groene nachtorchis
Orchid, Ghost	Epipogium aphyllum	Widerbart	Spookorchis
Orchid, Greater Butterfly	Platanthera chlorantha	Berg-Waldhyazinthe	Bregnachtorchis
Orchid, Heath Spotted	Dactylorhiza maculata	Geflecktes Knabenkraut	Gevlekte orchis
Orchid, Lesser Butterfly	Platanthera bifolia	Weisse Waldhyazinthe	Welriekende nachtorchis
Orchid, Musk	Herminium monorchis	Einknollige Honigorchis	Honingorchis
Orchid, Pink Frog	Neottianthe cucullata	Kapuzen-Nacktdrüse	Kapjesorchis
Orchid, Ruthe's Marsh*	Dactylorhiza ruthei	Ruthes Knabenkraut	Ruthes orchis*
Orpine, Large	Sedum maximum	Grosse Fetthenne	Bleke hemelsleutel
Parsley, Milk	Peucedanum palustre	Sumpf-Haarstrang	Melkeppe
Parsley, Mountain	Peucedanum oreoselinum	Berg-Haarstrang	Bergvarkenskervel

Pasqueflower, Eastern	Pulsatilla patens	Finger-Kuhschelle	Oostelijk wildemanskruid*
Pasqueflower, Small	Pulsatilla pratensis	Wiesen-Kuhschelle	Knikkend wildemanskruid*
Pea, Spring	Lathyrus vernus	Frühlings-Platterbse	Voorjaarslathyrus
Pine, Scots	Pinus sylvestris	Waldkiefer	Grove den
Pink, Carthusian	Dianthus carthusianorum	Karthäuser-Nelke	Karthuizer anjer
Pink, Maiden	Dianthus deltoides	Heide-Nelke	Steenanjer
Pink, Sand	Dianthus arenarius	Sand-Nelke	Zandanjer
Ragged-Robin	Silene flos-cuculi	Kuckucks-Lichtnelke	Echte koekoeksbloem
Rampion, Spiked	Phyteuma spicatum	Ährige Teufelskralle	Witte rapunzel
Ramsons	Allium ursinum	Bärlauch	Daslook
Rannoch-rush	Scheuchzeria palustris	Blumenbinse	Veenbloembies
Reed	Phragmites australis	Schilfrohr	Riet
Restharrow, Common	Ononis repens	Kriechende Hauhechel	Kruipend stalkruid
Rockrose, Common	Helianthemum nummularium	Gelbes Sonnenröschen	Geel zonneroosje
Rosemary, Bog	Andromeda polifolia	Rosmarinheide	Lavendelheide
Rowan	Sorbus aucuparia	Eberesche	Wilde lijsterbes
Sainfoin	Onobrychis viciifolia	Futter-Esparsette	Esparcette
Salomon's-seal, Angular	Polygonatum odoratum	Wohlriechende Weisswurz	Welriekende salomonszegel
Sanicle	Sanicula europaea	Sanikel	Heelkruid
Saxifrage, Marsh	Saxifraga hirculus	Moor-Steinbrech	Bokjessteenbreek
Scabious, Small	Scabiosa columbaria	Tauben-Skabiose	Duifkruid
Scabious, Yellow	Scabiosa ochroleuca	Gelbe Skabiose	Geel duifkruid*
Sedge, Fibrous Tussock	Carex appropinquata	Schwarzschopf-Segge	Paardenhaarzegge
Sedge, Slender Tufted	Carex acuta	Schlank-Segge	Scherpe zegge
Sermountain, Broad-leaved	Laserpitium latifolium	Breitblättriges Laserkraut	Breed lazerkruid
Sheep's-bit	Jasione montana	Berg-Sandglöckchen	Zandblauwtje
Soapwort	Saponaria officinalis	Gewöhnliches Seifenkraut	Zeepkruid
Spearwort, Greater	Ranunculus lingua	Zungen-Hahnenfuss	Grote boterbloem
Speedwell, Fingered	Veronica triphyllos	Dreiteiliger Ehrenpreis	Handjsereprijs
Speedwell, Long-leaved	Veronica longifolia	Langblättriger Ehrenpreis	Lange ereprijs
Speedwell, Spiked	Veronica spicata	Ähriger Ehrenpreis	Aarereprijs
Spruce, Norway	Picea abies	Gemeine Fichte	Fijnspar
St. John's-wort, Slender	Hypericum pulchrum	Schönes Johanniskraut	Fraai hertshooi
Star-of-Bethlehem, Yellow	Gagea lutea	Gemeiner Gelbstern	Bosgeelster
Stork's-bill	Erodium cicutarium	Gewöhnlicher Reiherschnabel	Gewone reigersbek
Sundew, Great	Drosera anglica	Langblättriger Sonnentau	Lange zonnedauw
Sundew, Round-leaved	Drosera rotundifolia	Rundblättriger Sonnentau	Ronde zonnedauw
Swallowtail	Vincetoxicum hirundinaria	Weisse Schwalbenwurz	Witte engbloem
Sweet-flag	Acorus calamus	Kalmus	Kalmoes
Tea, Labrador	Ledum palustre	Sumpf-Porst	Moerasrozemarijn
Thistle, Brook	Cirsium rivulare	Bach-Kratzdistel	Oeverdistel

English	Scientific	German	Dutch
Thistle, Cabbage	Cirsium oleraceum	Kohl-Kratzdistel	Moesdistel
Thyme	Thymus sp.	Thymian	Tijm
Thyme, Basil	Acinos arvensis	Feld-Steinquendel	Kleine steentijm
Toadflax, Common	Linaria vulgaris	Gewöhnliches Leinkraut	Vlasbekje
Toothwort	Lathraea squamaria	Gewöhnliche Schuppenwurz	Bleke schubwortel
Tormentil	Potentilla erecta	Blutwurz	Tormentil
Twayblade, Common	Neottia ovata	Grosses Zweiblatt	Grote keverorchis
Twayblade, Lesser	Neottia cordata	Kleines Zweiblatt	Kleine keverorchis
Vetch, Kidney	Anthyllis vulneraria	Gewöhnlicher Wundklee	Wondklaver
Vetchling, Pea-like*	Lathyrus pisiformis	Erbsenartige Platterbse	Erwtlathyrus*
Violet, Marsh	Viola palustris	Sumpf-Veilchen	Moerasviooltje
Viper's-bugloss	Echium vulgare	Gewöhnlicher Natternkopf	Slangenkruid
Water-lily, Fringed	Nymphoides peltata	Seekanne	Watergentiaan
Water-lily, White	Nymphaea alba	Weisse Seerose	Witte waterlelie
Water-lily, Yellow	Nuphar lutea	Gelbe Teichrose	Gele plomp
Water-plantain	Alisma plantago-aquatica	Gewöhnlicher Froschlöffel	Grote waterweegbree
Water-soldier	Stratiotes aloides	Krebsschere	Krabbenscheer
Water-violet	Hottonia palustris	Wasserfeder	Waterviolier
Willow, Downy	Salix lapponum	Lappländische Weide	Laplandwilg*
Willow, Goat	Salix caprea	Sal-Weide	Boswilg
Willow, Grey	Salix cinerea	Grau-Weide	Grauwe wilg
Willowherb, Great	Epilobium hirsutum	Zottiges Weidenröschen	Harig wilgenroosje
Wintergreen, Chickweed	Trientalis europaea	Siebenstern	Zevenster
Wintergreen, Common	Pyrola minor	Kleines Wintergrün	Klein wintergroen
Wintergreen, Round-leaved	Pyrola rotundifolia	Rundblättriges Wintergrün	Rond wintergroen
Wintergreen, Serrated	Orthilia secunda	Nickendes Wintergrün	Eenzijdig wintergroen
Wintergreen, Umbellate	Chimaphila umbellata	Dolden-Winterlieb	Schermwintergroen
Woodruff	Galium odoratum	Waldmeister	Lievevrouwenbedstro
Wormwood, Field	Artemisia campestris	Feld-Beifuss	Wilde averuit

MAMMALS

English	Scientific	German	Dutch
Aurochs	Bos primigenius	Auerochse	Oeros
Badger	Meles meles	Dachs	Das
Bat, Pond	Myotis dasycneme	Teichfledermaus	Meervleermuis
Bear, Brown	Ursus arctos	Braunbär	Bruine beer
Beaver	Castor fiber	Bieber	Bever
Bison, (European)	Bison bonasus	Wisent	Wisent
Boar, Wild	Sus scrofa	Wildschwein	Wild zwijn
Cat, Wild	Felis silvestris	Wildkatze	Wilde kat
Deer, Red	Cervus elaphus	Rothirsch	Edelhert
Deer, Roe	Capreolus capreolus	Reh	Ree

Dog, Raccoon	Nyctereutes procyonoides	Marderhund	Wasbeerhond
Dormice	Gliridae	Bilche	Slaapmuizen
Elk	Alces alces	Elch	Eland
Fox, Red	Vulpes vulpes	Rotfuchs	Vos
Hare, Mountain	Lepus timidus	Schneehase	Sneeuwhaas
Lynx	Lynx lynx	Luchs	Lynx
Marten, Beech	Martes foina	Steinmarder	Steenmarter
Marten, Pine	Martes martes	Baummarder	Boommarter
Mink, American	Neovison vison	Amerikanischer Nerz	Amerikaanse nerts
Otter	Lutra lutra	Fischotter	Otter
Polecat	Mustela putorius	Waldiltis	Bunzing
Shrews	Soricidae	Spitzmaus	Spitsmuis
Stoat	Mustela ermina	Hermelin	Hermelijn
Tarpan	Equus caballus gmelini	Tarpan	Tarpan
Voles	Arvicolidae	Wühlmäuse	Woelmuizen
Weasel	Mustela nivalis	Mauswiesel	Wezel
Wolf	Canis lupus	Wolf	Wolf

BIRDS

English	Scientific	German	Dutch
Bee-eater	Merops apiaster	Bienenfresser	Bijeneter
Bittern, Great	Botaurus stellaris	Rohrdommel	Roerdomp
Bittern, Little	Ixobrychus minutus	Zwergdommel	Woudaapje
Blackbird	Turdus merula	Amsel	Merel
Blackcap	Sylvia atricapilla	Mönchsgrasmücke	Zwartkop
Bluethroat	Luscinia svecica	Blaukehlchen	Blauwborst
Brambling	Fringilla montifringilla	Bergfink	Keep
Bullfinch	Pyrrhula pyrrhula	Gimpel	Goudvink
Bunting, Corn	Miliaria calandra	Grauammer	Grauwe gors
Bunting, Lapland	Calcarius lapponicus	Spornammer	IJsgors
Bunting, Ortolan	Emberiza hortulana	Ortolan	Ortolaan
Bunting, Reed	Emberiza schoeniclus	Rohrammer	Rietgors
Bunting, Snow	Plectrophenax nivalis	Schneeammer	Sneeuwgors
Buzzard	Buteo buteo	Mäusebussard	Buizerd
Buzzard, Honey	Pernis apivorus	Wespenbussard	Wespendief
Buzzard, Rough-legged	Buteo lagopus	Rauhfussbussard	Ruigpootbuizerd
Capercaillie	Tetrao urogallus	Auerhuhn	Auerhoen
Chaffinch	Fringilla coelebs	Buchfink	Vink
Chiffchaff	Phylloscopus collybita	Zilpzalp	Tjiftjaf
Coot	Fulica atra	Blässhuhn	Meerkoet
Cormorant, Great	Phalacrocorax carbo	Kormoran	Aalscholver
Corncrake	Crex crex	Wachtelkönig	Kwartelkoning
Crake, Little	Porzana parva	Kleines Sumpfhuhn	Klein waterhoen
Crake, Spotted	Porzana porzana	Tüpfelsumpfhuhn	Porseleinhoen

Crane	*Grus grus*	Kranich	Kraanvogel
Crossbill	*Loxia curvirostra*	Fichtenkreuzschnabel	Kruisbek
Crow, Hooded	*Corvus corone cornix*	Nebelkrähe	Bonte kraai
Cuckoo	*Cuculus canorus*	Kuckuck	Koekoek
Curlew	*Numenius arquata*	Grosser Brachvogel	Wulp
Diver, Black-throated	*Gavia arctica*	Prachttaucher	Parelduiker
Diver, Red-throated	*Gavia stellata*	Sterntaucher	Roodkeelduiker
Dove, Collared	*Streptopelia decaocto*	Türkentaube	Turkse tortel
Dove, Stock	*Columba oenas*	Hohltaube	Holenduif
Dove, Turtle	*Streptopelia turtur*	Turteltaube	Tortelduif
Duck, Tufted	*Aythya fuligula*	Reiherente	Kuifeend
Dunnock	*Prunella modularis*	Heckenbraunelle	Heggenmus
Eagle, (Greater) Spotted	*Aquila clanga*	Schelladler	Bastaardarend
Eagle, Booted	*Hieraaetus pennatus*	Zwergadler	Dwergarend
Eagle, Golden	*Aquila chrysaetos*	Steinadler	Steenarend
Eagle, Lesser Spotted	*Aquila pomarina*	Schreiadler	Schreeuwarend
Eagle, Short-toed	*Circaetus gallicus*	Schlangenadler	Slangenarend
Eagle, White-tailed	*Haliaeetus albicilla*	Seeadler	Zeearend
Egret, Great White	*Egretta alba*	Silberreiher	Grote zilverreiger
Falcon, Red-footed	*Falco vespertinus*	Rotfussfalke	Roodpootvalk
Fieldfare	*Turdus pilaris*	Wacholderdrossel	Kramsvogel
Firecrest	*Regulus ignicapillus*	Sommergoldhähnchen	Vuurgoudhaantje
Flycatcher, Collared	*Ficedula albicollis*	Halsbandschnäpper	Withalsvliegenvanger
Flycatcher, Pied	*Ficedula hypoleuca*	Trauerschnäpper	Bonte vliegenvanger
Flycatcher, Red-breasted	*Ficedula parva*	Zwergschnäpper	Kleine vliegenvanger
Flycatcher, Spotted	*Muscicapa striata*	Grauschnäpper	Grauwe vliegenvanger
Gadwall	*Anas strepera*	Schnatterente	Krakeend
Garganey	*Anas querquedula*	Knäkente	Zomertaling
Godwit, Black-tailed	*Limosa limosa*	Uferschnepfe	Grutto
Goldcrest	*Regulus regulus*	Wintergoldhähnchen	Goudhaan
Goldeneye	*Bucephala clangula*	Schellente	Brilduiker
Goldfinch	*Carduelis carduelis*	Distelfink	Putter
Goosander	*Mergus merganser*	Gänsesäger	Grote zaagbek
Goose, Bean	*Anser fabalis*	Saatgans	Rietgans
Goose, Greylag	*Anser anser*	Graugans	Grauwe gans
Goose, Lesser White-fronted	*Anser erythropus*	Zwerggans	Dwerggans
Goose, White-fronted	*Anser albifrons*	Blässgans	Kolgans
Goshawk	*Accipiter gentilis*	Habicht	Havik
Grebe, Black-necked	*Podiceps nigricollis*	Schwarzhalstaucher	Geoorde fuut
Grebe, Great Crested	*Podiceps cristatus*	Haubentaucher	Fuut
Grebe, Little	*Tachybaptus ruficollis*	Zwergtaucher	Dodaars
Grebe, Red-necked	*Podiceps grisegena*	Rothalstaucher	Roodhalsfuut
Grebe, Slavonian	*Podiceps auritus*	Ohrentaucher	Kuifduiker
Greenfinch	*Carduelis chloris*	Grünling	Groenling

238

English	Scientific	German	Dutch
Grouse, Black	*Lyrurus tetrix*	Birkhuhn	Korhoen
Grouse, Hazel	*Tetrastes bonasia*	Haselhuhn	Hazelhoen
Gull, Black-headed	*Chroicocephalus ridibundus*	Lachmöwe	Kokmeeuw
Gull, Little	*Hydrocoloeus minutus*	Zwergmöwe	Dwergmeeuw
Harrier, Hen	*Circus cyaneus*	Kornweihe	Blauwe kiekendief
Harrier, Marsh	*Circus aeruginosus*	Rohrweihe	Bruine kiekendief
Harrier, Montagu's	*Circus pygargus*	Wiesenweihe	Grauwe kiekendief
Harrier, Pallid	*Circus macrourus*	Steppenweihe	Steppekiekendief
Hawfinch	*Coccothraustes coccothraustes*	Kernbeisser	Appelvink
Heron, Grey	*Ardea cinerea*	Graureiher	Blauwe reiger
Heron, Night	*Nycticorax nycticorax*	Nachtreiher	Kwak
Hobby	*Falco subbuteo*	Baumfalke	Boomvalk
Hoopoe	*Upupa epops*	Wiedehopf	Hop
Jackdaw	*Corvus monedula*	Dohle	Kauw
Jay	*Garrulus glandarius*	Eichelhäher	Gaai
Kingfisher	*Alcedo atthis*	Eisvogel	IJsvogel
Kite, Black	*Milvus migrans*	Schwarzmilan	Zwarte wouw
Kite, Red	*Milvus milvus*	Rotmilan	Rode wouw
Lapwing	*Vanellus vanellus*	Kiebitz	Kievit
Lark, Crested	*Galerida cristata*	Haubenlerche	Kuifleeuwerik
Lark, Horned	*Eremophila alpestris*	Ohrenlerche	Strandleeuwerik
Linnet	*Carduelis cannabina*	Bluthänfling	Kneu
Magpie	*Pica pica*	Elster	Ekster
Mallard	*Anas platyrhynchos*	Stockente	Wilde eend
Martin, House	*Delichon urbicum*	Mehlschwalbe	Huiszwaluw
Martin, Sand	*Riparia riparia*	Uferschwalbe	Oeverzwaluw
Moorhen	*Gallinula chloropus*	Teichhuhn	Waterhoen
Nightingale, Thrush	*Luscinia luscinia*	Sprosser	Noordse nachtegaal
Nightjar	*Caprimulgus europaeus*	Ziegenmelker	Nachtzwaluw
Nutcracker	*Nucifraga caryocatactes*	Tannenhäher	Notenkraker
Nuthatch	*Sitta europaea*	Kleiber	Boomklever
Oriole, Golden	*Oriolus oriolus*	Pirol	Wielewaal
Osprey	*Pandion haliaetus*	Fischadler	Visarend
Owl, Barn	*Tyto alba*	Schleiereule	Kerkuil
Owl, Eagle	*Bubo bubo*	Uhu	Oehoe
Owl, Great Grey	*Strix nebulosa*	Bartkauz	Laplanduil
Owl, Little	*Athene noctua*	Steinkauz	Steenuil
Owl, Long-eared	*Asio otus*	Waldohreule	Ransuil
Owl, Pygmy	*Glaucidium passerinum*	Sperlingskauz	Dwerguil
Owl, Short-eared	*Asio flammeus*	Sumpfohreule	Velduil
Owl, Tawny	*Strix aluco*	Waldkauz	Bosuil
Owl, Tengmalm's	*Aegolius funereus*	Raufusskauz	Ruigpootuil
Partridge, Grey	*Perdix perdix*	Rebhuhn	Patrijs
Phalarope, Red-necked	*Phalaropus lobatus*	Odinshühnchen	Grauwe franjepoot

CROSSBILL GUIDES · NORTH-EAST POLAND

Pigeon, Wood	*Columba palumbus*	Ringeltaube	Houtduif
Pintail	*Anas acuta*	Spiessente	Pijlstaart
Pipit, Red-throated	*Anthus cervinus*	Rotkehlpieper	Roodkeelpieper
Pipit, Tawny	*Anthus campestris*	Brachpieper	Duinpieper
Pipit, Tree	*Anthus trivialis*	Baumpieper	Boompieper
Plover, Common Ringed	*Charadrius hiaticula*	Sandregenpfeifer	Bontbekplevier
Plover, Little Ringed	*Charadrius dubius*	Flussregenpfeifer	Kleine plevier
Pochard	*Aythya ferina*	Tafelente	Tafeleend
Quail	*Coturnix coturnix*	Wachtel	Kwartel
Rail, Water	*Rallus aquaticus*	Wasserralle	Waterral
Raven	*Corvus corax*	Kolkrabe	Raaf
Redpoll, Common	*Carduelis flammea s.l.*	Birkenzeisig	Barmsijs
Redshank	*Tringa totanus*	Rotschenkel	Tureluur
Redstart, (Common)	*Phoenicurus phoenicurus*	Gartenrotschwanz	Gekraagde roodstaart
Redstart, Black	*Phoenicurus ochruros*	Hausrotschwanz	Zwarte roodstaart
Redwing	*Turdus iliacus*	Rotdrossel	Koperwiek
Robin	*Erithacus rubecula*	Rotkehlchen	Roodborst
Roller	*Coracias garrulus*	Blauracke	Scharrelaar
Rook	*Corvus frugilegus*	Saatkrähe	Roek
Rosefinch, Common	*Carpodacus erythrinus*	Karmingimpel	Roodmus
Ruff	*Philomachus pugnax*	Kampfläufer	Kemphaan
Sandpiper, Broad-billed	*Limicola falcinellus*	Sumpfläufer	Breedbekstrandloper
Sandpiper, Green	*Tringa ochropus*	Waldwasserläufer	Witgat
Sandpiper, Marsh	*Tringa stagnatilis*	Teichwasserläufer	Poelruiter
Sandpiper, Terek	*Xenus cinereus*	Terekwasserläufer	Terekruiter
Scaup	*Aythya marila*	Bergente	Topper
Serin	*Serinus serinus*	Girlitz	Europese kanarie
Shoveler	*Anas clypeata*	Löffelente	Slobeend
Shrike, Great Grey	*Lanius excubitor*	Raubwürger	Klapekster
Shrike, Lesser Grey	*Lanius minor*	Schwarzstirnwürger	Kleine klapekster
Shrike, Red-backed	*Lanius collurio*	Neuntöter	Grauwe klauwier
Siskin	*Carduelis spinus*	Erlenzeisig	Sijs
Skuas	*Stercorarius sp.*	Raubmöwen	Jagers
Skylark	*Alauda arvensis*	Feldlerche	Veldleeuwerik
Smew	*Mergellus albellus*	Zwergsäger	Nonnetje
Snipe	*Gallinago gallinago*	Bekassine	Watersnip
Snipe, Great	*Gallinago media*	Doppelschnepfe	Poelsnip
Snipe, Jack	*Lymnocryptes minimus*	Zwergschnepfe	Bokje
Sparrow, House	*Passer domesticus*	Haussperling	Huismus
Sparrow, Tree	*Passer montanus*	Feldsperling	Ringmus
Sparrowhawk	*Accipiter nisus*	Sperber	Sperwer
Starling	*Sturnus vulgaris*	Star	Spreeuw
Stork, Black	*Ciconia nigra*	Schwarzstorch	Zwarte ooievaar
Stork, White	*Ciconia ciconia*	Weissstorch	Ooievaar
Swallow, Barn	*Hirundo rustica*	Rauchschwalbe	Boerenzwaluw

SPECIES LIST & TRANSLATION

Swan, Bewick's	*Cygnus bewickii*	Zwergschwan	Kleine zwaan
Swan, Mute	*Cygnus olor*	Höckerschwan	Knobbelzwaan
Swan, Whooper	*Cygnus cygnus*	Singschwan	Wilde zwaan
Swift	*Apus apus*	Mauersegler	Gierzwaluw
Teal, Common	*Anas crecca*	Krickente	Wintertaling
Tern, Black	*Chlidonias niger*	Trauerseeschwalbe	Zwarte stern
Tern, Caspian	*Hydroprogne caspia*	Raubseeschwalbe	Reuzenstern
Tern, Common	*Sterna hirundo*	Flussseeschwalbe	Visdief
Tern, Little	*Sternula albifrons*	Zwergseeschwalbe	Dwergstern
Tern, Whiskered	*Chlidonias hybrida*	Weissbart-Seeschwalbe	Witwangstern
Tern, White-winged	*Chlidonias leucopterus*	Weissflügel-Seeschwalbe	Witvleugelstern
Thrush, Song	*Turdus philomelos*	Singdrossel	Zanglijster
Tit, Bearded	*Panurus biarmicus*	Bartmeise	Baardman
Tit, Blue	*Cyanistes caeruleus*	Blaumeise	Pimpelmees
Tit, Coal	*Periparus ater*	Tannenmeise	Zwarte mees
Tit, Crested	*Lophophanes cristatus*	Haubenmeise	Kuifmees
Tit, Great	*Parus major*	Kohlmeise	Koolmees
Tit, Long-tailed	*Aegithalos caudatus*	Schwanzmeise	Staartmees
Tit, Marsh	*Poecile palustris*	Sumpfmeise	Glanskop
Tit, Penduline	*Remiz pendulinus*	Beutelmeise	Buidelmees
Tit, Willow	*Poecile montanus*	Weidenmeise	Matkop
Treecreeper	*Certhia familiaris*	Waldbaumläufer	Taigaboomkruiper
Treecreeper, Short-toed	*Certhia brachydactyla*	Gartenbaumläufer	Boomkruiper
Wagtail, Citrine	*Motacilla citreola*	Zitronenstelze	Citroenkwikstaart
Wagtail, Grey	*Motacilla cinerea*	Gebirgsstelze	Grote gele kwikstaart
Wagtail, Grey-headed	*Motacilla (flava) thunbergii*	Thunberg-Schafstelze	Noordse kwikstaart
Wagtail, White	*Motacilla alba*	Bachstelze	Witte kwikstaart
Wagtail, Yellow	*Motacilla flava*	Schafstelze	Gele kwikstaart
Warbler, Aquatic	*Acrocephalus paludicola*	Seggenrohrsänger	Waterrietzanger
Warbler, Barred	*Sylvia nisoria*	Sperbergrasmücke	Sperwergrasmus
Warbler, Garden	*Sylvia borin*	Gartengrasmücke	Tuinfluiter
Warbler, Grasshopper	*Locustella naevia*	Feldschwirl	Sprinkhaanzanger
Warbler, Great Reed	*Acrocephalus arundinaceus*	Drosselrohrsänger	Grote karekiet
Warbler, Greenish	*Phylloscopus trochiloides*	Grünlaubsänger	Grauwe fitis
Warbler, Icterine	*Hippolais icterina*	Gelbspötter	Spotvogel
Warbler, Marsh	*Acrocephalus palustris*	Sumpfrohrsänger	Bosrietzanger
Warbler, Reed	*Acrocephalus scirpaceus*	Teichrohrsänger	Kleine karekiet
Warbler, River	*Locustella fluviatilis*	Schlagschwirl	Krekelzanger
Warbler, Savi's	*Locustella luscinioides*	Rohrschwirl	Snor
Warbler, Sedge	*Acrocephalus schoenobaenus*	Schilfrohrsänger	Rietzanger
Warbler, Willow	*Phylloscopus trochilus*	Fitis	Fitis
Waxwing	*Bombycilla garrulus*	Seidenschwanz	Pestvogel
Wheatear, Northern	*Oenanthe oenanthe*	Steinschmätzer	Tapuit

Whinchat	Saxicola rubetra	Braunkehlchen	Paapje
Whitethroat	Sylvia communis	Dorngrasmücke	Grasmus
Whitethroat, Lesser	Sylvia curruca	Klappergrasmücke	Braamsluiper
Wigeon	Anas penelope	Pfeifente	Smient
Woodcock	Scolopax rusticola	Waldschnepfe	Houtsnip
Woodlark	Lullula arborea	Heidelerche	Boomleeuwerik
Woodpecker, Black		Dryocopus martius	Schwarzspecht
Woodpecker, Great Spotted	Dendrocopos major	Buntspecht	Grote bonte specht
Woodpecker, Green	Picus viridis	Grünspecht	Groene specht
Woodpecker, Grey-headed	Picus canus	Grauspecht	Grijskopspecht
Woodpecker, Lesser Spotted	Dendrocopos minor	Kleinspecht	Kleine bonte specht
Woodpecker, Middle Spotted	Dendrocopos medius	Mittelspecht	Middelste bonte specht
Woodpecker, Syrian	Dendrocopos syriacus	Blutspecht	Syrische bonte specht
Woodpecker, Three-toed	Picoides tridactylus	Dreizehenspecht	Drieteenspecht
Woodpecker, White-backed	Dendrocopos leucotos	Weissrückenspecht	Witrugspecht
Wren	Troglodytes troglodytes	Zaunkönig	Winterkoning
Wryneck	Jynx torquilla	Wendehals	Draaihals
Yellowhammer	Emberiza citrinella	Goldammer	Geelgors

REPTILES AND AMPHIBIANS

English	Scientific	German	Dutch
Adder	Vipera berus	Kreuzotter	Adder
Frog, Edible	Pelophylax esculentus	Teichfrosch	Bastaardkikker
Frog, Grass	Rana temporaria	Grasfrosch	Bruine kikker
Frog, Moor	Rana arvalis	Moorfrosch	Heikikker
Frog, Tree	Hyla arborea	Europäischer Laubfrosch	Boomkikker
Lizard, Sand	Lacerta agilis	Zauneidechse	Zandhagedis
Lizard, Viviparous	Zootoca vivipara	Bergeidechse	Levendbarende hagedis
Newt, Common	Lissotriton vulgaris	Teichmolch	Kleine watersalamander
Newt, Crested	Triturus cristatus	Kammolch	Kamsalamander
Snake, Grass	Natrix natrix	Ringelnatter	Ringslang
Snake, Smooth	Coronella austriaca	Schlingnatter	Gladde slang
Spadefoot, Common	Pelobates fuscus	Knoblauchkröte	Knoflookpad
Terrapin, European Pond	Emys orbicularis	Europäische Sumpfschildkröte	Europese moerasschildpad
Toad, Common	Bufo bufo	Erdkröte	Gewone pad
Toad, Fire-bellied	Bombina bombina	Rotbauchunke	Roodbuikvuurpad
Toad, Green	Pseudepidalea viridis	Wechselkröte	Groene pad
Toad, Natterjack	Bufo calamita	Kreuzkröte	Rugstreeppad
Worm, Slow	Anguis fragilis	Blindschleiche	Hazelworm

INVERTEBRATES

English	Scientific	German	Dutch
Admiral, Poplar	*Limenitis populi*	Grosser Eisvogel	Grote ijsvogelvlinder
Admiral, White	*Limenitis camilla*	Kleiner Eisvogel	Kleine ijsvogelvlinder
Apollo, Clouded	*Parnassius mnemosyne*	Schwarze Apollo	Zwarte apollovlinder
Argus, Brown	*Aricia agestis*	Kleiner Sonnenröschen-Bläuling	Bruin blauwtje
Argus, Geranium	*Aricia eumedon*	Storchschnabel-Bläuling	Zwart blauwtje
Argus, Mountain	*Aricia artaxerxes*	Grosser Sonnenröschen-Bläuling	Vals bruin blauwtje
Baskettail, Eurasian	*Epitheca bimaculata*	Zweifleck	Tweevlek
Beauty, Camberwell	*Nymphalis antiopa*	Trauermantel	Rouwmantel
Beetle, Bark	see, Engraver, Spruce		
Blue, Amanda's	*Polyommatus amandus*	Vogelwicken-Bläuling	Wikkeblauwtje
Blue, Chalkhill	*Polyommatus coridon*	Silbergrüner Bläuling	Bleek blauwtje
Blue, Cranberry	*Plebejus optilete*	Hochmoor-Bläuling	Veenbesblauwtje
Blue, Holly	*Celastrina argiolus*	Faulbaum-Bläuling	Boomblauwtje
Blue, Large	*Phengaris arion*	Schwarzgefleckten Bläuling	Tijmblauwtje
Blue, Little	*Cupido minimus*	Zwerg-Bläuling	Dwergblauwtje
Blue, Long-tailed	*Lampides boeticus*	Grosser Wanderbläuling	Tijgerblauwtje
Blue, Short-tailed	*Cupido argiades*	Kurzschwänziger Bläuling	Staartblauwtje
Bluetail, Small	*Ischnura pumilio*	Kleine Pechlibelle	Tengere grasjuffer
Brown, Arran	*Erebia ligea*	Weissbindiger Mohrenfalter	Boserebia
Brown, Dusky Meadow	*Hyponephele lycaon*	Kleines Ochsenauge	Grauw zandoogje
Brown, Large Wall	*Lasiommata maera*	Braunauge	Rotsvlinder
Brown, Woodland	*Lopinga achine*	Gelbringfalter	Boszandoog
Butterfly, Map	*Araschnia levana*	Landkärtchen	Landkaartje
Chaser, Blue	*Libellula fulva*	Spitzenfleck	Bruine korenbout
Chaser, Broad-bodied	*Libellula depressa*	Plattbauch	Platbuik
Chaser, Four-spotted	*Libellula quadrimaculata*	Vierfleck	Viervlek
Clubtail, River	*Gomphus flavipes*	Asiatische Keiljungfer	Rivierrombout
Copper, Large	*Lycaena dispar*	Grosser Feuerfalter	Grote vuurvlinder
Copper, Purple-edged	*Lycaena hippothoe*	Lilagold-Feuerfalter	Rode vuurvlinder
Copper, Scarce	*Lycaena virgaureae*	Dukatenfalter	Morgenrood
Copper, Sooty	*Lycaena tityrus*	Brauner Feuerfalter	Bruine vuurvlinder
Copper, Violet	*Lycaena helle*	Blauschillernder Feuerfalter	Blauwe vuurvlinder
Crayfish, Noble	*Astacus astacus*	Edelkrebs	Europese rivierkreeft
Crayfish, Signal	*Pacifastacus leniusculus*	Signalkrebs	Californische rivierkreeft
Darter, Banded	*Sympetrum pedemontanum*	Gebänderte Heidelibelle	Bandheidelibel
Darter, Black	*Sympetrum danae*	Schwarze Heidelibelle	Zwarte heidelibel

Darter, Moustached	*Sympetrum vulgatum*	Gemeine Heidelibelle	Steenrode heidelibel
Darter, Ruddy	*Sympetrum sanguineum*	Blutrote Heidelibelle	Bloedrode heidelibel
Darter, Yellow-winged	*Sympetrum flaveolum*	Gefleckte Heidelibelle	Geelvlekheidelibel
Demoiselle, Banded	*Calopteryx splendens*	Gebänderte Prachtlibelle	Weidebeekjuffer
Demoiselle, Beautiful	*Calopteryx virgo*	Blauflügel-Prachtlibelle	Bosbeekjuffer
Emerald, Brilliant	*Somatochlora metallica*	Glänzende Smaragdlibelle	Metaalglanslibel
Emerald, Downy	*Cordulia aenea*	Gemeine Smaragdlibelle	Smaragdlibel
Emerald, Northern	*Somatochlora arctica*	Arktische Smaragdlibelle	Hoogveenglanslibel
Emerald, Yellow-spotted	*Somatochlora flavomaculata*	Gefleckte Smaragdlibelle	Gevlekte glanslibel
Emperor, Blue	*Anax imperator*	Grosse Königslibelle	Grote keizerlibel
Emperor, Lesser	*Anax parthenope*	Kleine Königslibelle	Zuidelijke keizerlibel
Emperor, Lesser Purple	*Apatura ilia*	Kleiner Schillerfalter	Kleine weerschijnvlinder
Emperor, Purple	*Apatura iris*	Grosser Schillerfalter	Grote weerschijnvlinder
Engraver, Spruce	*Ips typographus*	Buchdrucker	Letterzetter
Featherleg, Blue	*Platycnemis pennipes*	Blaue Federlibelle	Blauwe breedscheenjuffer
Fritillary, Assmann's	*Melitaea britomartis*	Östlicher Scheckenfalter	Oostelijke parelmoervlinder
Fritillary, Cranberry	*Boloria aquilonaris*	Hochmoor-Perlmutterfalter	Veenbesparelmoervlinder
Fritillary, Dark Green	*Argynnis aglaja*	Grosser Perlmutterfalter	Grote parelmoervlinder
Fritillary, False Heath	*Melitaea diamina*	Baldrian-Scheckenfalter	Woudparelmoervlinder
Fritillary, Glanville	*Melitaea cinxia*	Wegerich-Scheckenfalter	Veldparelmoervlinder
Fritillary, Heath	*Melitaea athalia*	Gemeine Scheckenfalter	Bosparelmoervlinder
Fritillary, High Brown	*Argynnis adippe*	Feuriger Perlmutterfalter	Bosrandparelmoervlinder
Fritillary, Lesser Marbled	*Brenthis ino*	Mädesüss-Perlmutterfalter	Purperstreep-parelmoervlinder
Fritillary, Nickerl's	*Melitaea aurelia*	Ehrenpreis Scheckenfalter	Steppeparelmoervlinder
Fritillary, Niobe's	*Argynnis niobe*	Stiefmütterchen-Perlmutterfalter	Duinparelmoervlinder
Fritillary, Pallas'	*Argynnis laodice*	Östlicher Perlmutterfalter	Tsarenmantel
Fritillary, Pearl-bordered	*Boloria euphrosyne*	Frühlings-Perlmuttfalter	Zilvervlek
Fritillary, Queen of Spain	*Issoria lathonia*	Kleiner Perlmutterfalter	Kleine parelmoervlinder
Fritillary, Scarce	*Euphydryas maturna*	Eschen-Scheckenfalter	Roodbonte parelmoervlinder
Fritillary, Silver-washed	*Argynnis paphia*	Kaisermantel	Keizersmantel
Fritillary, Small Pearl-bordered	*Boloria selene*	Braunfleckiger Perlmutterfalter	Zilveren maan
Fritillary, Spotted	*Melitaea didyma*	Roter Scheckenfalter	Tweekleurige parelmoervlinder
Fritillary, Weaver's	*Boloria dia*	Magerrasen-Perlmutterfalter	Akkerparelmoervlinder
Grasshopper, Blue-winged	*Oedipoda caerulescens*	Blauflügelige Ödlandschrecke	Blauwvleugelsprinkhaan
Grayling, Baltic	*Oeneis jutta*	Baltischer Samtfalter	Baltische toendravlinder
Grayling, Rock	*Hipparchia hermione*	Kleine Waldportier	Kleine boswachter
Hairstreak, Blue-spot	*Satyrium spini*	Kreuzdorn-Zipfelfalter	Wegedoornpage
Hawker, Blue	*Aeshna cyanea*	Blaugrüne Mosaikjungfer	Blauwe glazenmaker

Hawker, Bog	*Aeshna subarctica*	Hochmoor-Mosaikjungfer	Noordse glazenmaker
Hawker, Brown	*Aeshna grandis*	Braune Mosaikjungfer	Bruine glazenmaker
Hawker, Green	*Aeshna virides*	Grüne Mosaikjungfer	Groene glazenmaker
Hawker, Green-eyed	*Aeshna isosceles*	Keilfleck-Mosaikjungfer	Vroege glazenmaker
Hawker, Hairy	*Brachytron pratense*	Frühe Schilfjäger	Glassnijder
Hawker, Moorland	*Aeshna juncea*	Torf-Mosaikjungfer	Venglazenmaker
Heath, Chestnut	*Coenonympha glycerion*	Rostbraunes Wiesenvögelchen	Roodstreephooibeestje
Heath, Large	*Coenonympha tullia*	Grosses Wiesenvögelchen	Veenhooibeestje
Heath, Pearly	*Coenonympha arcania*	Weissbindiges Wiesenvögelchen	Tweekleurig hooibeestje
Heath, Scarce	*Coenonympha hero*	Wald-Wiesenvögelchen	Zilverstreephooibeestje
Horseflies	*Tabanidae*	Bremsen	Dazen
Midges	*Ceratopogonidae*	Gnitzen	Knutjes
Moth, Winter	*Operophtera brumata*	Kleiner Frostspanner	Kleine wintervlinder
Pincertail, Small	*Onychogomphus forcipatus*	Kleine Zangenlibelle	Kleine tanglibel
Redeye, Large	*Erythromma najas*	Grosses Granatauge	Grote roodoogjuffer
Redeye, Small	*Erythromma viridulum*	Kleines Granatauge	Kleine roodoogjuffer
Ringlet	*Aphanthopus hyperanthus*	Brauner Waldvogel	Koevinkje
Ringlet, False	*Coenonympha oedippus*	Moor-Wiesenvögelchen	Goudooghooibeestje
Sedgling	*Nehalennia speciosa*	Zwerglibelle	Dwergjuffer
Skimmer, White-tailed	*Orthetrum albistylum*	Östlicher Blaupfeil	Witpuntoverlibel
Skipper, Chequered	*Carterocephalus palaemon*	Gelbwürfeliger Dickkopffalter	Bont dikkopje
Skipper, Large Chequered	*Heteropterus morpheus*	Spiegelfleck-Dickkopffalter	Spiegeldikkopje
Skipper, Northern Chequered	*Carterocephalus silvicolus*	Schwarzfleckiger Golddickkopffalter	Geelbont dikkopje
Snaketail, Green	*Ophiogomphus cecilia*	Grüne Flussjungfer	Gaffellibel
Swallowtail	*Papilio machaon*	Schwalbenschwanz	Koninginnenpage
White, Eastern Bath	*Pontia edusa*	Östlicher Resedafalter	Oostelijk resedawitje
White, Marbled	*Melanargia galathea*	Schachbrett	Dambordje
White, Wood	*Leptidea sinapis*	Senfweissling	Boswitje
Whiteface, Dark	*Leucorrhinia albifrons*	Östliche Moosjungfer	Oostelijke witsnuitlibel
Whiteface, Lilypad	*Leucorrhinia caudalis*	Zierliche Moosjungfer	Sierlijke witsnuitlibel
Whiteface, Ruby	*Leucorrhinia rubicunda*	Nordische Moosjungfer	Noordse witsnuitlibel
Whiteface, Small	*Leucorrhinia dubia*	Kleine Moosjungfer	Venwitsnuitlibel
Whiteface, Yellow-spotted	*Leucorrhinia pectoralis*	Grosse Moosjungfer	Gevlekte witsnuitlibel
Yellow, Moorland Clouded	*Colias palaeno*	Hochmoor-Gelbling	Veenluzernevlinder
Yellow, Pale Clouded	*Colias hyale*	Goldene Acht	Gele luzernevlinder

GLOSSARY

Central European Plain Sometimes called northern European plain. This is an extensive lowland area north of the Alps and the Carpathians, and south of the North Sea and Baltic Sea. It has a temperate climate, with strong Atlantic influences in the west and a continental character in the east.

Dystrophic A dystrophic environment is an environment that is very poor in nutrients.

Eutrophication Process of nutrient enrichment. When an environment eutrophicates, nutrients are added to it. As a result, the vegetation changes. Competitive species that require a lot of nutrients, take over from species that are able to cope with less nutrients, but are also less competitive. Eutrophication is a big problem in nature conservation. Nutrient enrichment through modern agricultural techniques have destroyed many valuable vegetations.

Improved meadow Meadow that underwent the process of agricultural intensification – better drainage and better fertilized. Note that the term 'improved' fits the perspective of economic yield. From an ecological perspective, 'degraded meadow' could apply to exactly the same as improved meadow.

Lek A lek is a courting arena. The males of some bird species (e.g. Ruff, Black Grouse, Capercaillie, Great Snipe) congregate to compete, through display, over the females.

Old-growth Forest Natural forest that has been undisturbed longer than the life span of individual trees. Old-growth stands are characterised by trees of different ages (so not just old trees), a mosaic structure of old and young trees and a lot of dead wood, both standing and on the forest floor. Because of these features, old-growth is something altogether different from a forest with mature trees. Old-growth forms a rare ecosystem with a very high ecological value.

Succession The gradual transformation from one assemblage of plants and animals to another. Succession typically moves from a pioneer stage, through a grassland stage and a scrubland stage, to the forest stage. The type of pioneer, grassland, scrubland and forest vegetations depends on factors such as soil, hydrology, nutrients, minerals and human influence.

Suchary Polish word for dystrophic bog lakes, fringed by a raised bog vegetation.

PICTURE CREDITS

Bosma, Henk: 49 (b)
Crossbill Guides / Cate, Bouke ten: Cover, 4 (tl)+(br), 5(bl), 25, 28, 32 (b), 33 (t), 35 (b), 39 (t), 41 (t), 43, 44, 47, 50, 58, 63, 68, 75, 85, 96, 101, 105 (b), 110, 119, 127 (t+b), 130 (b), 138 (t), 145, 148, 150, 154, 156, 157 (t+b), 164 (b), 165 (t), 167, 171 (t+b), 174, 175 (b), 176 (b), 178 (t), 179, 182, 184 (t), 185, 188 (t), 190 (t), 191, 192, 193, 199, 201 (t), 205 (t), 206
Crossbill Guides / Hilbers, Dirk: Cover, 5 (tr), 10, 14, 15, 23, 26, 27, 31, 32 (t), 34, 37 (t), 39 (b), 45, 46, 48, 52 (c+b), 53, 54, 57, 72, 76, 77, 78, 79, 86, 88 (t+b), 107 (t), 116, 122, 125, 128 (t), 130 (t), 131, 135 (t+c+b), 139, 141 (b), 146 (t), 155 (t+b), 159 (b), 161 (t), 164 (t), 170 (b), 180, 188 (b), 195 (t), 196, 202, 204 (t+b)
Crossbill Guides / Lotterman, Kim: 107 (b)
Crossbill Guides / Vliegenthart, Albert: 109 (b), 123 (b)
Fikkert, Cor (www.kina.nl): 128
Gebuis, Hans: 42 (b)
Greef, Jan van der (www.insightintonature. com): 89, 93 (t)
Hierck, Martin (www.martinhierck.com): 97, 126
Holten, Jan van: Cover, 29, 35 (t), 41 (b), 49 (t), 80, 91, 94, 95, 100, 103, 105 (t), 109 (t), 111, 134, 143, 146 (b), 152, 158, 161 (b), 165 (b), 168, 175 (t), 176 (t), 178 (b), 184 (b), 195 (b), 200, 210
Holten, Wilma van: 36 (b)
Hulscher, Rikus (www.agronatura.nl): 4 (bl), 5 (tl), 5 (br), 52 (t), 123 (t), 170 (t), 197
Huskens , Kim: 36 (t)
Karjalainen, Sami (www.samikarjalainen.fi): 112
Kempers, Rob (www.robkempers.nl): 151

Lachmann, Lars: 66, 67 (t+b)
Mazurek, Lukasz (www.wildpoland.com): 162
Morkvenas, Zymantas: 99
Olthof, Sonja: 102
Saxifraga / Bouwman, Jaap: 106
Saxifraga / Hoogenstein, Luc: 159 (t)
Saxifraga / Knijff, Arie de: 38
Saxifraga / Mollet, Martin: 93 (c), 172
Saxifraga / Uchelen, Edo van: 42 (b)
Saxifraga / Zekhuis, Mark: 190 (b), 205 (b)
Sierdsema, Henk: 33 (b), 59, 115, 149
Szymura, Mateusz (www.bialowieza.info.pl): 4 (tr), 93 (b), 186, 201 (b), 207
Termaat, Tim: (37 (t)
Verhart, Frank: 62, 140
Wild, Angela de: 141 (t)

All illustrations by Crossbill Guides / Horst Wolter

In the references that follow the numbers refer to the pages and the letters to the position on the page (t=top, c=centre, b=bottom with l and r indicating left and right).

ACKNOWLEDGEMENTS

247

Like all Crossbill Guides, this book has been produced in close collaboration with many people. Local experts, non-local experts, photographers and many others have helped us create a guide that lives up to the standards set by previous guides. We would like to thank some of these people here. First of all we would like to thank our Polish proof-readers Gosia Gorska, Piotr Marczakiewicz, Łukasz Ławrysz and Łukasz Mazurek. They have helped us eliminate the last errors and added valuable information. We have also received a lot of help from the different National and Landscape Parks in the region. We would like to thank Anna Gierasimiuk, Renata Krzyściak-Kosińska, Czeslaw Okolow, Tomasz Kolodziejczak, Matteusz Szymura, Andrzej Karczewski and Gosia Karczewska of Białowieża National Park, Monika Olszewska, Joao Matos da Costa and Iwona Laskowska of Narew National Park, Agnieszka Henel, Krysztof Frackiel, Helena Bartoszuk and Cezary Werpachowski of Biebrza National Park, Paulina Pajer-Giełażys, Maciej Romański, Adam Januszewicz and Wojciech Misiukiewicz of Wigry National Park, Teresa Swierubska of Suwałki Landscape Park and Rafał Michniuk of Knyszyn Landscape Park. We have also received enthusiastic support from some nature conservation organisations. Of OTOP, we would like to thank Marcin Dudek and Lars Lachmann, of PTOP we would like to thank Jarek Banach, Gabriela Kulakowska, Marta Potocka and Adam Zbyryt. A great many others have helped us in many ways. We would like to thank Grzegorz Blachowski, Grzegorz Grzywaczewski, Rikus Hulscher, Théo Phyle Havard dit Duclos, Wilma van Holten, Jan van Holten and Frederike ten Cate for their assistance and support in the creation of this guidebook. For the many splendid photographs in the book we thank the Saxifraga Foundation and the many photographers who selflessly made their photographs available to us. Within our own ranks we owe gratitude to Alex Tabak, Albert Vliegenthart, Kees Hilbers, Riet Hilbers, John Cantelo and Sam Gobin for the timely completion of the book. Furthermore, we welcome Gino Smeulders (de biogeoloog) within our ranks. Gino has provided us with information about the geology of the region. Finally, we would like to thank Swarovski Optik (Dale Forbes) and the Polish Tourist Organisation (Magdalena Stoch) for their financial support. Without them, this book would not have been possible.

Dirk Hilbers and Bouke ten Cate
Crossbill Guides Foundation, March 2013

CROSSBILL GUIDES

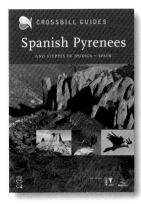

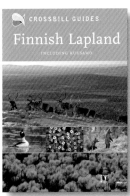

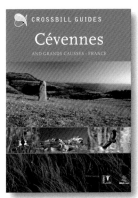

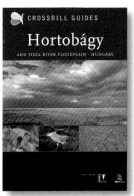

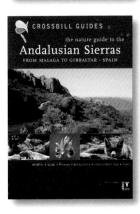

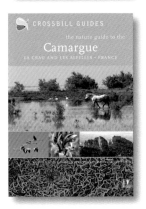

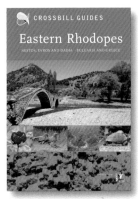

More titles are in preparation. Check our website for further details and updates.

WWW.CROSSBILLGUIDES.ORG